S0-EFN-760

OMNIVM LVX CIVIVM

BOSTON
PUBLIC
LIBRARY

PAPERS DELIVERED AT THE SMITHSONIAN INSTITUTION ANNUAL SYMPO-
SIUM, FEBRUARY 16–18, 1967

Robert McC. Adams
Wolfgang Braunfels
Asa Briggs
Hiroshi Daifuku
Bertrand de Jouvenel
René Dubos
Paul Goodman
Edward T. Hall
Hubert H. Humphrey
Philip Johnson
Rt. Hon. Miss Jennie Lee
Ian L. McHarg
Leo Marx
S. Dillon Ripley
Robert C. Wood

Smithsonian Annual II

# THE FITNESS OF MAN'S ENVIRONMENT

With an Introduction by
The Right Honorable Jennie Lee, P.C., M.P.

SMITHSONIAN INSTITUTION PRESS
CITY OF WASHINGTON

THE SUPPORT OF THE FORD FOUNDATION AND THE TACONIC FOUNDATION, INC., IS GRATEFULLY ACKNOWLEDGED.

The first volume in the Smithsonian Annual Series, *Knowledge Among Men,* was published by Simon and Schuster in 1966.

SMITHSONIAN PUBLICATION 4728

© 1968 SMITHSONIAN INSTITUTION

LIBRARY OF CONGRESS CATALOG CARD NUMBER: 68-20988

"BOSTON PUBLIC LIBRARY"

# FOREWORD

HUBERT H. HUMPHREY

FOR MOST OF man's long sojourn on this planet, he has been—to paraphrase the words of the poet A. E. Housman—a stranger and afraid in a world he never made. But I think we can say now that man is no longer a stranger. Modern science and technology have brought to him the blessings, or at least the facts, of modern communication. Man is a member of the human family *in fact,* and is not a mere spectator in today's world; he is an actor, a participant. It may not be the best of all possible worlds, but it is in large part the world that man himself has made. At least, he has placed his hand upon it, taken that which was given to him by nature, and has designed it somewhat for himself; sometimes to his betterment and sometimes to his detriment.

There are a number of people today who seem to be thinking along the lines of the song from that musical, *Stop the World, I Want to Get Off.* The problem is that we haven't learned how to stop the world and very few of us are going to get off. Thus, our problem and our challenge is to try to do something about it as long as we are here. Whether deliberately—as in the building of structures or cities—or inadvertently—as in the pollution of the air and the water—man has drastically altered his physical environment.

Throughout the world, leaders in government and in society are asking evermore how we can improve the physical environment of man's home. That is a theme in this country and this is an era when we speak of beautification—of our countryside, of our cities. This is a time when we are giving greater emphasis to architecture and design, a time when this nation has finally given official recognition to the arts

5

and the humanities by act of Congress and by the establishment of such a commission or council. We are deeply concerned about our physical environment.

We know that conventional attitudes and yesterday's methods for dealing with the physical environment must be reconsidered; not necessarily cast aside, but possibly recast for the needs of modern man. We cannot ignore the tremendous impact of urbanization, of mechanization, of the new means of transportation. All of these have added a new dimension to our environment and to the problems inherent in such drastic and rapid changes as we now experience from science and technology. The fragmented approach of the past must, therefore, be replaced by a broader and a more comprehensive view of our environment seen as a whole. For this, we need to call not only on people who work day-to-day in architecture or in city planning, but also on men and women concerned with the broadest possible scientific and humanistic considerations.

I have been deeply concerned about the quality of life in our nation; in our cities and, of course, in rural America. I have often wondered whether the obsolescence and the deterioration of our cities reflect what has happened to people in our culture or whether the deterioration of our cities has resulted in the deterioration and the deprivation of the human spirit. It is my personal view that we must not only help to rehabilitate the physical structure of this world in which we live but also help to rehabilitate those who are the denied, who have become despairing, deprived, and who have been regrettably the victims of inadequacy of environment and opportunity. So we approach this important subject of man's physical environment. I must say, as one who is concerned with matters of some scientific importance in the Government, that the environment of the earth is not fully known. We know so little even about this terrestrial ball on which we live. We have examined piecemeal its crust; we know very little about the rest of it. We know something about the atmosphere; mainly that it is polluted. We know a bit about the seas; primarily the surface and beneath that only to limited depths. We are now busily engaged in the exploration of what we call this earth—the land mass and its seas—in a program that is identified throughout the world as oceanography.

We also are exploring space, which is a part of man's physical environment. And man should know all about this environment—the earth, the atmosphere, the seas, the infinity of space. When I am asked if it is worth our time and effort, I can only say this: since we are inhabitants of a world—of a globe—that is a part of the solar system, the least that we can do is to become acquainted with our home. Our home is the solar system of which we are one infinitesimal part and we need to know even that fragment called the world. And in the world we need to know that minute, ever so minute, area that we call our neighborhood.

The papers contained in this volume represent a group of carefully selected experts who, over the past six months, have prepared statements concerning the principles which should guide the development of the physical environment of man. I think this is the right approach. To these contributors, I say: we want you to dream boldly, courageously (I might even add the term "far out"), because we need to have people who can break through the traditional pattern of the redesign of our cities. I imagine there is another form besides the rectangular. If you can discover it, we will be most appreciative. If you can sell it, we will be ever in your debt.

I wish all of you well and I, for one, look forward to reviewing the results of your labors. I am so pleased that the Smithsonian Institution has seen fit to take on this responsibility. We welcome your counsel and advice. We not only welcome you, we frankly say we need you.

7

# PREMISE

S. DILLON RIPLEY

THE PAPERS in this volume testify to the extraordinary interest created by the present public realization that something is somehow wrong with man's relations with his environment. And yet this is not a particularly new subject nor one in itself startling for Americans. For two generations we have been aware that the last frontier has been crossed in our Nation, that the land was not expendable, that man was no more defenseless and at war with nature. Yet the war continues. If the Industrial Revolution seemed to encourage the dream of man's total victory over nature, the fateful fact has been as Eric Hoffer says, "that man was not inventive enough to automate his second creation, that his machines were half-machines lacking the gears and filament of thought and will, setting in motion a process of mass dehumanization." In the process, nature suffers continually in an undeclared war. Man animated by hunger for profit or for spectacular action, continually erodes our landscape. Many feel that this is appropriate, that man and nature can never live in harmony. Thomas Hardy said, "nature and man can never be friends." Curiously enough our increased command over nature has not reinforced our humaneness. As Hoffer comments, "On the contrary, in many parts of the world the taming of nature by rapid industrialization gave rise to degrees of social barbarization." Man has neither learned to shut out nature—to defend himself from it, as it were—nor indeed has he learned to live in cities as a humane individual.

In these essays we have attempted to create relatedness; to relate biologists and anthropologists—students of the human ecosystem—with planners and architects. As Edward Hall points out, the hidden

9

structures of culture are among the most consistently ignored features of 20th-century life. People of different ethnic groups perceive space differently and respond differently to crowding. What will overload and sensorily deprive one culture will understimulate another. As he indicates, architects may talk only to architects. There may be a lack of feedback, of reportage on experiences without which conclusions cannot be drawn. Architects suffer, as do many intellectuals, by being literate persons who feel themselves members of the educated minority. How often such an elite suffers from less than valid claims to superiority! How often superiority produces what Hoffer describes as a "colonial official" mentality. In New Mexico and nearby areas the Pueblo Indians have developed an indigenous and adaptive architectural style. Lack of cultural reportage, however, prevents them under the Federal Housing Administration standards from constructing what they would like. As nonintellectuals they presumably have to take what they can get. Designers for the masses tend not to see people, only prizes from other architects and planners. Dr. Braunfels, too, stresses this theme of feedback. People do vary. The ethnic German desires a "corner," a private space. The ethnic Italian takes pleasure in relative crowding, less privacy, and vocal situations. Variety is the key to the system. And to this René Dubos adds his wise observation that, in spite of the consistency of this genetic heritage, the physical environment of the maturing individual closely affects his responses throughout life. An experimental infant monkey, deprived of the sight of his own hands, will suffer a measurable loss by that deprivation in the total conceptualization of the fact of grasping and, mayhap, understanding objects. The linkages of the neural pathways of sight and touch are clear to see in the end result, though still demonstrable to science today as "through a glass darkly."

But certainly architects might well team up with anthropologists to study the types and varieties of crowding in urban life; the vivid patterns, the deprivations, the pleasures. Last summer in Ireland I watched scores of lovely blocks of Georgian flats in Dublin being demolished as part of a long-range plan involving moving many impoverished people into new sugarloaf shaped blocks of flats, what Hall calls, "paternalism by high rise." These are the blocks of flats which are identical, outside Paris, in Beirut, near Rio de Janeiro, in

10

New Delhi, in New Haven, Conn. There are surely measurable degrees
of trauma for very poor people in being so moved. Certainly the complexity of large scale planning is such that virtually all academic disciplines must be involved, not only in universities but in independent
institutions. But let us do all this with great care. Remember the stric-
tures about intellectuals. Let us not "engineer" people, masses, as we
would a mass of statistics. Let us not become neo-colonialists.

Some of you may wonder why the Smithsonian Institution would
sponsor a volume on environmental quality. It has been a central
theme in our interests since 1851. Joseph Henry developed the *Registry of Periodical Phenomena*—a series of coordinated observations on
meteorological and biological phenomena—in order to understand
climate in America. Inductively such a registry would lead to a better
understanding of the total environment. In conjunction with his atmospheric studies, Professor Henry was concerned with the first
"smog"—byproduct of the Industrial Revolution—the coal smoke
which hung like a pall over our own greatest developing cities.

In the setting up of the Hodgkins Fund in 1891, whose purpose
was to study the properties of the atmosphere, the Smithsonian first
developed a modern approach to present-day environmental problems.
In 1913 a report published under that Fund by a medical research
team of the Physiological Laboratory of the London Hospital Medical
College showed that temperature, air movement, relative humidity,
and generalized environmental factors were important causes in physical deterioration suffered by humans in certain slums, mines, and excessive crowds. Chemical changes in the atmosphere were extensively
studied. As the authors stated, "life is the reaction of the living substance to the ceaseless play of the environment." Other research was
on tuberculosis, on the cloud and fog precipitation devices of Cottrell,
on Michelson's interferometer in spectroscopy, and included the development at M.I.T. of the first wind tunnel in the United States by
a team which included a present Smithsonian Regent, Jerome
Hunsaker. In addition, our first architectural publication was that by
Robert Dale Owen in 1849, *Hints on Public Architecture*. Currently,
we desire to collect and centralize architectural renderings to delineate certain central environmental themes.

The psychological influence of modes and styles of architecture has been too little studied. Some of the authors refer to this effect. Is New York vital and electric partly because of the stimulus of its vertical clusters of lines, like erect sheaves of arrows? Is there a certain monolithic solemnity about Washington Federal architecture which creates a sense of brooding calm? Sometimes the great Government buildings all of a certain height, massive, flat, inert, make me think of a large pride of lions lying out in the grass after a kill. Only a distant male rears his heavy head and mane to create the domed effect of the Capitol. There is a discipline in all this. The pride needs it to achieve its dynamic team objective. The vitality and elan are harnessed.

The need is great. The environment is changing as perhaps dictated by simple natural evolution. We show in these pages a few examples of the past and some dim pathways for the future. The Smithsonian Institution, insofar as it represents a museum to most people, must behave more like Harold Lasswell's *social planetarium* where all is possible. If the machine can be reversed to delineate the path of Halley's Comet fifty years ago, we can with our demonstrations exhibit the present and decry the future. For these purposes the museum exists, ready to be an educational tool for all the people.

# CONTENTS

13

# THE FITNESS OF MAN'S ENVIRONMENT

# INTRODUCTION

RIGHT HONORABLE JENNIE LEE, P.C., M.P.

THE RT. HON. MISS JENNIE LEE, P.C., M.P., has been Minister for the Arts in her Majesty's Government since October 1964. Miss Lee was made a member of Her Majesty's Privy Council in June 1966 and was elected Vice-Chairman of the Labour Party in October 1966 and Chairman in October 1967. Since March 1965 she has also been Joint Parliamentary Secretary of State and subsequently Minister of State for Education and Science. Miss Lee was appointed Parliamentary Secretary, Ministry of Public Building and Works in October 1964. She is Labour Member of Parliament for Cannock, a Midland constituency, and has been since 1958 a member of the National Executive Committee of the Labour Party. She was, for many years, a director and member of the editorial board of the left-wing weekly, *Tribune*. Miss Lee has been a member of the Ministry of Health's Central Advisory Committee on Housing and her special interests in Parliament center on housing as well as on international and Commonwealth affairs.

Miss Lee is the widow of the Rt. Hon. Aneurin Bevan, whom she married in 1934. She was born at Lochgelly in Fife in 1904, daughter of a Scottish miner from whom she inherited a strong tradition of service to the miners' cause. Miss Lee distinguished herself at school, winning a scholarship to Edinburgh University where she took her M.A., LL.B., and also qualified as a teacher. At the same time, she was one of the leading members of the Labour Club and became a frequent speaker for the Independent Labour Party. In 1928 she was nominated as prospective Parliamentary candidate for North Lanark and was elected at a by-election in 1929. After the formation of the National Government in 1931, Miss Lee lost her seat at the general election. Then came the split between the I.L.P. and the Labour Party, in which she sided with the former. She remained an I.L.P. supporter until 1942 when she resigned because she was unable to accept its anti-war attitude. Two years later she rejoined the Labour Party, and it was as a Labour candidate that Miss Lee returned to Westminster as M.P. for Cannock in July of 1945.

During World War II, Miss Lee was a lobby correspondent in the House of Commons and liaison officer to factories for the Ministries of Aircraft Production and Information. It was during this period that she wrote *Our Ally, Russia*. In addition to her book on Russia, Miss Lee has written two autobiographical works, *To-Morrow is a New Day* and *This Great Journey*.

I HAVE TO BEGIN with a confession. When first I received the invitation to compose an introduction for this volume I sent a polite (I hope a *very* polite) negative reply. Now this was not because I did not appreciate the honor, but rather because of a kind of spiritual critique. I said to myself, "Why go over all that old stuff again?" It is now more than fifty years since Patrick Gettys, in my own beloved Edinburgh, was preaching about the quality of man's environment and how he should seek to achieve it. Since then there have been so many dreamers and so many planners and so many plans that it seems to me that the thing that now matters is to win some major victories in the field of power politics in order that we can begin to implement the plans that we have all talked about so much.

Nevertheless, we have this contemporary dream and in any planning for our environment we have got to think of not just some of us but of all of us. There have been some extremely stratospheric phrases used recently by people in this field—one in particular to the effect that technological progress and scientific problem solving could only improve the quality of man's life if controlled and guided by a worldwide vision of the common good. Now that is using a very broad brush indeed, and that sentiment is of the kind that can very easily be caricatured and distorted. But I am essentially very conscious of the fact that while we discuss the quality of man's environment, the majority of mankind is not discussing quality; it is discussing whether it can keep alive at all. But that does not exempt us from our specific task, in our particular qualities, to address ourselves to this problem of the fitness of our environment. I feel that it is extremely heartening that, in the midst of all his pressing duties, the Vice President of the United States has taken the time to prepare a Foreword to this volume and to wish us well. I hope he's got a lot of friends among the Congressmen and the Senators! At least you've got bridges with government in your country, in America. We, too, have bridges in my country, but our jobs are certainly far from done. Without immodesty surely we can claim that the one common task we all have is to guide, inspire, badger, and pressure our respective governments into leading us forward into this new stage in social evolution.

First we must ask ourselves what it is we are trying to do. Where are

19

we trying to go? How far does poor humanity have any control over its destiny or are we blind creatures facing social and economic forces that care nothing for your private judgment or prejudices or for mine? Of course, any fool can be a defeatist. It is easy to accept a defeatist's views. But that kind of attitude toward life has never impressed me. Our historic task in this century is plainly to find a way forward to the classless society based on the democratic principles that most of us have been brought up to believe in. Of course, as yet we are only groping. We've not yet succeeded in making ourselves comfortable and at home in our 20th-century technological age. But if we can avoid the horror, the unspeakable tragedy of a third world war, why shouldn't we win through? We've all got an element of defeatism in us; we have our gloomy moments. But other generations, other times, have built civilizations that have conformed to their closest ideals. I consider that the real measure of man is a willingness to confront the world around him, with all its agonizing complexities, and still retain the principle of action. In the very act of considering the quality of life, we are at once striking an optimistic note. We know at least many of the things we want to reject. I imagine that there is a wide measure of agreement among us concerning the noise, the squalor, the air pollution, and the traffic jams that engulf so much of city life. But it is when we come to consider the remedies for our social ills that the real fun will begin. Because we come from different countries, varied environments, and we each have our own distinctive relationships to the problems of our community. You know what this means: I will tell you my problems, now you tell me yours. We shall each bring our own particular truths, but those truths will inevitably be colored by our backgrounds, by our jobs, by our own environment. I think one thing will be evident from these papers; a spirit of humility. I don't think even our most distinguished experts seek to claim that they know all the answers even for any one city or any one part of the problem. Of course, we know that no previous civilizations had the technical resources of today. We keep saying to ourselves that the machines are our servants—let's hope they remain our servants. But this very fact underlies the multitude of the contemporary problems. If only a few of us drove to work, no problem would arise. But when your neighbor, indeed all your neighbors, insists he has the same right to four wheels under him that you have, a radically new situation arises that cannot be solved by looking to past civilizations.

No one should underestimate what we are really seeking to do. We are seeking, all of us, to make a seemingly stimulating environment not for a privileged minority but for the whole family of man. It is quite possible to be a realist and an idealist at the same time. Secretary Ripley told me recently that he had been in South Africa and had been drilled rather severely by questioners who said, "Now, what's the difference? In America you're no different from South Africa. All your racial problems and distinctions and the rest. . . ." But he was able to say to them that, in America, whatever might be the weaknesses of human nature, social differences, etc., the government of the day held a philosophy which did not believe in segregation or inequality. He was able to tell them that the ethos of America is this seeking after brotherhood—this seeking after governing together the family of man. This then is the modern problem: not to build the grandeur of the ancient civilization, but to build the 20th century for the whole family of man. In this century, whenever we approach the problem of the quality of man's environment, we are always embarrassed by the size of the family of man. Now if we could only leave most of them outside, how much simpler it would be! But in this great America you never had and you never will escape your democratic ethos. You will never, never get away from the fact that you were founded by those who came from the old world to break away from feudalism and class distinctions and start again. However much we may admire the cities of the ancient and medieval world, we cannot forget that the vast majority of mankind in those days lived in bitter bondage, the many serving every vicious whim as well as every inspired dream of the privileged few. The core of the matter is that the great princes of the past could command all the talents and resources of the world around them to build for the glory of a god they unquestionably believed in, and to build for their own greater glory. They planned not only their own individual dwellings but often the whole countryside around them, including complete towns and villages.

Today, even if we should wish to create and renovate our environment in this way, the road is barred to us. The last great period of domestic architecture in England vividly illustrates what I am seeking to say. We are very proud of our Regency terraces in London and Bath. They are a joy to look at and we are doing all we can to preserve the best of them. But these great houses, in all their architectural beauty, assume a rigid class structure. Servants slept in the bleak, cold attics and worked in the gloomy basement kitchen. The masters and mistresses were able to live graciously on the principal floors but only so long as the servant and master relationship remained. But what modern architects could build in that fashion?

Let me here put in a modest word of criticism. Sometimes our architects and our town planners can be distressingly derivative. I'm thinking, for instance, of many of the huge blocks of flats in my own hometown—and this applies, I know, to all other countries—huge blocks of flats that no doubt look splendid on the drawing board, complete with pretty green grass around them. In use, however, some of these flats have become a kind of mocking caricature of what we ought to do. We had our wonderful city squares in Edwardian and Victorian days. The garden in the center was a real garden and the purpose of the railing around it was to give exclusive possession to the surrounding families; the vulgar multitudes were kept outside. But when we take some of those tall domestic blocks of flats now, alas, the railings around the gardens are not there to keep the children of the tenants safe and happy. Very often we find that they are there to keep the children out, to keep them from trampling over the grass. Now, this has not been a deliberate act of unkindness. It is simply that numbers have become the enemy of many types of amenity. Thus we have to do a great deal of fresh thinking.

I have read with a great deal of respect and interest much of what has been written about how people should live, the sort of house they should have, and the transport and social amenities that should be available to them. But, you know, I think that we can only plan for ourselves, our family, and our friends. Whenever we plan not for us but for them, everything goes wrong. I can take an illustration right from my own constituency right in the heart of England. In all kindness, at the end of World War II, we thought in our rehousing schemes it was a splendid thing to set apart a group of houses for elderly people in their retirement years. Well, they weren't saying what they wanted. We were deciding what *we* thought *they* should have. Then we discovered that they were bored to death watching one another's funerals. The last thing in the world they wanted was this kind of age segregation. So we got a bit better. We decided that we should have the groundfloor flats for elderly couples, with the young couples up above. They weren't so keen on the noise from up above—once again we superior people were deciding what other people should have. Now I think by a process of trial and error that we are getting near to something which is pretty ideal. I am very proud of some of our houses where there is privacy and dignity for the individual in addition to companionship and security. In other words: the little unit where you can lock your front door, have a friend in, do your own shopping, come and go as you please, retire and arise when you want, go off and stay with friends for the weekend—but also feel secure in the knowledge that if you are ill in the middle of the night, you need only ring a bell to bring help.

If we plan a future in which extremes of wealth and poverty have been eliminated, in which we get rid of our slums, in which at the same time we get rid of over ostentatious private dwellings which the contemporary citizen is simply refusing to service, then we must keep still one more thing in mind. To the extent that we are prepared to live in our homes, pleasantly but modestly, we must remember that in our civil capacity we must not apologize whenever a community—whether our greatest city or our smallest village—seeks to build splendid public buildings. This will be a way forward when we are trying to rebuild the unity of our communities: the wonderful town centers, the halls, the theaters, the museums, the galleries. Far from being discarded, our artists must be made to feel that they are going to become our most precious asset—that we are not going to apologize for public expenditure on either a national or local level. In seeing to this, we do more than simply build a utility future. When some of my own countrymen say to me that the arts are the fringe activities, I remind them that the added priority which we are giving to the arts in Britain today is not a byproduct of super affluence. I think it is a deep instinctive

23

sense of history and self-preservation that one finds it is often in times of stress that you most need your poems, your music, your songs, satire, jokes, and invincible dreams. London has never forgotten that it was in the midst of the blitz that Dame Myra Hess was playing in the National Gallery. It was during the war that my Arts Council had its beginning.

But now I must apologize because—being a Scots pedant—I am beginning to trespass on the territory of some of our distinguished contributors to this volume. We are most fortunate in having been brought together from so many different countries and walks of life—academicians, town planners, historians, architects, etc.—to appear collectively in one volume. It is very wonderful for me not only to learn of the points of difference between our countries but also to learn how very, very much we all have in common—both in the ills we seek to be rid of, and in the dreams we have for the future.

# TWO POINTS OF PHILOSOPHY AND AN EXAMPLE

PAUL GOODMAN

ON MAY 25, 1911, Porfirio Diaz, president of Mexico, resigned from office following a successful revolt led by Francisco Madero on behalf of the masses living in poverty and seeking the restoration of communal lands and better living conditions. In that same year, Paul Goodman was born in New York City. Although the two events have little apparent connection, Goodman has spent much of his professional life as a social critic speaking out against precisely those conditions that fomented the Mexican socioeconomic upheaval.

He has carried his views, as a professor, to the University of Chicago, New York University, Sarah Lawrence College, Black Mountain College, the Institute of Gestalt Therapy in New York, and, as Knapp Professor in 1964, to the University of Wisconsin. Since 1964, he has been a Fellow of the Institute for Policy Studies in Washington, D.C.

As a social commentator, Paul Goodman has written poems, plays, novels, and numerous nonfiction articles and books as diversified in their subject matter as their titles indicate: *Growing Up Absurd; Kafka's Prayer; The Structure of Literature; The Community of Scholars; The Facts of Life; The Break-Up of our Camp; Parent's Day; Stop Light; The Empire City; Making Do; Compulsory Mis-Education; Communitas; People or Personnel; Utopian Essays and Practical Proposals; The Lordly Hudson; Like a Conquered Province;* and, most recently, *Hawkweed.*

Throughout his works, Paul Goodman affirms his beliefs in an ideal America, a true democracy, and the return of decency to our lives.

IN PRINCIPLE, technology, the use of instruments, is a branch of moral philosophy, subject to the criteria of prudence, efficiency, decency, and so forth. I need not demonstrate, in 1967, that those who abuse our technology at present are not interested in moral philosophy, are certainly not being prudent and decent, and are only in a narrow sense careful of efficiency and costs—they altogether neglect social costs. But even if we are interested in moral philosophy and want to use our technology prudently and decently, there are modern dilemmas that are hard to solve. So here let me make two small points of philosophical analysis that are usually overlooked.

In the first place, as technology increases, as there is a proliferation of goods and as civilization becomes more complex, there is a change of the scale on which things happen. Then, if we continue to use the concepts that apply to a smaller scale, we begin to think in deceptive abstractions. There are certain functions of life that we think we are carrying on, and that *were* carried on on a smaller scale, but which now on a larger scale are only seemingly being carried on. Sometimes, indeed, because of the error in our thinking, we get an effect opposite from that which was intended.

Consider penology, a poignant example. When some fellows sat in stocks in the town square and people passed by and jeered at them or clucked their tongues, it is possible, though the psychology is dubious, that the effect might have been reform or penitence. (In my opinion, public confession on the square was more likely to lead to penitence and social integration.) But the Tombs in New York, a jail for many thousands locked up in cages, obviously has no relation whatever to penitence, reform, or social integration. In fact it is a school for crime, as is shown by the rate of repeaters who come back on more serious charges. This kind of penology on this scale has the opposite effect from that intended: it produces crime. Yet we have come by small steps from the fellow in stocks on the town square up to the Tombs or San Quentin. It seems to be "penology" all along the line, but there has been a point at which it has ceased to be penology and has become torture and foolishness, a waste of money and a cause of crime. And even the social drive for vindictiveness, which is probably the chief

27

motive for punishment, is not satisfied; instead, there is blotting out of sight and *heightening* of social anxiety.

The change of scale has produced the same contrary effect in schooling. When there was academic instruction for many for a short time, or for a few for a longer time, it is possible that some academic education occurred. To be sure, most education for most people happened by means other than schools. Society functioned very well and many people became very expert and learned without going to school—in 1900, 6 percent graduated from high school and less than half of 1 percent went to college. Now, however, 100 percent are forced to go to high school and last year 75 percent graduated. Nearly 40 percent now go to college and by 1970 we are planning for 50 percent. On this scale, it is my observation as a reporter, very little education is occurring. For academic purposes, we might do just as well if we closed all the schools, though of course they serve for baby sitting, policing, and so forth. We could surely provide all the academic instruction that is achieved by far simpler and cheaper methods. Yet by small steps we have come to the present, using the same framework of administration and the same language, although the reality has entirely changed with the change of scale.

Take communications, as it is called. Newspapers, public speaking, and vaudeville meant one thing when they occurred in a simpler context, with the means of communication generally available to all. They mean another thing when we have mass media, semimonopolist broadcasting, licensed channels. The effect, by and large, has been homogenization and brainwashing—that is, precisely to prevent communication. We speak of our mass media as communications, yet they are importantly the preventing of communication. There is certainly very little talk back. Indeed, since television time is so expensive and by law the networks must give equal time on "controversial issues," the inevitable effect has been to avoid controversy altogether.

Grimly, the same damaging abstraction has been occurring in medicine. Since the doctors are swamped, there is a tendency in urban medicine to deal in vital statistics rather than health. I was recently at a conference in San Francisco concerned with the contraceptive pill. The doctors agreed that the pill was a heroic means of contraception

28

and in private conversation they were dubious about its use because of the different effects on different women. Most of them felt, however, that since the pill's contraceptive effects were sure and since there was population pressure and economic pressure among the poor, it was a good policy publicly to promote its use. Classically, though, medicine was primarily concerned with the health of each individual. I am sure each of us is very much concerned about his own health. Vital statistics and the welfare of society 10 years from now are other kinds of questions, also very important, but because of the change in scale of operation, medicine has begun to lose its classical function and practice begins to have only an approximate relation to that function. This process can go very far, as it has already done in schooling. For instance, hospitals that are very large because of technological advantages may come to be run for administrative convenience even to the disadvantage of patients.

To conclude with a global example that includes the previous ones, we now see that city planning has turned into something called "urbanism," planning for urban areas. In this planning there is no such word as "home," but only dwelling units and housing. Yet it is a real question whether it is possible to have good housing, to provide people with homes, if we slip into thinking of dwelling units. It is a question whether urban areas are governable as cities, or whether just this way of thinking does not worsen anomie. Historically, when the city's functions occurred on a smaller scale and with smaller bureaucracies, an average citizen could understand their integration, even when he did not control it. There was shape and style, something to belong to and be loyal to. Vandalism and neglect were not indifferent. It was not possible for large segments of the population just to drop "out of society." And the sense of citizenship is indispensable for the high culture that is one of the most interesting functions of cities. Florence in its heyday had a hundred thousand inhabitants, Athens about the same; Goethe's Weimar had twenty-five thousand. In New York, a metropolitan region of fifteen million, I doubt that there are more than one hundred thousand who take part in the city with the feeling that in some sense it is theirs, that they understand its integration and control it or try to control it. The others just live there.

29

But of course there *are* changes in scale, brought about by new technologies and increased populations. How to cope with these? One suggestion has been that instead of pretending to education, communication, health, and so forth in a mass context that makes these things impossible, it would be better if we began to provide two entirely distinct sets of services: the old (and indispensable) professions with a personal responsibility to clients, and the disciplines of social engineering (a term I here use uninvidiously) working mainly on background conditions and treating persons in respects where individual differences are unimportant and personal response is not called for. Our present procedure, however, both destroys the old professions and embarrasses forthright social engineering. Thus, the ancient academic ritual of text, examination, and commencement, that made sense with academic types in a community of scholars, makes no sense in mass universities; yet we also cannot forthrightly use teaching machines and television for brute instruction and provide other means of usefully occupying the time of the nonacademic. Physicians are not trained for home visits, family medicine, and preventive psychiatry, and the conditions of medical practice become more and more routine; yet we cannot forthrightly provide mass routine checkups, and it is only a few specialists in Public Health who show any medical concern for the background conditions of physical and mental disease.

Architecture and neighborhood planning are determined by bureaucrats according to abstract standards rather than the preferences of inhabitants, and all planning is subordinated to highway planning: yet we do not use our technology to clean the air and the rivers or rationalize transportation.

Local and competing newspapers have lapsed, town meetings and ward politics have lapsed, political oratory is ghost-written and not subject to cross examination, there is no vaudeville or local live theater except in a few metropolitan centers. Instead, we have packaged opinion and bland controversy on the mass media. Yet with these, there is no effort either to raise the cultural level by high-standard fare or to open the media to searching extremes that question the usual premises. The mass media can be used only to discuss mass-acceptable options, and then no new wisdom can enter the arena. For instance, instead of the usual spectrum from doves to hawks in a television panel on Vietnam, we ought to consider the views of those who think we have entered the phase of a universal American empire that should regulate the world and, on the other hand, of those who hold that the entire structure of sovereignty and power is long outmoded and unworkable.

I have spoken of the "disciplines of social engineering . . . working mainly on background conditions." This brings me to the second philosophical issue I want to raise. In fact, at present we do not really have these disciplines. The social-psychological, anthropological, and ecological studies that are necessary for good social engineering and the right use of new technology are not sufficiently developed. We do not know the remote effects of what we institute in education, medicine, or urbanism; I have given a few examples to show how the remote effects might be the opposite of our intentions. We may use computers to estimate requirements, costs, and benefits, but in the fields we are discussing the theories on which the programs are based are puerile.

Let us suppose, however, that we do have better studies and better programs. There then arises the philosophical question: can we directly apply our best theories to human and social situations? I think not, for to preplan too thoroughly is to kill life; and the more subtle the theory, the more dangerous the attack. This is the invidious sense of "social engineering." Prudence and science are one thing, determining how people are to live and breathe is quite another. It is probably best just to open a space in which they can live and breathe in their own way. That is, we should aim at decency, not excellence. We cannot draw the lines a priori, but in every case there is something to plan for and much to refrain from planning for. This often means when to technologize, to achieve a decent background, and when not to technologize, to achieve freedom.

Contrast an ideal forest preserve with a real State park. The forest preserve would be a kind of museum. We would put a hedge around a piece of the past, the antiquity of the globe untouched, saying that this place is not to change. You would come there by car but enter on foot. You may camp where you choose but there are no campsites and you

31

don't need a permit—only be prudent and don't set the trees on fire.
The forest preserve would be a kind of wilderness area with no rules
whatever. But the State park is part of the urban complex; it is an
extension into the green places of the rules of the city. You need a
permit to camp and must camp at the specified places. This has
advantages; you have a platform, and wood and water are provided.
The fee is nominal, but there *is* a fee.

When I was young, we could freely pitch a tent on Fire Island
Beach and freely build our fires or build a shack and squat. Because of
the pressure of real estate developers, this has been forbidden and you
now cannot squat in the sun and wind; many more cops patrol the
beach and it is part of their duties to see that you do not. One feels
trapped. One must make social arrangements and pay rent. But it is
not the money that is onerous, it is that one has to obey their rules.
They have planned for us, no matter how benevolent the plan.

The possibility of an escape into freedom from social rules is, of
course, the pastoral ideal, as well described by Leo Marx. But the
pastoral ideal can apply also in urban places. (Some of my novels
have been called urban pastorals, and so they are.) One of the objec-
tions to much recent architecture and public housing is that it presents
an impenetrable glass front; there are no holes and basements to creep
into for games and sex. The waterfront has been improved into a
concrete wall or a lovely promenade; there are no railroad yards or
abandoned piers where one could hide from truant officers or fish. It is
interesting that Jane Jacobs, who is a zealot against the new architecture because she wants to preserve neighborly sociability, nevertheless
balks at the pastoral ideal of dark places and nooks. She wants everything bright and public, for safety. And to be sure, urban life has
become more dangerous than the jungle. But I doubt that safety can
be assured by architectural design or doormen. People who feel
trapped and powerless will follow you home or finally assault you in
public.

The philosophical point I wish to make is that there must be a kind
of constitutional limit to planning, even at the expense of efficiency
and the "best" solution. An analogy is the protection of freedom of

speech in the Bill of Rights. In the interpretation of the "absolutists," Justices Black and Douglas, freedom of speech is not to be balanced in terms of its social aspects, it is anarchic, prior to law—you can say what you damned please, up to the limits of actual emergency, however troublesome, violent, or conflictful your speech may be. And as a writer, let me say that unless I have this freedom of speech, I do not have freedom at all. I cannot know beforehand what words will come to me, and if I feel that there is a limit to what I can say, then nothing new will ever come to me.

A realistic method of guaranteeing freedom from excessive physical planning and social engineering is to condone or even encourage people's resistance to them. I say "realistic" because there is in effect a rising wave of popular protest in the country. The courts can encourage resistance by a tolerant attitude toward sit-ins, certain kinds of trespass, and civil disobedience. Bureaucratic control can be largely delegated away to "black power," "student power," etc. And it would be advantageous to replace many bureaucratically-run social services with a guaranteed income, which would enable powerless people to form their own cooperatives and suit themselves. These countervailing factors would then have to be taken into account in the programs of the social engineers. At present, needless to say, politicians who have to cadge votes are acutely conscious of inarticulate popular resistance and do draw the line. But planners disregard it because it is inarticulate, and since they—organized, rational, and well-financed—have more staying power than the populace, there is steady encroachment on freedom.

Another method of guaranteeing freedom from excessive planning brings me back to my first point, the revival of old-fashioned professionals responsible to clients and the immediate community rather than to society and social trends. Unless people become things, they will always live in the small scale as well as the big scale, and more intensely in the small scale than in the big scale. It is the role of their professionals, whom they ought to be able to hire and fire, to articulate, interpret, and design for them their small-scale needs in education, medicine, law, and housing. These will inevitably include spontaneity, individual differences, personal response, local options, and the need for freedom. Big-scale planners and social engineers will then have something articulate to cope with.

With this much introduction, let me launch into some remarks on rural reconstruction as interpreted in modern conditions. I want to propose a new look at rural-urban symbiosis.

It is important to understand that the present urbanization throughout the world is not a result of technological advance. Indeed, the thrust of modern technology has been against urbanization; consider electrification, power tools, telephone, radio and television, the automobile. And automation implies, if anything, the concentration of a great plant in a small space with a few workers, and the freedom of location of the programmers and the managers. Patrick Geddes assumed that with electrification the cities, amassed around steam power, would cease to grow. Ralph Borsodi thought that power tools would lead to dispersal, and Frank Lloyd Wright thought that the automobile would do it. Marx and Engels and Kropotkin blamed excessive urbanization on the power structure and looked to a better rural-urban symbiosis.

As has always been the case, our present urbanization is the consequence of a policy of enclosure. Poor people and farmers never leave home willingly. The young leave the land for adventure and bright lights; the especially gifted have to seek out the centers of culture and opportunity. But the mass of country people stay as long as they can make a living. Enclosure takes place in various ways. In the 18th century they shut off the commons to raise sheep; at the same time the city factories were developing and needed cheap labor, so there was a place for desperate farmers to find work, beginning at age nine. This combination of the "squirearchy" and the new capitalists is described in *The Deserted Village* and by Wordsworth. In our own century, during the 70 years that we have had control in Puerto Rico, we have destroyed this beautiful and fertile land by another classical method; old-fashioned mercantilism of the genre of George III. We have forbidden the Puerto Ricans to ship and travel directly without touching at United States ports, we have imposed severe quota restrictions on the processing of Puerto Rican sugar, we have ruled out coffee, and we have sequestered the more fertile plain for industrial use. Thus we have destroyed the agricultural base. But in the past two decades we have imposed on the top a thin crust of high technology and now the country is ravaged. Thirty-five percent of the population is on relief. People flee a thousand a week to New York, and flee back a thousand a week to the slums of San Juan. In other parts of the world, for example the Virgin Islands or Latin America, enclosure occurs by the importation of some industry, e.g. oil or hotels, with a wildly inflationary standard. A few natives are paid $70 a week where the average cash income was $70 a year. Then the *campesinos,* in sheer self-respect must flock to the city where there is no provision for them; they settle in thousands in tin shacks and die of cholera. Meantime, there is no effort to subdivide the land and get rid of feudal landowners; when there is such an effort, we dispatch the Marines.

Our American enclosure—the rural population is now 6 percent actually farming—has come about through cooperation in the American cash style amounting virtually to a conspiracy among chaingrocers, big plantations, suburban developers, and highway bureaucrats, steadily abetted by public policy. It is said to be efficient, and, indeed, one farmer can now feed thirty. Nevertheless, the price of food has *not* fallen (during the war in Vietnam, of course, it has risen), although the farmers' take has declined by about 8 percent a decade. Nor indeed do the retailers make much—at A & P wages are low and still the profit on store sales is 1 percent; 11 percent of A & P's 12 percent profit goes to their own middlemen, packagers, processors, transporters, jobbers. Thus it seems clear that the new "agrindustry" is not all that efficient. At present, 70¢ of the food dollar is spent in national chains and, naturally, food technology has been developed according to this pattern. If the technologists had put their wits to intensive agriculture by small growers, as in Holland, no doubt that method too would have become much more efficient.

The result has been depopulation of vast areas of the country at the same time that there are evident signs of overpopulation in the urban areas. As John Calhoun puts it, there are too many social signals in urban centers, so that the circuits are clogged and normal development is impossible; there is not enough social space for trying out, there is too much noise, there is no solitude to develop personality, all experience is preprocessed, there is no relief from chronic anxiety. Of one million Negroes in New York, more than half came during the last 20 years as a result of the failure of southern sharecropping. Seven hundred thousand Puerto Ricans have come to New York City in the past 30 years. Of course, since New York has a housing shortage, it is necessary to provide public housing. This costs $20,000 a unit—which money could have been spent to keep the immigrants in the country. Clearly if the Negroes had wanted to come north, they would have done so 40 years ago, for they were not well treated in Mississippi and Alabama.

At present, however, or certainly during this generation, there is no chance of rural reconstruction on an agricultural base; indeed, the skills are rapidly vanishing. Possibly there may be a revival of specialized intensive farming, selling fresh food to nearby cities, if people can begin to demand a quality standard of living. This cannot occur in the ring surrounding the cities, for that has been suburbanized, but conceivably it might happen in the next ring.

But there is a chance of rural revival on a different principle: to help solve urban problems that are not easily or cheaply soluble in urban conditions. Such a principle would bring the country into the mainstream of modern problems, which are urban, and it would channel urban cash into rural areas now depopulating. Consider some possibilities.

It is advantageous for city children to spend a year or two at a country school and live on a family farm. Something similar is not uncommon for the upper middle class, but it would be profoundly awakening for slum children who have not, by age 13, been half a mile from home. Cost per child in a New York school is $850 a year; for little more than this sum one could help support the failing rural school and provide worthwhile cash for a farmer (perhaps three children to a farmer, who need merely feed them well and not beat them). The Farmers' Union and the 4-H clubs have offered to administer such a program.

It is advantageous to allow urban welfare money to be used for living in a rural neighborhood. Twenty-five hundred dollars buys destitution in a big city, but in a depopulating area, where one can also farm for part of subsistence, it provides a very decent life, including running an old car. Indeed, if we had a rational world, it would be possible for welfare recipients to use urban welfare money in foreign regions which have noninflationary prices, e.g., parts of Mexico, Crete, Sicily.

In our present system of enclosure, country vacations in motels and resorts have become part of the urban system. It would be advantageous to try to revive something more like the old visiting of country cousins at the farm.

The majority of patients in big mental institutions are harmless but cannot cope, or would hurt themselves and stop traffic, in urban environments. Very many are really getting no treatment and are just rotting away, though at great social expense. For the same money they could be boarded with rural families, and there is evidence that in such conditions there would be more remissions.

In functions like these, I am drawing on the classical pattern of regionalism, the capital and its country in symbiosis, each with a contrasting but complementary set of conditions and functions. This is, of course, the opposite of our homogenizing "conurbation" and regional planning. And the meaning of contemporary endless suburbanization is that one is never really in the city or in the country. The center becomes blighted and decays; the country is depopulated and returns to swamp. In the conurbation, regional planning means highway planning, smog planning, or efforts to equalize taxation; these are necessary, of course, but hardly sufficient for human needs.

The symbiotic conception of an urban-rural region requires administrative changes, e.g., to use New York City school money or welfare money in Vermont, central Pennsylvania, or the northern counties of New York. Or to use urban public housing money for improving farms in Mississippi or Alabama.

Rural reconstruction on this basis could well be culturally administered by revived Land Grant colleges, whose functions have now entirely been perverted to teaching urban know-how (usually in a second-rate fashion). Likewise there ought to be a renascence of local newspapers, which are now nothing but advertising and gossip sheets.

And there ought to be established numerous local radio and TV stations—each region can have 17 television channels, of which usually only two are in use. There cannot be rural reconstruction unless one's home place stands for something and is worth remaining in; but there are ways to strive for this.

In conclusion, let me repeat that I do not think there can be a significant cutback in urbanization in this generation. Nevertheless, the kind of rural reconstruction proposed can alleviate urban problems in terms of 2 percent of this and 5 percent of that. More important, it recreates options in an increasingly monolithic society. And finally, the pattern of rural subsistence with sources of cash from providing useful social services is tranquil and beautiful in itself.

# THE NATURAL HISTORY
# OF URBANISM

ROBERT McC. ADAMS

ROBERT MCC. ADAMS

DR. ROBERT MCC. ADAMS brings to his essay on urbanism some 17 years of archeological fieldwork in Iraq, Iran, and Mexico where his researches centered on irrigation, land use, and urban settlement. His prime interests are reflected in his major published works: *Land Behind Baghdad* (1965) and *The Evolution of Urban Society* (1966). Dr. Adams has also edited, with C. H. Kraeling, *City Invincible: a Symposium on Urbanization and Cultural Development in the Ancient Near East.*

At the age of 29, Dr. Adams joined the faculty of the University of Chicago in 1955. Since 1962 he has been the Director of the Oriental Institute of the University of Chicago. In 1966–67, he was the Annual Professor at the Baghdad School of the American Schools of Oriental Research.

Dr. Adams is a fellow of the American Academy of Arts and Sciences, the American Association for the Advancement of Science, Sigma Xi, and the American Anthropological Association. He is also a member of the Society for American Archaeology and the German Archaeological Institute.

THE UNDERLYING BOND between cities and their hinterlands is that the existence of the former depends upon their capacity to mobilize and deploy the latters' agricultural surpluses. Perhaps this is a truism, but like all truisms it obscures a complex reality. Does it imply that major steps in urban development have depended upon prior improvements in agricultural productivity rather than vice versa? What meaning can be ascribed to the concept of an agricultural surplus that is independent of the social system in which it is voluntarily brought forward as offerings, forcibly extracted as taxes, or exchanged for other goods and services in an urban market? How much, in fact, of the whole range of interactions between city and countryside is accurately epitomized by a statement of their purely economic relationship?

Merely to ask these questions evokes a less constrictive approach. To understand the origins and evolution of urban centers, including the diversity of their institutional arrangements and physical forms, we must deal with city and countryside not only as opposed abstractions on an economic plane but as intimately interacting parts of an embracing cultural and ecological system.

Granting that such an undertaking may be of some historical or philosophical interest, what relevance does it have today as we grope for solutions to an unprecedented urban crisis? One argument, of course, is that the past continues to exercise a subtle but pervasive influence upon our perception of present realities. In this sense, as Benedetto Croce observed, all history is contemporary history. It must be studied if the patterns of thought and action we inherit are to be understood or even recognized and, in any case, these patterns cannot simply be excised at will from our present lives.

Equally important, the technological destruction of distance that characterizes our epoch is rapidly tending to fuse all of the metropolises of the world into instances of a single type. Hence some thought about earlier cities that were less closely in interaction with one another may help to clarify the basic attributes of cities generally. If we stress the positive and negative features of urbanism as a broad category of settlement and adaptation, features which in some cases have preserved an uneasy balance over millenniums, it may help us also to modify the sense of complete and wasteful novelty with which all too frequently current problems are regarded.

In long term evolutionary perspective, the growth of cities very closely followed the introduction of agriculture. No more than four to six millenniums seem to have separated the first reliance on domesticates—for even a minor proportion of the diet—from the emergence of settlements whose size and complexity unambiguously attest to their full urban status. In contrast to the many hundreds of millenniums of man's earlier biological and cultural development, this is a relatively insignificant interval. About the same interval, it might be noted, separated the Urban Revolution from the Industrial Revolution. Industrialism followed and was dependent upon certain concomitants of urban life: the accumulative growth of technology, the elaboration of economic systems permitting the support of craft specialists, and the appearance of a class of entrepreneurs able to mobilize capital for ends not previously sanctioned. It is hardly very useful, however, to say that the latter development was a *consequence* of the former. In the same way, the Food-Producing and the Urban Revolutions also must be distinguished from one another, even while we recognize that the order in which they occurred was a necessary and inevitable one.

What is more important about both agriculture and urbanism is that both originated independently in a number of widely separated centers in the Old and New Worlds rather than diffusing outward from a single source. This complicates the task of generalizing about their interrelationships, in that both similarities and differences between the separate instances need to be taken into account. On the other hand, the fact that there were essentially independent sequences of change culminating in roughly similar institutional arrangements highlights regularities in the processes of change and lends importance to the search for causal explanations of them. A systematic analysis of these regularities is severely limited, to be sure, by the narrowly specialized concerns and inherent obscurity of the early written sources. Prior to the advent of writing—generally, but not in all cases, closely associated with the onset of urban civilization itself—we are confronted with the still more severe shortcomings of a purely archeological record. Given such evidence, the fact that there were indisputable regularities is not as helpful as it might seem. Only an irrepressible optimist would assume that wide consensus and a real sense of closure are soon to be realized on even the basic processes involved.

Within the limitations of our data, conditions antecedent to the first appearance of urban centers can be quickly sketched. Although the beginnings of agriculture closely followed the end of the Pleistocene, they cannot be explained as merely the consequence of a new set of environmental conditions. To be sure, the introduction and spread of agricultural techniques was almost explosively far-reaching and rapid in comparison with the earlier, almost imperceptible, pace of increasing hunting-gathering efficiency and cultural complexity. Yet all the potential domesticates were confined to regions far removed from the marked climatic and life-zone changes associated with the advance and retreat of the glaciers. And such environmental changes as there were, differed little from those that occurred repeatedly during earlier, warmer intervals of the Pleistocene. Having crossed some ill-defined threshold of complexity, what was apparently different some nine or ten thousand years ago was man's capacity to rapidly elaborate new responses to long preexisting environmental potentials.

Examples of this enhanced adaptive capacity can be found in many regions of both the Old and New Worlds. Perhaps the widest and most easily observed development was in the direction of increasing sedentism. Particularly favored were environmental niches in which different food resources complemented one another, permitting substantial enlargement of the local group through the full turn of seasons while at the same time reducing dependence upon migration. Technical innovations also played a part. While naturally there were differences from region to region, such improvements regularly included composite tools and weapons: the bow and arrow; ground stone utensils appropriate for carpentry, food preparation, and other uses; and new devices for transport with a potential importance by no means confined to the food quest.

The independent origins of agriculture in the Near East, Mesoamerica, and probably other regions can be thought of as manifestations of these widely occurring developments under circumstances in which the local biota included species of plants and animals that could be domesticated and utilized with the foraging, extractive, and culinary technology at hand. Retrospectively, the line between hunting or harvesting wild resources and consciously planting or breeding them appears to us as a Rubicon, but the portents of crossing it must not have been apparent to those who first did so. In the early post-Pleistocene milieu of increasingly assured manipulation and control of local food resources of all kinds, the elaboration of techniques we deem agricultural must have taken the form of intensified experimentation and a resultant sequence of small, locally variable improvements along already familiar lines.

The major initial effect of an agricultural mode of subsistence was the extension of the zones of settled life far beyond the restricted niches in which the potential domesticates originally were at home. Spreading outward from numerous local centers for particular species, such zones soon overlapped extensively. Agriculture was rendered more secure as a mode of subsistence through this increase in the varieties of domestic resources, and its seasonal cycle and requisite techniques were increasingly differentiated from those for hunting and gathering. The extent of the divergence between early agricultural economies and their precursors, however, should not be overestimated. Given still primitive techniques, the limited caloric value of many of the early cultigens, and almost uncounted natural hazards, the relative security and productiveness that we associate with agriculture was not within reach. As a way of life it was perhaps more continuously demanding than hunting and gathering, with the participation of all but the very young and very old being required in subsistence pursuits. Percentage calculations of dietary intake are possible only in rare instances, but the general pattern clearly was one of a necessary, continuing reliance on a broad spectrum of domesticates, weeds of cultivation, and naturally occurring foods.

With the establishment of a settled, agricultural, way of life, a new set of ecological processes can be discerned. To generalize from the Mesopotamian and Mesoamerican cases in which the data is most abundant, the regions of earliest urban growth were *not* identical with those in which agriculture had originated. One of the essential features of this geographical shift probably was the development of more

44

intensive agricultural techniques for which previously marginal areas now became optimal, although we remain very poorly informed about the nature and timing of major innovations like irrigation, complementary planting of mixed crops to assure fertility, and the plow. Such innovations would permit the formation of greater food surpluses by individual agricultural producers. Perhaps more important, they also freed certain members of the community for at least part-time specialization and encouraged the accumulation of stores with which to meet periodic shortages.

On this basis a trend toward increasing population seems fairly certain. It is difficult, however, to confirm such a trend from the limited and indirect evidence of changing settlement patterns and the minuscule portions of archeological sites that generally are excavated. Thus, all that can be said with confidence is that the frontiers of agriculture continued to expand rapidly. And at the frontiers, of course, we must reckon not only with natural increases in population resulting from agriculture but also with the direct conversion to agriculture of former hunter-gatherers.

Perhaps the most reasonable demographic reconstruction at present is that, while there was some increase in population density generated by the shift to more intensive forms of cultivation, the scarce resource in early civilizations generally remained people rather than land. Accordingly, movement was relatively easy and there was little demographic inducement for the emergence of stable polities. Periodic reshufflings prevented the sharp polarization of society into small groups exercising a tight monopoly of productive resources and the resultant reduction of other groups to the permanent status of dependent retainers. If this is so, other factors must have been the primary motive forces behind the formation of early states: chronic inequalities in productivity between different regions; the selectively impoverishing effects of the numerous natural hazards to agricultural subsistence; the accumulative growth of redistributive institutions once they had passed beyond a certain critical threshold of size; and, perhaps, the military advantages conferred on those types of social organization best able to equip and mobilize large bodies of militia or professional soldiery.

45

Viewed from the standpoint not of labor productivity but of land productivity, the effects of agricultural intensification may have been equally significant. Means of transport remained primitive; in most of the New World only human portage was available, but even in the Near East the economic use of wheeled vehicles apparently followed the appearance of urban civilization only after a long interval. Hence, long-distance movements were confined to strategic raw materials and luxuries. Those agricultural hinterlands whose surpluses could be economically brought in to sustain the growth of population centers were of very limited radius. Techniques leading to increased output per unit area therefore directly permitted an increase in settlement size.

In short, increased size and density were perhaps the crucial characteristics of early urban centers. Numerous general treatises on cities notwithstanding, there is no evidence that the onset of urbanization was accompanied—much less caused—by rapid, significant changes in the prevailing division of labor. The overwhelming proportion of the population continued for some time to be engaged primarily in agricultural pursuits, as was still the case until very recently with many African cities. Congregated in large settlements, city dwellers were more easily subject to political control, taxation, military service, and corvee labor, but the contribution of specialized, urban crafts to the satisfaction of their primary needs remained extremely small. The small handfuls of craftsmen, scribes, and other specialists found in early cities were, for the most part, in the service of the major institutions and were employed primarily in the production of military equipment and ritual articles required for cult observances.

There was another feature of the newly emergent, intensive agricultural regimes which was central to the ensuing growth of urban societies. The areas in which independent civilizations originated seem to have been characterized by a series of specialized microenvironments for which different, equally specialized, subsistence pursuits were appropriate. Such was the case, for example, with the lateral succession of fishing, farming, and herding as one moved away from the major watercourses in the Near East, or with the replacement of one crop complex by another with increasing altitudes in the Mesoamerican and Andean highlands. The existence of interdependent zones of this type

46

fostered the formation of "symbiotic regions" within which the complementary distribution of subsistence products could be effected. To deal with this new order of complexity, it is not suprising that writing systems were invented or independently elaborated, in turn permitting further increases in administrative complexity and lending formality and continuity to urban traditions. To the extent that these developments contributed to the formation of centralized institutions, the personnel and facilities of the latter could only contribute to the further growth of the principal settlements in which they were located.

The tempo and sequence of these ecological trends in relation to the onset of urban life still is largely obscure. There are at least a few well-documented cases to suggest that the initial growth of cities was generally rapid, sometimes even being the outcome of conscious policies applied within a single generation. Hence the achievement of the forms of civilized, urban life was relatively sudden; nevertheless, the fashioning and consolidation of the base that could support an urban superstructure may have been a much longer process. Almost certainly, for example, there were mechanisms of interzonal exchange and redistribution available and functioning on some level before new urban elites arose to redirect and administer them. To judge from comparable societies studied by recent ethnographers, somewhat similar purposes can be served by a variety of devices that do not presuppose the submission of scattered communities of agriculturalists to some paramount leadership. Bride-wealth payments linking exogamous, differently specialized communities are among such devices. So also are cycles of cult observances in shifting localities, which provide not only for the movement of religious ideas and pilgrims but also of goods.

In addition, there was undeniably at least some ordinary trade in items that were hardly luxuries long antedating the appearance of cities; obsidian for the manufacture of finely chipped stone tools is a widely occurring case in point. "Trade" in this sense, however, is a gross, essentially uninformative term that does nothing to clarify the relationship between the participating prehistoric communities or the manner in which such relationships were affected by the subsequent rise of urban centers. Fortunately, recent advances in archeological

47

methodology suggest that we can soon move beyond the mere recognition of exotic materials to a quantitative analysis of some of the components of social behavior by which that material was circulated.

It may be useful at this point to restate the ecological role of early cities at the time of their origins. They seem fairly generally to have functioned as junction points or nodes in the appropriation and redistribution of agricultural surpluses. In addition, they provided a permanent base for the operation of new institutions that no longer merely mediated but, instead, authoritatively administered the interrelationships between specialized producers occupying adjacent eco-niches. Such institutions were embedded in realms of cultural meaning not confined to their primary ecological functions, including attempts on many levels to unify, symbolize, and stabilize the newly emergent, urban-dominated social patterns. Cities became focal points not merely for the safe storage of surpluses prior to their deployment, but for conspicuous expenditures for public building programs, for the maintenance of elites in luxurious surroundings, and for the enhancement of military power. With the concentration of wealth, early urban centers became both proponents of expansionism and powerful incentives for external attack. Massive fortifications accordingly became one of their dominant architectural forms.

A summary like the foregoing is necessarily abstract and generalized. It emphasizes recurrent features at the expense of known variations and lacunae in the evidence, hence perhaps seeming to imply that early cities everywhere were the outcome of a tightly interconnected, uniform set of causal processes. It may be taken to imply further that the superior adaptive potential of the city led in some direct fashion to its origin and contributed decisively to the spread of urbanism. What could be more advantageous, after all, than state-protected, rationally allocated stores of surpluses to compensate for year-to-year fluctuations in harvest? Or centralized investment in and control of irrigation canals and other facilities for intensive agriculture and the improvement of transport?

Although perhaps not incorrect at some fairly high level of abstraction, both implications are misleading. The subsequent growth and spread of cities cannot be understood as the irresistible sweep of a set

48

of innovations which were obviously superior in socioeconomic terms. Instead, the process by which cities assumed the ecologically dominant role we now associate with them consisted of a shifting, complex, quite unstable, adjustment of environmental, economic, technological, political, and even ideological factors. Cumulatively, of course, the trend was irrevocably toward urbanism, but contained within this worldwide trend extending over millenniums were repeated advances and reverses at the local level. To understand this irregularity we must consider not just later increments in urbanism but also some of the attendant costs and dangers.

Perhaps the most informative single index of the subsequent evolution of cities is the increase in size. Early direct testimony on this is notoriously untrustworthy, so that historical demographers must depend on the convergence of secondary, approximate, probabilistic lines of reasoning. Even the order of magnitude of the population of particular cities often remains a matter of sharp debate, although there is broad agreement that older claims of immense size must be viewed with increasing skepticism. As a generalization for the Old World, probably no city was larger than several tens of thousands of inhabitants before the first millennium B.C., while by the Middle Ages cities of several hundreds of thousands occurred at intervals in the Mediterranean basin and across Asia to China. The picture is somewhat more obscure in the civilized areas of the aboriginal New World; the earlier stage certainly had been attained by not long after the time of Christ, while the onset of the second stage may have been close at hand when the independent sequence of development was ended by the Spanish Conquest.

Undoubtedly these parallel, decisive increases reflect improvements in the subsistence economy, but it is important to note that any such improvements rested on technical innovations only to a limited degree. In the aboriginal New World, in fact, crop complexes and methods of cultivation both seem to have remained remarkably stable. The Andean area offers partial exceptions, but at least in Mesoamerica there is no evidence for any significant advance in the technology or organization of agriculture from remote precivilized times until the flourishing urban societies so vividly described by the Spaniards.

49

To be sure, some new, specialized crops like sugar and silk were brought under cultivation in the Old World, many of them for the first time of a highly labor-intensive character suitable to increasing populations. With the exception of the westward spread of irrigated ricelands, however, few of the new items became subsistence staples. The harnessing of wind and water power for rotary movement was important in the spread of agriculture into arid areas and in reducing the costs of milling and similar operations, but its direct contribution to urban growth was hardly a major one.

The introduction of iron presents a somewhat more complicated case, although not a basically dissimilar one. With the rapidly spreading adoption of iron during the first millennium B.C., into the hands of agriculturalists came implements that were not only more durable than bronze but that could be produced much more cheaply and from more widely scattered bodies of ore. The availability of iron, however, led only very slowly to the development of more efficient tools and processing techniques. Probably its primary effects on urban life were associated instead with its low cost. Iron tools now became available to ordinary workmen deployed in large numbers on major public works directed toward the extension and improvement of agricultural lands. Partly as a consequence, the intensity of agriculture in the neighborhood of cities was increased through the formation of encircling "green belts" of irrigated, continuously cultivated orchards and truck gardens. Some areas of formerly limited agricultural potential also were transformed, including the Iranian plateau and parts of North Africa, with corresponding effects upon their political importance.

If the immediate hinterlands of cities were not converted by this process into metropolitan areas in the modern sense, they were nonetheless integrated into an urban-centered society to an unprecedented degree. To take only economic features for which the evidence is least ambiguous and most durable, there was a—not steady but, on the whole, cumulative—reduction in the self-sufficiency of even outlying peasant communities. To the eye of the reconnoitering archeologist, for example, a litter of iron, glazed pottery sherds, glass, and fired brick fragments, immediately distinguishes Near Eastern sites of all sizes occupied after roughly the time of Alexander from any earlier ones. All of these remains were the products of urban specialists which, after more than a millennium of having been largely restricted to official or luxury use, passed into general circulation with dramatic suddenness and irreversible effect. Coinage was perhaps the most important of the widely circulated new features, and it was also the only recent innovation among them. Its crucial significance lay not in any contribution to advancing technology but in the networks of economic interrelations that it facilitated: it was through these networks that other craft products reached wider, peasant markets.

As this suggests, the increase in urban size by a full order of magnitude was primarily a reflection of developments in political economy rather than in technology. The earlier, territorially consolidated unit was the city state, which either maintained itself as an island in a barbarian sea or else contended periodically with neighboring units of the same kind within a framework of regional rivalries and ephemeral alliances. In time, larger administrative units—of which the Third Dynasty of Ur and the Dynasty of Hammurabi in Babylon (and perhaps the Egyptian Old Kingdom, at an even earlier period) are good examples—began to make their appearance. Wider conquests were extended outward from a firmly pacified if not unified heartland, until, after a few generations, the thinness of the centralized administrative veneer became apparent. Then the old fissures reopened in the home territory and the assertions of hegemony over distant areas gradually were dropped.

By contrast, the great cities of classical and later times characteristically came into being as components of large, relatively long-lived, continental empires. Such cities were creatures of strong patrimonial regimes to a degree quite unmatched earlier. They directly depended on royal largesse for the support of the now predominant proportion of artisans, tradesmen, soldiers, and petty officials. Not infrequently, royal intervention was even more tangibly reflected in their planned, overall layouts.

As part of a wider spectrum of efforts to maintain or enlarge the central power and to prevent its devolution into the hands of a newly emergent landed nobility, these later cities were founded, manipulated, and (at times) even abandoned almost by royal whim. Behind numerous instances of capricious exercise of power, however, lay conscious policies of shifting populations to destroy parochial loyalties and of strengthening the administrative fabric over the whole realm. Unprecedented emphasis was attached to improvements in communications, with the development of "Royal Roads," post routes, and local garrisons and caravansaries to assure security of movement. With the relative success of these policies for long periods, warfare for the most part could be limited to distant frontiers with barbarians or to zones of contention with rival powers of like magnitude. This, in turn, permitted more intensive, long-range development of the vital central regions of empires, aided by the flow of refugees and captives inward from the frontiers.

Under circumstances like these, the ecology of cities no longer can be understood in terms of their immediate sustaining areas. By medieval times, many individual Old World cities were widely identified with particular specialized products—Damascus blades, Mosul muslins, Bokhara carpets, Venetian silks—confirming the existence of highly institutionalized, long-distance trade for which the stimulus and setting had become a genuinely international one. Rome in the first century A.D. was probably exceptional, in that a third of its wheat had to be shipped in from Egypt. To judge from studies of relatively recent examples of the same kind, virtually all of the necessary food supplies for most other preindustrial cities continued to be drawn from very limited, adjacent areas. But the raison d'être of all these imperial centers, as well as the explanation for the periodic rise and decline in their fortunes, lay in the policies and problems of patrimonial regimes which, like the cities themselves, had attained a new order of size.

We must return, however, to the price that had to be paid for these achievements. To begin with, for all but the most recent chapter of urban history, cities have not been sources of population growth but of severe population loss. It is uncertain whether preindustrial urban life was normally associated with lowered birth rates, but there is no doubt that urban mortality rates were much higher than rural ones prior to the very recent introduction of effective measures for public health. The increased density and aggregate size of settlement, in relation to primitive techniques of sanitation and other means of controlling vectors of disease, could only lead not just to greater periodic losses in epidemics but also to heightened mortality, particularly of infants and children, as a regularly prevailing feature. The growth of cities, and even their continuing existence, accordingly was always dependent on an inflow of population from rural districts and smaller towns.

The founding or expansion of cities that was repeatedly boasted of by strong rulers in antiquity could have been either an expression of the accelerated movement of urban immigrants in search of the prosperity that followed in the wake of conquest, or a consequence of the extension of more coercive forms of royal control over the countryside. Neither alternative substantially affected the urban-rural differences in mortality rates, except in the sense that exceptionally short-sighted and acquisitive regimes could compensate to a degree by substantially depressing the living standards of the rural peasantry. Attitudes of conscious and sustained encouragement for rural well-being on the whole are distinguished in historical records by their rarity, seldom occurring except at times of unusual political stability. Under most circumstances, there were practical difficulties in drawing off so large a surplus that the agricultural producers were reduced to or below a bare subsistence margin. But it is noteworthy that, at least in the Near East, general movement in time of famine was toward cities and not away from them. With absentee landlords and predatory officials, as well as with sustained high levels of banditry and periodic nomadic incursions, it would appear from this that reserves of food adequate to meet prolonged crises seldom could be accumulated in smaller settlements.

While the concentration of surpluses in urban centers brought some relative immunity from fluctuations in the harvest, this boon frequently was accompanied by an exposure to new perils. Traditions associated with urban institutions have a force and continuity of their own, limiting the mobility of city populations in response to disastrous changes in local environmental conditions. Any tendency toward increased full-time specialization in nonagricultural pursuits, of course, would have the same effect. Intensified urban pressure on agricultural resources can, and in some important cases evidently did, lead to soil

53

exhaustion or, as a consequence of over-irrigation, to crippling increases in soil salinity. The substitution of monocrop cultivation for diversified agriculture, apparently as a dependent rural extension of urban, market-oriented economies, is widely known for its attendant impoverishment of both the land and the husbandman. Policies of excessive taxation made necessary by overextended urban establishments sometimes led to the abandonment of villages and farmlands, further accentuating the imbalance between rural capacities and urban demands.

There were drawbacks even where the positive contribution of the state seems most apparent. For example, the substitution of large-scale, state-run irrigation works for smaller, locally maintained systems enlarged the agricultural base on which cities could depend and placed new powers of control in the hands of their elites. However, because such systems were beyond the capacity of local agriculturalists to administer and maintain, they were dependent on the—altogether unlikely—permanent conjunction of urban economic strength, political stability, and favorable attitudes toward rural investment. Moreover, the truly large-scale systems of the last twenty-five hundred years or so, through the increased supplies of water they assured and their disruption of natural drainage patterns, vastly increased the dangers of salinization and consequent land abandonment.

What all of these processes have in common is the increased systemic fragility to which they led. Perhaps the clearest, most dismal reflection of that fragility was that both rural and urban population curves apparently were characterized by a succession of marked peaks and troughs, quite in contrast to the steady and rising curves of the last few centuries. The approach of an urban ecological climax, in other words, was only attained—prior to the Industrial Revolution—at the cost of a dangerous narrowing of ecological alternatives.

"Rural" and "urban" generally are employed as polar opposites, but the examples just cited suggest that from an ecological standpoint this is seriously misleading. Both categories represent a conflation of related and unrelated features, not all of which correspond neatly to the more or less assumed gross differences between the two. In fact, it would appear that the most essential characteristic of urban and rural

adaptations was not their mutual isolation but their historic comple-
mentarity and interdependence. At best, they are somewhat arbitrarily
defined components of a single, embracing, cultural-environmental
system, each changing only in close response to changes in the other.
The dichotomy between "rural" and "urban" which still persists in our
thinking probably reflects an even deeper failure to understand that
developments both in city politics and subsistence economics ultimately converge in their effects upon the success or failure of a society's whole pattern of adaptive responses to its environmental setting.
Embodied in written traditions that formerly were largely limited to
and inculcated by urban elites unfamiliar with agriculture, this misun-
derstanding continues to exert a negative influence on academic judgment and administrative policy.

The special biases and limitations of written traditions preserved by
urban elites have seriously distorted our understanding of the historical ecology of cities in a number of other respects. Most important is
the narrowness of the recorded tradition itself, with its concentration
on urban politics and state administrative records, cults devoted to city
deities, and military struggles between rival polities. From such
sources, very little can be learned of the relationship between town
and countryside, since what lay outside the walls simply was not felt to
be worthy of notice. This bias persists even in the accounts of literate
travelers familiar with rural districts. For example, there are many
descriptions of ancient and medieval Near Eastern cities, often quite
detailed and almost modern in their objective quality, but it is not until
the European accounts of the last few centuries that we begin to find
commonplace references to conditions in smaller towns and villages
along the caravan routes between the major centers.

To make matters worse, this absence of written reference to rural
conditions has been accentuated by the concentration of archeological
excavations in the same major centers from which the textual sources
stem. Until quite recently the principal motivation for archeological
research on historic periods has been the finding of monumental buildings and tombs, with the hoped-for association of luxury goods and
written records. Fortunately, this objective has now broadened in
conformity with the interests of the social sciences: there is an awak-

ening interest in regional studies, for example, in which entire settlement patterns are scrutinized with the aid of sampling procedures. But it will be many years before archeological data from minor settlements begins to permit an understanding of their nature and importance.

Even insofar as early urban chronicles are indirectly relevant to their wider, extramural context, there are serious distortions somehow to be overcome. Literary stereotypes abound, with the individual husbandman regarded patronizingly as ignorant and docile while the aggregate of rural dwellers, on their own ground, were pictured as brutish and terrifying. Such stereotypes, lumping together diverse interests and modes of life, conceal important roots of change in rural society. To some degree, they probably also overstress its passivity in contrast to urban initiative. Not unnaturally, mention was more likely to be made of sporadic urban contributions to rural well-being than to continuing interrelations which prevailingly ran the other way. Responsibility is claimed repeatedly for the initiation of irrigation projects, for example, but their subsequent neglect by urban administrators seldom receives mention and the assignment of blame for their abandonment solely to external enemies usually is more than doubtful. Only the rare and usually ineffectual reformer speaks of the oppressive affects upon the countryside of the manipulation of urban credit. Yet in the dangerously uncertain world of the peasant, the need for credit was endlessly renewed and always vital.

The traditional character of literary sources deriving from largely illiterate societies leads to assertions of continuity which are also doubtful. Neither changes in basic institutional patterns nor major cycles of urban growth and abandonment penetrated this stream of recorded consciousness in any necessary proportion to their effects upon the society at large. Furthermore, there is always a problem with observations or statements which applied not to whole regions or countries but to privileged groups in the principal cities alone. After the breakdown of the authority of the Egyptian Old Kingdom, for example, there are literary dirges uniformly attesting to widespread destruction, unrest, and impoverishment; yet contemporary provincial cemeteries contained luxuries that were previously monopolized by the capital and court.

56

In a larger sense then, literary sources oriented toward the interests of narrow social elites probably have permanently obscured the character of the societies in question. It is not merely the rural peasantry but large segments of the urban population about whom we learn only indirectly or not at all. And with regard to the full spectrum of their interests and activities, our information is even more selective. Except for rare, almost anecdotal instances—Thales of Miletus is said to have speculated in olive oil; the great Egyptian vizier Imhotep took pride in his skill as a carpenter and sculptor—little place was given or value attached to technical knowledge and empirical observation.

The equivalent uncertainties for urban patterns are obvious. The generality of the acceptance of the many unprecedented controls upon social behavior that, to us, are mandatory in an urban setting—the real extent of legitimation of authority, the degree of flux in employment and residence, and the depth of penetration of the great traditions of urban civilization into the lives of both the urban and the rural populace—all are enigmatic everywhere prior to classical times. Except in the Mediterranean basin, they remain so until much later still. The provisional, at times even conjectural, character of what it has been possible to say here about the natural context within which urbanism emerged as a viable and ultimately dominant pattern thus is only an aspect of the prevailing ignorance about our more remote historic antecedents in general.

In spite of this obscurity, it is clear that the conditions we face today are profoundly different ones. A single American farmer produces for 37 of his fellow citizens, not to mention supporting Indian cities halfway around the world with Kansas wheat. High storage dams of reinforced concrete, chemical fertilizers, and agricultural machinery have mitigated the onerous conditions of husbandry as an occupation, multiplied its productivity, and transformed the position of its practitioners in our society. Palaces, cities, literati, the stuff of traditional history, once could be expressions only of the continuing, brutal exploitation of the agricultural masses. They need be so no longer.

Diffidently, with mutual suspicion and at times with sharp conflict, we nonetheless are moving gradually toward an awareness of the new conditions. A continuing reliance on policies of exploitation has be-

57

come overwhelmingly dangerous. In the long perspective of history, it is perhaps equally important that such policies have become ineffi-cient. Comprehensive programs of economic development, whatever their political coloration, increasingly tend to focus on liberating pro-ductive forces and stimulating the widest possible demand. The static opposition of rich and poor over the distribution of a limited surplus accordingly is giving way—at any rate in the developed, metropolitan countries—to progressively wider involvement of the whole society in the processes of production and consumption, for only in this way can the growing objectives of any segment be satisfied.

With circumstances so radically different, exploration of the remote past becomes more than ever an academic exercise. Yet if it is ever valid to seek relevance through retrospective generalization, two les-sons suggest themselves. The first is that the isolation of urban prob-lems as a separate genre is a legacy of thought from times in which city and countryside were in irreconcilable opposition over the same, piti-fully small surpluses with which to sustain life and affirm its human qualities. This is an increasingly unfortunate legacy in a new age when entire nations have become urban "fields." Extended to the interna-tional scene, it is reflected in the gap that continues to widen omi-nously between a handful of metropolitan powers and most of the remainder of the world. We must learn to approach problems of urban life through a succession of widening contexts that override political boundaries and that impose no artificial separations between industry and agriculture, between the needs of cities and those of their support-ing areas and hinterlands, and between policies of economic develop-ment and policies aimed at extending social integration.

The second lesson flows less from what I have said than from what I have taken for granted. The historic role of cities has been as prime creative centers: seats of learning; sources of artistic and philosophical ferment; initiators and exponents of ecumenical ideas; and forges in which have been fashioned most of our persuasive symbols of, and common aspirations for, a fuller life. This has been so in spite of harsh ecological pressures and consequent repeated interruptions of cultural continuity, and in spite of the thinness of the veneer of even the urban population which formerly could be supported in such "secondary"

58

activities by the subsistence pursuits of others. It would be tragic, as we contemplate the massive urban problems all around us now, to lose sight of cities as the locus of this cumulative achievement. Our task is to save our cities, not to resign ourselves merely to cataloging their defects.

# INSTITUTIONS AND THEIR CORRESPONDING IDEALS: AN ESSAY ON ARCHITECTONIC FORM AND SOCIAL INSTITUTIONS

WOLFGANG BRAUNFELS

WOLFGANG BRAUNFELS was born in Munich on October 5, 1911. After studying history of art in Florence, and at the universities of Paris, Munich, and Bonn, he worked as an independent scholar in Florence.

At the termination of World War II, he began his formal career by reorganizing the museums of Cologne at the request of Konrad Adenauer. His first major published work, *Mittelalterlich Stadtbaukunst in Toskana* (1952), dealt with Tuscan town planning in the Middle Ages and was largely responsible for his appointment to the chair of History of Art in the Department of Architecture at the Rheinisch-Westphälische Technische Hochschule at Aachen. It was while he was at Aachen that Professor Braunfels organized the 1965 10th Exhibition of the Council of Europe on Charlemagne. This Exhibition, in addition to his scholarly reputation as a specialist in the theory of art, led to his appointment to the chair of History of Art at the Ludwig-Maximilian Universität in Munich in 1965.

During the past 20 years, Professor Braunfels has published many articles dealing with Italian architecture, with sculpture, painting, and iconography, and with the theoretical aspects of art and their interpretation. He is also the author of *Die Heilige Dreifaltigkeit* (1954), *Meisterwerke Europäischer Plastik* (1958), *Der Dom von Florenz* (1964), and *The World of Charlemagne* (1968). He edited (1967) *The Lorsch Gospels* and the four-volume *Karl der Grosse, Lebenswerk und Nachleben* (1965–66) to which he also was a contributor.

I MAY ADMIT at the start that I have only one idea to contribute on the subject of this symposium, and I do not claim that it is a particularly new or original idea. Nevertheless it is one that has formulated itself slowly within me during my thirty years of studying architecture in the old historical settings of Europe, and my hope is that within the framework of this symposium it will take on a new significance and be of some service to the architecture of the future.

May I first be allowed to present my theme in its German form, not only because that was the language in which I formulated it but also because the idea itself may be found rather Germanic. *Die Idealität der Institutionen und ihre Bedeutung für die architektonische Gestaltung.* This is my title. The attempt to translate it gives it a slightly different character because there is no exact English equivalent of "idealität"; both "idea" and "ideal" mean something slightly different. I have therefore chosen to call it "Institutions and their Corresponding Ideals," though it might have been better to choose the more exact rendering of "Architectural Form as an Expression of the Ideals and Underlying Conceptions of Human Institutions." Behind this title is hidden an entire sum of historical fact and from this we are able to deduce a historical law. In my language this would run: *Jedes architektonische Kunstwerk hat zur Voraussetzung eine festgefügte Institution, für die es notwendig ist. Es wird dadurch zum Kunstwerk, das es zugleich die Idealität zur Anschauung bringt, aus der diese Institution lebt. Vom Rang der Idealität hängt auch der Rang der Kunstwerkes ab, wo immer es ihn erreicht. Idealitäten einer Institution waren in der Vergangenheit nicht auf einandere übertragbar. Deshalb sind auch Bauformen, die im Dienste einer Idealität gewonnen wurden, nicht unverändert auf andere übertragbar.* I shall first translate this formula and then enlarge on it and seek to justify myself in going so far as to describe it as a law. In English it runs: "Every architectural work of art pre-supposes the framework of a strongly defined institution, for which it is essential. It becomes a work of art in giving a visible form to those ideals on which the life of the institution depends. The standing of the work of art is in direct relation to the importance of the underlying ideals of the institution, wherever it represents them faithfully. The underlying ideals of different institutions were never in the past interchangeable. Hence, it follows that architectural forms created in the service of one set of ideals can never be adopted unchanged in the service of any other."

Perhaps I may be permitted in describing the relationship between architectonic form and the ideals which give rise to an institution to make use of a definition drawn from a different and more important context; it is "The outward and visible sign of an inward and spiritual grace"—the definition of a sacrament in the catechism of the Anglican Church. It is the ideal or spiritual conception on which the institution depends that gives the artist the possibility of creating living forms, speaking forms, or even sometimes symbolic forms. Just as the nature of the ideal determines the character of the institution, so does the ideal desire to express itself in terms of architectural form.

In order to illustrate my thesis, I have had to decide whether to make use of general types, without describing any specific building, or to choose such well-known examples that everybody may be expected to know them. My decision has been to use some of each. In two of my institutions, the farmhouse and a Benedictine monastery, I shall be speaking generally, while to illustrate the other three I shall call upon specific examples, the city-state of Siena, the Palace of Versailles, and the Farnese palace in Rome, which are all famous.

I shall begin with the simple farmhouse, which arises from that most ancient of institutions, a family working on the land. Just as an old proverb tells us that a priest may be known from the state of his church roof, so does the exterior of the farmhouse indicate whether the farmer is prosperous. As soon as you enter you are aware of a special ideal, which expresses itself not only in the layout but in the decorative details—in the timber-work of the roof, the windows, the doors, and even in the fireplace. As long as it goes on serving its proper purpose, the house is, as it were, a living being with its own personality, and to turn it into a restaurant, with a kind of spurious cosiness, as is so often done now in Europe, is to desecrate it. In these attempted reconstructions the fabric is preserved but, deprived of its true *raison d'être,* of the ideal and necessity it was built to serve, the farmhouse is reduced to a dead body, to which its new function can give only an artificial semblance of life.

64

Let me now act as your guide on a visit to a Benedictine monastery. Still today, when you enter a monastery of the Middle Ages, even if it has fallen into ruins, it is at once clear not only to which order the monks who built it belonged but also how they interpreted their rule, whether they lived the strict religious life as conceived by their founder or had fallen into luxurious and even licentious ways: only good monks were able to create good monastic architecture, and only as long as the rule was being lived were they able to give their interior life a clear external form. In fact we must study not only the Rule of St. Benedict but have some knowledge of the history of the interpretation of the rule in order to understand a Carolingian monastery as shown in Walter Horn's model based on the Plan of St. Gall or of Conant's reconstruction of Cluny in all its glory. The monks not only prayed, worked, washed, ate, and studied together but together they walked in long, slow-moving processions from one building to another. For each of their activities there was a special room, each with its own form and decorative scheme. If they gave the richest form, as was fitting, to the church, where they read the Gospel and chanted the Psalter, next in importance was the Chapter House, where the monks met to listen to the chapters of their rule, and the refectory, where, as they ate, readings from the Fathers of the Church reminded them that the corporeal nourishment taken through the mouth was symbolic of the spiritual nourishment entering through their ears. We could describe a Benedictine monastery as a highly functional arrangement, with special buildings for the abbot, guests, doctors, the sick, and novices, as well as service blocks for workers and cattle. Like Noah's ark it was independent and well provided for against whatever storms the times might bring. It can be said that the clear juridical language of the rule was mirrored in the building program and architectural style of the Benedictine monasteries. The building of all good monasteries of the High Middle Ages can be taken as so many interpretations of a Roman rule in Romanesque forms.

For an example of a free-town, let us turn to Siena at the end of the 13th or the beginning of the 14th century. This was a period when the city-state of Siena was at the height of her prosperity, acting as banker to the Church and flushed with self-confidence after her victory

65

over Florence in the battle of Montaperto, which was described by Dante. It was also the moment of her highest artistic achievement, when painters such as Duccio, Simone Martini, and Ambrogio Lorenzetti and such sculptors as Giovanni Pisano and Tino da Camaino were making their contribution. Like most Tuscan towns, Siena was then governed by a democratic assembly, with so many separate committees that the majority of well-born citizens were occupied for the greater part of the year in the process of governing themselves and in changing the forms of their constitution; this they did as often as did Florence, which Dante described as a sick man who could not rest in the same position for half an hour at a stretch.

Both the assembly and each of the committees kept an annual record of all their decisions. These records took the form of a bound collection of laws and of future projects known as *statuti,* and this book was handed every year to the podestà or president, whose duty it was to put them into effect. Under the constitution, the podestà was never a citizen of Siena and his term of office was limited to one year. Since it was the authorities' wish that everything be recorded with the utmost accuracy, we also know which projects were actually carried out, as they appear again in the financial records of the 'Biccerna,' which, with the pertinacity of other tax offices we know personally, never seems to have lost a single paper for over seven hundred years.

In the first days of May every year the citizens of Siena held a great assembly in the town hall devoted to building and public works. And, out of the many, many paragraphs of the proceedings I shall summarize what took place on May 4th, 1297. The assembly succeeded that day in discussing and passing no fewer than fifty-four resolutions concerning the town; these dealt with the enlargement of the cathedral, a completely new project for the Palazzo Pubblico—which laid down norms for all the facades with double-arcaded windows on the Campo or main square—and such minor matters as strengthening the town gates, paving the streets, improving the drainage system, and constructing new fountains.

The agenda of that meeting testifies that the citizens of Siena considered each project within the framework of the town as a whole. Many of the resolutions make it clear that no one was free to build at

66

will, and that very strict regulations were enforced. But, from the wording of the texts, we learn that this sense of order in town planning arose from a general ideal of what a strong, good, beautiful, and pious city should be. For the Sienese, the ordering of the town was directly connected with the order of life which, in its turn, was a mirror of the order of the Celestial City. If we look deeper into the sources of these ideas, we shall find that all the podestàs and most of the lawyers responsible for framing the statutes had studied in Bologna, and that, through the Justinian legal code, they had absorbed antique theories of Greek thought which had passed into Roman law. One of these was the conception of *decor publicus* or beauty in public life, and the evidence goes to show that the officials of Siena thought well about how and by whom it could best be manifested in their own city. The right to build in stone and to erect towers, like churches, was confined to a few of the most powerful families, while other citizens had to use brick. In three or four of the streets, no house might be of timber and a rich facade was obligatory. There existed a special body, known as the Officio del Ornato, or office for beauty, staffed by three citizens, one of whom was always a notary. Every Saturday they made a visitation to a different part of the town, and where a building was found not to conform to the regulations, the owner was often obliged to rebuild it. We know this because it sometimes happened that the owner pleaded lack of means and, in these cases, the committee would arrange for a member of the family to be appointed podestà in a smaller, conquered town and to contribute from his earnings to the cost of a new building.

Siena would never have become the city we see today without, *first,* the belief that the ordering of the town was a mirror of the cosmos and so of life itself, *secondly,* that this order could be manifested in symbolic form and, *thirdly* that it was incumbent on every citizen to collaborate in the establishment of this order. If the Sienese never achieved the perfect city, it was because they changed their ideas every five or ten years. As a result, in the place of a perfect city, we have a living city, which is something more. It was a long and sustained effort to reach a Utopian perfection and every stage of the way gave rise to new impetuses for art.

After the monastery and the city-state, let us enter the blue *grille du roi* of the court of honor of Versailles. Modern rationalism would find it absurd that a king should almost ruin his country for the sake of building a palace or laying out a park. Nor would any Secretary of State today agree with Colbert in advising the king or president that nothing could better ensure his fame than victories on the battlefield or monumental buildings. But Versailles was not built for the personal glory of the king; it was to be a symbol of his position in the state and in the world. We find that the central room in the palace was not a grand staircase for receiving other princes, as in German Baroque palaces, or, as in Italy, a vast salon for great feasts, but the bed-chamber of the king. There, attended by the ladies and gentlemen of his court, the king rose every morning like the sun, and in the evening, still in their presence, he retired again to bed, like the sun sinking below the horizon. Thousands of emblems in every room signify that the king was at once Apollo, Hercules, and Jove, and every column of the palace demonstrates that we are in the realm of Apollo. The whole architecture speaks Greek or Latin with a French accent. With the first day of the Regency, the beginning of the reign of Louis XV and the appearance of the first shell on the walls, everybody knew that the reign of Apollo was over. Venus, of whom the shell is a symbol, now reigned supreme and soon the Marquise de Pompadour would give the whole building a new character. We call the style rococo.

For my last example, let me take you to 16th-century Rome where, in the middle of the city, Pope Paul III built a huge family palace, the Palazzo Farnese, for his sons and grandsons. The gardens ran down to the Tiber and were connected by a bridge to the Villa Farnese, which the Pope had bought from the Chigi and which lay on the other side of the river. Antonio Sangallo had almost finished the building when Michelangelo took it over and, with a few changes and additions, gave it its present famous form.

The family for whom this mansion was built was not by origin either very old or very grand or honorable. Their new residence was designed to show that as a result of the activities of the Pope, the marriage of one of his grandsons to a daughter of Charles V and the adroit politics of Cardinal Alessandro Farnese, they were now to be considered not only very great and honorable but even of ancient descent. They could never have built such a palace if they had not been determined to show that the House of Farnese was every bit as great as the House of Hapsburg or of Bourbon. Michelangelo, himself, was unimpressed by the House of Farnese and did not intend to make his art subservient to the glory of this central Italian pack; accordingly he needed another ideal in order to achieve his building.

Now it so happened that in 1545, the same winter in which Michelangelo took over the task of remodelling the almost finished building, the Farnese bull was dug up in Rome. Michelangelo admired this work, just as forty years before he had admired the Laocoön, and he decided to transform the entire courtyard into a frame for this masterpiece of antique sculpture. His scheme was to place it beneath the central archway leading into the garden, between the Farnese Hercules and another Roman work. It was a grand concept in which architecture was used both as a background and as a frame for one of the most admired masterpieces of the past. Although the project was abandoned by Michelangelo's successors, it deeply influenced later Roman palaces, which, as the Palazzo Borghese shows, reached their highest achievement in the interconnection of palace, courtyard, and gardens decorated with Greek and Roman statues. Thus it was that two separate ideals gave rise to the Palazzo Farnese: it was to be a symbol of the greatness of the House of Farnese and a fitting setting for the famous Farnese collections of art.

If we study the influence of these five building types, we shall find that two—the farmhouse and the monastery—developed their forms in the course of centuries, evolving from simpler to more differentiated structures. And, in the process, it might happen that one of a group of farmhouses or a single monastery would make a sudden step forward, carrying with it the whole surrounding civilization. By contrast, the Palace of Versailles and the residence of a noble Roman family were from the very first the creations of the greatest artists of their time and exemplified the highest perfection which the century could achieve. As such, they had the effect of influencing and raising the level of minor building types, such as ordinary houses, and even of churches and monasteries. Perhaps the best example of an architectonic setting which, once having achieved a position of preeminence, influenced all other building types of the age, is the Gothic cathedral.

Between these two categories, one of the buildings that evolved gradually and the other of buildings that from the first were the deliberate and perfected creation of a great artist and which influenced all around it, stands our fifth example: the free-town of Siena. Here, the two opposite tendencies are found so closely interwoven and in such an interesting manner that a detailed study of the tendencies would be most illuminating for the understanding of the close interconnection between institutions and their ideals.

My purpose is not to plead the cause of any special theory of art. I should describe it as an invariable fact, however, drawn from our experience, that great architecture has never existed independently but has always been found in the service of an institution fulfilling the function of giving visible definition to the underlying ideals. Even an isolated detail—the fragment of a Greek column, a stained glass window from a Gothic cathedral, part of a rocaille decoration from an 18th-century *chateau de plaisance*—tells us something special about the individual ideals. I have spoken of it as a law that architecture exists in conjunction with institutions, which have changed continually in the course of history, and certainly all good architects of the past observed the principle as they would a law. Sometimes it was the artists themselves who first perceived, defined, or even brought into being new conceptions which changed the whole aspect of a civilization. But, in these cases too, the identification of the form with the ideal held true.

It is always dangerous to assess the present situation in terms drawn from a study of the architectural settings of bygone times with respect to the reasons for the fundamental differences between modern architecture and the architecture of the past. Again, however, it is not my task to evolve theories. My twelve years of lecturing in an architectural department taught me that it is as wrong to interpret the architecture of our ancesors in the light of modern notions as it is to demand of contemporary architecture that it fulfil the longings of an earlier age. And in trying to establish eternal, unchanging principles, which have

70

remained unmodified in the course of centuries, we at once enter a very narrow defile. There are, nevertheless, some observations about the direction of modern architecture in the light of the past that we are perhaps justified in making.

If we study the two principal impulses from which modern architecture developed in the twenties, we find the objectives of both realized to the highest possible degree in the crystalline forms of Mies van de Rohe and in the plastic forms of Le Corbusier. These are, however, forms that can be adopted for almost every type of building, irrespective of the function it is intended to fulfil in society. It is true that Le Corbusier realized this fact and that he developed extremely precise ideas of the style of contemporary life which his architecture is intended to represent. Nevertheless, most of his buildings remain perforce as isolated monuments in the midst of hostile surroundings.

In the case of a few modern institutions, functionalism and pure form have united to express something new in the service of a new ideal. We can see this at work in the better constructions and buildings created to serve our communications system, in the bridges, road networks, airports and railway stations. One might even interpret a single railway-line, cutting its way in simple geometric figures through the undulations of a hilly landscape, as an expression of the fusion of pure form and functionalism. It could be regarded as the symbol of national or international unity and it is this symbolism that we find so beautifully expressed in many of our airports and other centers of communication.

I must emphasize that even the forms and structures of the most utilitarian and technical works of architecture are determined by the underlying ideals. A point that might profitably be discussed is whether it would not be worthwhile to try to make these ideals part of the conscious thinking of architects. Plato suggested that whereas it is in our power to create beauty in details, the beauty of the whole is something of which we are so much a part that we are unaware of it. But we are now so far removed from the time of Plato that we can no longer trust our unconscious instincts.

I would still like to cite an example of the symbolism of a piece of public works construction in ancient Rome. Most of the drainage

71

system of the historic city is probably still intact today, that is to say some of the sewage canals which end up in the Cloaca Maxima, which had a height of just over seven feet and a width of fourteen and a half feet. Most of the vaulting of this main canal was finished in the second century B.C., and the rest under Augustus. Pliny in his "Natural History" gave a completely inaccurate account of it because he himself saw in it one of the main manifestations of the power of the Romans to dominate the forces of nature. He speaks of seven great streams flowing into the Cloaca, of their rapid course, of the waterfalls, of the struggle with the waters of the Tiber where the two meet, and tells us that this sewer was even capable of carrying away huge slabs of stone from the debris of burnt-down houses. And, in fact, when we see pictures of the vaulting of the Cloaca Maxima it does look as if it had been constructed to deal with such colossal tasks, even if, in fact, it was only filled with a rather sluggish flow of—what sewers are usually filled with!

Other symbols of the Roman power to dominate Nature are the aqueducts, of which the Pont du Gard in Provence and the Aqua Claudia near Rome are the most famous examples. That the Romans did not know the laws of hydraulics and the principles of kinetic energy is only a legend; they proved their knowledge of these sciences on many occasions. They could have learned it from the Greeks, who, at Pergamum, succeeded in piping water to their capital, bringing it for more than ninety kilometers over a difficult range of hills with a maximum rise at one point of over 600 feet, which means that the pipes would have had to withstand a pressure of 20 atmospheres.

I have used the word "legend," but what may very well *not* be a legend is that Hadrian is said to have condemned an architect to death for daring to suggest that by using high-pressure piping he could dispense with the aqueducts, which, for Hadrian, served to demonstrate the power of the Romans over Nature. The aqueducts stand out in Roman architecture as visible symbols of the *Virtù Romana,* and that is exactly why they are so beautiful.

Similarly, in modern factories rationalistic functionalism is found united to pure form, under conditions which express the objective of maximum output at minimum cost in the course of the working day.

72

But the factory building also serves as an image in advertising media, where it appears as a symbol of the social and hygienic conditions of the workers and is, above all, intended to create a picture of efficiency and standard of precision of what is produced within. It cannot be said that these objectives are of the highest order compared with what a Gothic cathedral sets out to express, and it must be realized that, although a factory or an airport may possess beauty, this can never be of the highest order because the warmth of a human situation and the recognition of a divine order are lacking in it.

Completely different conditions apply in the building of a housing project. It is reasonable that a factory should be governed by the principle of maximum return on invested capital but when this is the first consideration in housing, it must result in buildings of a very mediocre standard designed at the expense of beauty. And beauty in this sense includes all the human longings which lead to culture. Even when a building of a certain architectural merit is erected in a modern suburb, the effect is likely to be spoiled by the buildings on either side, which belong to quite a different or to no aesthetic category. In contrast to Siena and to other medieval towns, it is rare to find two buildings side by side, by different architects, which do not figuratively spit at each other! The desire of individuals to create for themselves personal settings with a certain picturesque charm can be satisfied in our days only by building something that stands quite alone in the landscape.

Because there are so few examples of individual planning by individual architects for individual ends which have led to the creation of a higher architectonic order, it is clear that architectural planning of the future should be on a much larger scale. What was achieved in the old cities through the existence of a hierarchical order of society cannot be achieved in a society where all that can be expressed is variations in the size of the family income. As it is inevitable that we should live together in much larger communities than in the past, great community centers are now among our leading institutions; and this is what the satellite towns of London must develop into when they have passed beyond the stage of being mere dormitory areas. The best architecture of the future is likely to be achieved in the creation of

73

larger and larger housing projects, but the ideals that alone can give life to these institutions must be found in new formulas for communal life. Mankind must devote a great deal more thought and imagination to this end. It is not enough to create crystalline forms and to build blocks of varying heights on a proportional system. We must also evolve new forms of buildings for the life of the community, though these will surely be other than the cathedral, town hall, market, and streets such as those in which various professions lived and worked together in old Siena.

The reasons why it is so difficult to give a new town of today the architectural unity and the meaningful order of the past are known to all of us. A Greek *polis* or an Italian city-state formed a unit in which all free citizens had more or less the same life, the same interests, and a belief in the same ideals. And for most of them life passed by without interruption within the city walls; even when they went out to war, it was together they left and together they returned. In our pluralistic society we see everyone dispersing over a wide area every morning to join completely different communities in which to perform quite different tasks. Probably the strongest common bond in their lives is the firm or enterprise for which they work, and, possibly for this very reason, office buildings and factories are usually superior to the residential centers to which their inmates return in the evening. As we have already noted, factories and offices are symbols of the working objectives of the enterprises within. With regret it must be said that the vast majority of residential centers are quite simply symbols of nothing.

The problem with our principal institutions is to establish the contemporary ideals which hold them together. It often seems that there are now no common ideals capable of arousing the same enthusiasm as is felt for a football match or its equivalent by at least three-quarters of the population of a modern city—though even a sports center can serve as a meeting point for a community, where all can feel a share in the same victories and defeats. In my view, one of the main tasks of the future must be the unceasing search for adequate ideals which can give a sense of purpose and unity to the lives of the citizens of our modern cities. We cannot leave this dilemma in the hands either of the architect or of the man who commissions the building. It is good to know that already in many countries considerable efforts are being made to provide facilities for people to develop their own community life.

If it is true, as I have attempted to show, that good architecture can only be created within the framework of an institution and that it is a visible symbol of the ideals on which the institution depends, we must make the greatest possible effort to define which institutions correspond to our present needs and which ideals best embody the aspirations of our century.

Let me end with another comparison. In many of the eastern monasteries the monks lived the life of hermits, each in his own little cell, meeting together only at rare intervals. It was St. Benedict who induced western monks to live together in community for twenty-four hours a day. The great danger is that our housing centers will become more and more like those eastern monasteries. Added to this, we should bear in mind that with modern industrial methods and the growth of automation, the working day, and indeed week, is bound to become shorter year by year, so that more and more people will be able to spend longer and longer in their anchoritic cells. It is not for me to pronounce on whether the daily television of our times or the daily prayers of the past are the best method of making the individual a useful member of society. Both involve gazing fascinated into an outside and distant world, in which one is called upon to play only the smallest of parts. What I fear is that it will be much more difficult to create a community out of the anchoritic television viewers than it was for St. Benedict to build up his monastic cities, based on his classic rule.

# THE SENSE OF PLACE

ASA BRIGGS

FROM KEIGHLEY, YORKSHIRE, where he was born in 1921, Asa Briggs has traveled to three continents lecturing and writing on the social and cultural history of urban forms and ways of life.

After serving in World War II with the Intelligence Corps, he was a Fellow of Worcester College, Oxford (1945–55), and Reader in Recent Social and Economic History, University of Oxford (1950–55). During these same years, he was a member of the Institute for Advanced Study at Princeton, N.J. (1953–54), and a Faculty Fellow of Nuffield College, Oxford (1953–55). In 1955, he was appointed Professor of Modern History at the University of Leeds. While still a member of the faculty at Leeds, he served as Visiting Professor to the Australian National University (1960). He was also (1966) Visiting Professor at the University of Chicago. In October of 1961, Dr. Briggs joined the faculty of the University of Sussex in Brighton as Professor of History, Dean of the School of Social Studies, and Pro-Vice Chancellor. He assumed the appointment of Vice Chancellor in October of 1967.

He has written numerous articles and books since 1945, foremost among them being: *Patterns of Peacemaking; The History of Birmingham (1885–1938); Victorian People; Friends of the People; The Age of Improvement; A Study of the Work of Seebohm Rowntree, 1871–1954; The Birth of Broadcasting; Victorian Cities;* and *The Golden Age of Wireless.* He has also edited: *Chartist Studies* and *They Saw it Happen, 1897–1940.*

DISCUSSIONS ON THE quality of man's environment have revealed at least as much diversity in the approach to the study of the subject as there is diversity in the actual environments which men have tried to fashion for themselves. And what holds for study holds also for the problems of environmental planning. It is fitting to recall the words of Patrick Geddes in his plan for Colombo, Ceylon, in 1921 that "neither the most practical of engineers nor the most exquisite of aesthetes can plan for the city by himself alone, neither the best of physicians nor of pedagogues, neither the most spiritual nor the most matter-of-fact of its governing classes."[1] Understanding cities or countrysides, like planning them, requires a combination of insights and techniques and a convergence of disciplines. Neither the combination nor the convergence is usually there.

My own contribution is the by-product of experience—of living in different kinds of environment and of traveling, usually quickly, sometimes slowly, from one environment to another—as much as of systematic study. This is how I, at any rate, felt that I could best approach the problems of this symposium. Yet in general terms, also, whatever the difficulties involved in the approach, there is much to be said for an emphasis on "experience"—a term to which I must return—in relation to environment. Individual cities provoke bold and controversial statements, like V. S. Pritchett's remark that "if Paris suggests intelligence, if Rome suggests the world, if New York suggests activity, the word for London is experience."[2] Remarks of this kind are an invitation to argument. At the same time, there are also conflicting declarations about each particular city. Mrs. Siddons, the actress, thought Britain's Leeds "the most disagreeable town in His Majesty's dominions" and Dickens, two generations later, described it as "a beastly place, one of the nastiest places I know," yet G. S. Phillips, a local writer strongly influenced by Emerson, called it "one of the grandest poems which has ever been offered to the world."[3] Behind the literature of each particular city—and there often is a literature as well as a collection of texts and documents—there is divergent experience, reflected in divergent response. The same environment is not necessarily experienced in the same way by different individuals or, extending the argument, by different groups.

79

For the most part, the element of study behind and within this paper has been concerned with the rich literature of particular cities—and with other expressions of urban styles—considered as an extension of and as a stimulus to my own experience. Such an element of stimulus—from reading or from travel—should be more generally present in concern for the contemporary city. It is, indeed, as important as the element of extension, since so many people have become so well used to the actual environment they live in that they are starved and deprived in the employment of their senses, unable not only to compare or to criticize, but, more seriously, to appreciate. Our urban environments are and have been characterized by manifest inequalities of education, of income, of health, and of opportunity. In such circumstances both deprived and privileged groups find it impossible to think and feel outside the limits of their own subenvironment. D. H. Lawrence more than any other modern English writer realized this in relation to English industrialism. My own studies, which begin in an industrial environment, have been directly concerned not so much with the present as with the past, with the social and cultural history of urban forms, rhythms, and textures, and of urban ways of life.

In patches, this study has been detailed and systematic—especially in relation to the 19th-century environment of Victorian cities—and I would claim, just because I am laying emphasis on experience and not despite it, that such historical study—modern, medieval or ancient—must be detailed and systematic and not highly generalized and philosophical if it is to be of much practical use at all. It is of little use talking about ideal types. What is more challenging even in relation to the ancient or medieval city, is to examine actual situations and processes. Such detailed examination is always intricate, often difficult, sometimes impossible, and far more complex than the study of the relationships between architects and their clients in relation to individual buildings. It should relate to the tangled nexus of decisions, conflicts, and compromises (public and private), whether concerned with money, power, ideas or techniques, which have fashioned particular environments, shaping not merely external appearance but individual and group experience and to the reactions and interreactions to those environments of real people, individuals, and groups. It should concern itself with "whole" environments—their interrelatedness and coherence (or lack of it) and not with catalogs of individual buildings or of separate features, however impressive—and it should always involve seeing and feeling as well as reading. A directness of approach is a precondition of understanding. Rasmussen emphasizes this point in the 20th century when, for example, he writes that the many tourists who visit Sta. Maria Maggiore in Rome on sightseeing tours "hardly notice the unique character of the surroundings. They simply check off one of the starred numbers in their guide-books and hasten on to the next one. They do not experience the place."[4] Long ago Hazlitt rightly made fun of the painter Benjamin West who when asked if he had ever been to Greece replied, "No I have read a descriptive catalogue of the principal objects in that country, and I believe I am as well conversant with them as if I had visited it."[5]

There are at least four good reasons for introducing a historical dimension into a symposium devoted to the quality of man's environment, even when—perhaps because—we are living in a period when we have visions of a future vastly different from our past and there is relentless pressure to consider questions of contemporary environment exclusively in functional and quantitative terms. First, we extend our range and strengthen our perspectives if we select from past as well as present revealing examples from many different societies and cultures of "successful" and "unsuccessful" human environments, including not only "planned" but what may be called "spontaneous" environments, both successful and unsuccessful, which owed little or nothing to expert guidance or to deliberately planned design. Second, there is more to be gained from comparing actual experience, past and present, common or distinctive, and the factors which molded it, than from thinking of environmental problems in a utopian mold, as they often have been and still often are considered. In this context the study of relationships in the past can be just as useful an analytical exercise as the study of relationships in the present, particularly when an attempt is made to set out all the relevant relationships; technical, social, political, and visual. Third, many of our environments, particularly in Europe, cannot be thought of at all, let alone "planned," without bringing the past into the reckoning; the ambivalent past, which carries with it both a rich heritage of buildings and vistas and a depressing legacy of blight, squalor, and decay. We do not start afresh. How to deal with this inheritance poses us with not one problem or with one choice but with a whole series of interrelated problems and choices. Fourth, the study of history enables us to understand more fully some aspects of contemporary experience in developing countries which are undergoing strains and tensions in their contemporary processes or urbanization. The stresses and strains of a developing nation have more in common with 19th-century or earlier urban strains and tensions in what are now developed or overdeveloped countries than they have with 20th-century strains and stresses of contemporary American cities as described in articles and features in widely read current periodicals. Where there are differences—as there often are—these, also, often lend themselves to historical analysis.

To put all this into focus, I shall concentrate on one aspect of environment—an aspect which can be examined both historically and in its contemporary setting, through a very interesting, though as yet limited, series of recent books and articles—the sense of place and how it has changed and is changing. "Utopia" means "no place." I shall be mainly concerned with particular places, chiefly cities, and how they are regarded. I want to talk mainly about cities in my own country, in the United States, and in Europe, although there are many extremely interesting non-American, non-European deviations and parallels.

I regard places, as Susanne Langer does in her *Feeling and Form,* as "creative things," "ethnic domains made visible, tangible, sensible." In this connection, a ship, constantly changing its location, is nonetheless a self-contained place, and a gypsy camp is far different from an Indian camp, although geographically it may be where the Indian camp used to be.[6] Given this approach, it is essential to note that cities are collections of places as well as places in themselves. White there has been only one Paris, one Rome, one New York, one London—to go back to Pritchett's great quartet—each of these cities in itself has been a collection of distinct places, each with its own ecology and history, sometimes with its own subculture. There have always been

82

some citizens who have thought primarily within the content of the city of a part rather than the whole. In Paris, Professor de Jouvenel does not visit the Champs Elysées, although he knows that it exists. His "experience" of Paris is quite different from people who do.

This phenomenon of disassociation has sometimes been a subject of amusement, sometimes a subject of concern. "I have often amused myself," wrote James Boswell in 1741—and he is quoted with approval by Jane Jacobs in *The Death and Life of Great American Cities*—"with thinking how different the same place is to different people." In the 19th century most people were shocked rather than amused by the fact that within the great cities populations coexisted in separation from each other, some "belonging," some "alienated." Social changes had taken place which had turned the city into a "problem" and which implied that in order to understand "the other population" or populations an effort of exploration within the city was necessary; an effort as great as that entailed in exploring foreign lands. "A hovel in one of the suburbs which they know least would be as strange to most Londoners as a village in the African forests."[8] The simile recurs relentlessly. Much modern sociology had its origins in this setting. The contemporary "problem" is to retain the sense of variety within the city—the invitation to explore—while eliminating social "blackspots." To do this it is necessary to be sensitive to urban processes. As the cities have grown, environmental change has necessarily affected different groups within the city in different ways. Some favored individuals and groups have been able to shape their environment—the places they knew best belonged to them—by taking private decisions for themselves. Others have had no freedom to do so. While this has been as true in medieval Siena as in 19th-century Manchester or in 20th-century Chicago, the consequences, social as well as aesthetic, have been different. To understand the relationships, therefore, between cities as "places" and the "places" within them, it is necessary to turn in detail to urban history, to changing social patterns, to changing notions of "private" and "public" property. In each historical city, the relationship has expressed itself both in social terms and in urban forms. The relationship, moreover, has so many different layers

83

that some historians have doubted whether great cities with historic names, as they exist today, can be treated "merely, or even primarily, as the descendants of the earlier ones."[9]

There are other approaches, of course, some of them very rewarding, to the relationship between the city as a place and "places" within it. Anthropology offers clues to men's deep attachment to the minor parts of the environment they live in, and to their willingness to name them.[10] "Likeability research" has concerned itself with the topological psychology of "spatial orientation," of the processes by which individuals and groups are always turning "spaces" into "places," "attaching" themselves to them through habit, memory, mood, and association. It has often mattered little whether the "spaces" were actually planned as "places." Within every city, indeed, there are "places" that were never planned. Rewarding as these approaches are in themselves, they can often be illuminated by the historian concerned with the central problem of "particularity," granted that he is willing to examine the problem not only in relation to the great cities of history—Pritchett's quartet or Athens or Florence or, for that matter, Chicago—but also in relation to cities of lesser reputation (off the main trade routes or travel routes of the world) or with only a very recent history.

Obviously, where the question of "particularity" now stands—or where we think it stands—influences our views about where it once stood. Almost all books on *the city* now begin with 20th-century "placelessness." Here are several examples of recent comment on it. "Mobility, communication, and the broadly distributed fruits of rising productivity are generating a society dispersed and heterogeneous, organized by functional relations rather than by proximity."[11] "The crime of subtopia is that it blurs the distinction between places."[12] "We reach for some vague concept of metropolis to describe the release of urban potential from its recognised ambit."[13] "Oakland: when you get there, there is no there, there," so Gertrude Stein is reputed to have said.[14] And in these judgements Nature comes into the reckoning as well as the man-fashioned environment. "The richly varied places of the natural world are structured in an ordered relationship that is yet full, for people, of drama and surprise. They are rapidly being obliterated under a meaningless pattern of building monotonous and chaotic.

The new structures will fall down one day but the obliteration of the natural order is permanent. We are in urgent need of understanding *places* before we lose them, of learning how to see them and to take possession of them."[15]

The so-called 20th-century shift from "place" to "placelessness," like all such so-called shifts, is feared by some, welcomed by others, both sides sharing strong feelings and powerful language. To most writers it is a *fait accompli,* as the industrial revolution once was: "spatial dispersion" and all that seems to go with it is treated as "a built-in feature of the future."[16] To many others it is also a source of melancholy and nostalgia. "The great positive values of an urban civilization stem from its 'togetherness,' " it is said, "from the concentrated variety that a Manhattan typifies, not from the endless, monotonous homogeneity which middle-class suburban dispersion [and an English writer, with Richard Hoggart's picture of recent English social history in the back of the mind might add working-class suburban dispersion] has produced."[17] Other writers, however, salute the emergence of the new, seeing in it not environmental chaos but the birth pangs of a newly-forming order with complexity and diversity as its main characteristics.[18] They have even found pleasure in seeing the distinctive landmarks disappear, a point of view not generally expressed in this symposium. As one English reviewer put it cryptically only a few weeks ago, "One of the most priceless boons our civilization has to offer is the realisation that we do not know where we are, provided we know where we are going."[19]

To a historian, much of this writing, whatever its angle, cryptic or downright, seems to contain an element of exaggeration which is very familiar throughout the long running debate about cities, a debate which can be traced back before the advent of industrialisation in the late 18th and 19th centuries. In fact, the contrast between past and present may not be quite as sharp as it is often claimed to be. Cities, however strong their sense of identity, have never been quite the autonomous self-contained places clear to those who draw sharp contrasts. It has never been possible to view them in isolation—either socially or culturally (usually not even visually)—from the countryside or the society in which they sprang up. "If you think of the city as a fixed place, fixed people, everything else just fits," a historian of medieval cities has written, "whereas there has always been flow in and flow out. In the Greek *polis* and in every other kind of city people live in the city only because they can get out of it. Even the high Renaissance Italians spent the summer in the country and they found the city liveable only for this reason."[20] In 18th-century England the pattern was systematized and established. Of course, it related then—as it still does—only to those favored individuals and groups who could make private decisions for themselves about their environment. Most city dwellers had a sense of place which owed nothing directly to any feeling either of contrast or of interdependence between city and country.

Likewise, while travelers' tales are full of comparisons and contrasts between cities—like early emigrants' letters—most city dwellers had little experience of travel to other cities which would have afforded them alternative sources of contrast between their own cities and other "places." Now a far greater number of them have, even though travel, as it extends, often means not the recognition of other places but the superimposition on them of institutions and patterns of life with which they are already familiar. As long ago as 1887, Frederic Harrison complained of a tendency among travelers to make places abroad as much as possible like places "at home." "In things spiritual and temporal alike" he wrote, "our modern mania abroad is to carry with us our own life, instead of accepting that which we find on the spot. The generation which planted London-on-the-Sea is succeeded by the generation which has planted Paris-on-the-Alps, Paris-on-the-Riviera, and Paris-on-the-Bay-of-Naples . . . *Coelum non vitam mutant qui trans mare currunt*. We go abroad but we travel no longer."[21]

Travelers through time have not made the recent history of "place" and "placelessness" any clearer than most travelers through space. Thus Lewis Mumford, in my view, quite wrongly argued that "placelessness" was a by-product of the industrial revolution. In the wake of coal and steam, he has maintained, the same kind of urban industrial community proliferated all over the world, Dickens's "Coketown," alias Smokeover, Mechanicsville, Manchester, Birmingham, Essen,

Elberfield, Lille, Roubaix, Newark, Pittsburgh, or Youngstown, the same place with different aliases.[22] In fact, in its early stages, the industrial revolution encouraged many new aspects of urban differentiation—in social and economic structure, even in buildings— sharpening the distinction between Birmingham and Manchester, for example, and directing public attention not to what they had in common but to their differences. There was no period of urban history when more attention was devoted to the "identity" of particular places. At the same time, Nature was seen in different perspective—with a special sense of "place" here also (as, for instance, in the "discovery" of the Lake District)—while the "special" distinctiveness of the older historic places of the past was emphasized. Few of these cities, indeed, were swallowed up in industrialisation, and it is fair to say that Florence, Venice, and Athens—to take three only of the great cities of the past—were rediscovered in detail as "places" during this period. Travelers were particularly sensitive to identity in this age of exploration, not least in America where the differentiation of American cities had been stressed by many travelers long before Lord Bryce made his well-known complaint that all American cities were alike, except that some were built in stone and some in brick. Charles Dickens's *American Notes* deserve to be set alongside Henry James's *Notebooks,* brilliant in their pictures of London and Paris, for sensitive, highly individualized comment on cities. "Every thoroughfare" in Boston, according to Dickens "looked exactly like a scene in a pantomime. . . . I never turned a corner without looking for a clown or a pantaloon, who, I had no doubt, were hiding in a door way or behind some pillar close at hand." Philadelphia was handsome but "distinctly regular. After walking about it in an hour or two, I felt that I would have given all the world for a crooked street." Washington was the city not of "magnificent distances," as it claimed, but of "magnificent intentions." "To the admirers of cities it is like a Barmecide Feast: a pleasant field for the imagination to rove in. . . . Such, as it is, it is likely to remain."[28] Dickens is well-known for his "symbolic" picture of Coketown, taken over by Mumford, and for his imaginative insight into the rich street life of Victorian London, well noted by Rasmussen: his impressions of American and Italian cities, which emphasize "particularity," deserve to be studied also for themselves and alongside his English examples.

There is much to be said when searching for city "identity" for turning to those books which provide evidence of a very special kind of distinctive personal experience and express it in such memorable form that the verbal statement in itself conveys the "mood" of the city as well as the mood of the artist to people who have never even seen a picture of it. I am in complete harmony with Professor Marx in his emphasis on the role of the writer and the artist (much more could be said of the latter) and more recently of the filmmaker in forging the sense of place, adding that it may be very particular as well as typal. To me such verbal or visual accounts are usually far more relevant than architects' photographs or planners' models. As V. S. Naipaul has put it in his fascinating book on India, "No city or landscape is truly rich unless it has been given the quality of myth by writer, painter or by its association with great events."[24] The "great events," however, are not strictly necessary. The sense of place, indeed, as expressed in words and pictures encompasses feelings that particular places are nasty as well as beautiful, hateful as well as lovable. One of the most remarkable documents of the British industrial revolution is called *A Gazeteer of Disgusting Places* published in 1843. In contemporary settings, there is sometimes a twist as far as the "nasty" is concerned. Twentieth-century travelers from Europe—in certain moods, at least—have often felt a sense of exhilaration in moving rapidly through the "placeless," brightly-lit, super-highway, motel, gas-station, used-car fringe of the United States. They have caught a sense of the United States as a different "place" even when the local environment is most "placeless" and even when the generalized features of areas of sprawl and blight have rightly been condemned by all writers, American and foreign, on the quality of environment.

A basic distinction must be drawn, of course, between impressions of the identity of places as set out in travelers' tales and the sense of identity felt by those who live in an environment and experience it directly and continuously. The problem of city identity can be fully understood, therefore, only if we pass from artistic expressions of

88

highly distinctive experience (often shot through with myth and symbol) to manifestations of common experience—to the identification of people with their environment and to the processes by which they become so identified or fail to become identified. Some people, whether or not they live in suburbs, have always been more interested in their own homes as "places" than in the cities in which their homes are situated. Others, however, including those who have had little chance to shape their private environment, have treated either their own "neighborhood" environment or the city as a whole as the focal "place," enjoying the "contagion of numbers," the bright lights, the noise and the bustle, as Charles Booth's East Londoners, who had a very strong sense of "place," enjoyed the East End. Some cities have always had a "lure" as "places," and a sense of attraction has been converted into a sense of belonging. There have been times in history, moreover, when for most of its inhabitants the sense of the city has seemed to be stronger than the sense of class (if not usually of ethnic division), and civic pride, on the one hand, and civic challenge to solve urgent "problems," on the other hand, have inspired large-scale environmental change, sometimes with a sense of civic gospel. Behind such a sense of the city there has often been not only a feeling of caring but a strong element of rivalry, of competitiveness with other "places." "The true grandeur and prosperity of our town," wrote one Birmingham man comprehensively in 1881, "is such as no competition can diminish, no jealousy malign, and no lapse of time make dim."[25] Even when the suppositions of civic loyalty have not been stated so explicitly, they have often been felt strongly.

We know very little in detail of the phenomenon of civic pride—less, indeed, than we know of city conflicts and of the urges, democratic or autocratic, to solve civic problems—although it is obvious enough first, that to "outsiders" civic pride often seems disproportionate and ill-founded (there is often an immense consequential credibility gap which affects even historians) and second, that civic pride can be manipulated and exploited by "booster" interests. Nonetheless, while so-called 19th-century "monumentalism" in architecture often contributed to civic pride in collective possession, there was pride also in drains and sewers; in what was hidden beneath the ground as well as

89

in what was displayed above it. Since the quality of environment in terms of basic health indices improved in some places while it was not improving or actually deteriorating in others, there was scope to express local pride in terms of the "Sanitary Idea."

How effective civic pride was in influencing the attitudes of those who were "not protected from the welfare impulses of others"—to employ a useful phrase of Professor Burger[26]—can only be examined in relation to particular cases. Yet when civic pride is absent, attempts to replace it by national programs of urban development—either from above or from below—often lose not only in lack of grasp of "local place" but in strength of feeling. Nineteenth-century experience is certainly misjudged if all industrial cities are thought of as being "the same," just as twentieth-century experience is also misjudged if all suburbs are thought of as being the same. In both cases varieties of economic and social structure have to be taken into the reckoning along with cultural differences associated with them. The sense of place, indeed, is not necessarily destroyed in suburbia even when suburbs look alike: in some cases it may even be enhanced in 20th-century versions of collective pride which may be as disproportionate as older forms of civic pride.

Against this historical background, what have been the changes which have influenced modern attitudes toward the distinctiveness of places? "Looking alike" is certainly part of the story, insofar as it has diminished visual variety, the variety of "features," and insofar as it has registered "feeling alike."[27] There has certainly been a tendency within architecture itself to search for what C. W. Moore has called "general" solutions as distinct from "specific" solutions which start with particular places. "The general solution whether curvily sculptured or puritanically cubed, is the diagram of an independent idea, conceived in isolation" or in creative fantasy or in somebody's—not necessarily the architect's—utopia.[27] Second, there has been a technical displacement of local materials and an exploitation of universal materials, a long-term shift which had its origins in the healthy desire to experiment as much as in the need to cut costs. Historians of architecture can doubtless point to other factors also, particularly in

90

the education both of architects and planners and in their sense of their own role, which have influenced this story.

The social forces, however, have been complex. First, local initiative has been limited not only by lack of imagination but by the increasing power of central government. This power has often been expressed bureaucratically in terms of standard setting, usually with the help of quantitative formulas, the standard turning into the norm. Care for "place" has been little considered, other national social goals being treated as primary. The new public housing program in France, for example, has led to standardized building of identical large blocks of (ugly) flats on the outskirts of provincial cities which had survived into the mid-20th century as visually and socially distinct and integrated "places." Likewise when London grows the plain quantitative question is put 'How can we get land for our surplus population?', and planners often answer it by riding roughshod over local issues associated with "place." Second, much that is "distinctive" in individual buildings and—more important—in whole *milieux,* has been destroyed not only through the pressure of market forces but through public action. Thus in Britain, for example, the historic city of Worcester has been massacred since 1945, with acres of medieval streets near the cathedral razed. Market forces have been responsible for the proliferation of subtopia, but those who wish to "control" them are often more concerned to "preserve" rural amenities than to maintain the sense of place. Ian Nairn, for example, having argued that "the crime of subtopia is that it blurs the distinction between places" goes on to state that it does so" by smoothing down the difference between types of environment—town and country, suburb and wild—rather than directly between one town and another." His sharp formal distinction between metropolis, town, arcadia, country, and wilderness leads him to advocate not means of directly maintaining the particular sense of place but rather of channeling "the existing mess into these legitimate environments."[29] Third, changes in the scale of business organization have led to a multiplication of the same kind of institutions everywhere—hotels, shops, banks, insurance offices—with far less "local" variety in typal form than there can be seen, for

91

example, in the typal forms of parish churches. Very little local initiative has been left to the architects of most of these buildings and, at most, concessions have been made to "local flavor," as in the case of some of the biggest chains of international hotels. Fourth, however, it is not simply "organization man" who is to be "blamed" for what has happened. Consumers' expectations—their sense of "urban amenities" —have become increasingly set in a national or international matrix.[29] Urban response has become generalized in quite different local environments. What is wanted is not to be different but to be the same. Fifth, the modern communications system, physical and cultural, registers all this even when it does not add new elements of its own. The automobile obviously changes the dimensions of "place," but as long ago as 1836 Emerson foretold a future when "regions" would become "neighborhoods" and "roads" "streets." Before the building of great highways tore into the heart of cities and introduced a new "placeless" geography, the railways were accused—even though they led directly from one "place" to another—of destroying the sense of "place." Now Professor Buchanan has written eloquently and forcefully—with little immediate hope of winning his case—of "the conflict between towns and traffic" in such distinctive places as Bath.[30]

Where the sense of place has survived it has been for deliberate reasons of history or for historical reasons which are concealed from view. Warsaw was rebuilt as it had been after 1945—a triumph of historical feeling not only for place but for the particular visual forms associated with that place—because its rebuilding was a magnificent gesture of pride and hope. Other smaller "places" in the world which have retained their visual identity in the 20th century and are now treasured for their distinctiveness, are places, like my own town of Lewes, which escaped some of the 19th-century social processes. They escaped because they were "off the map." Because they were "undeveloped" in the past, they have a special interest as "places" now. Other "places" have gained (paradoxically it may seem) from the care of commuters to protect environments in which they have acquired first a private stake and then gone on to develop a public concern. A sense of identity of this kind has been reinforced even within cities themselves—in Foggy Bottom and Georgetown in Washington, D.C., for instance, or in Islington in London—as interest in the part has been extended to commitment to the whole.

What more can policy do in the light of study? First, a strong imaginative sense of particular urban possibilities, based on an appreciation of the complex relationships between social facts and urban forms, needs to be an ingredient in all plans for environmental change. Plans couched in quantitative terms do no more than set frames, and they contain no kind of guarantees. When London looks for overspill solutions in old places like Bury St. Edmunds or Kings Lynn, the problems posed need imaginative answers sensitively worked out in terms of place. The South East plan of 1964, which is set out in purely quantitative terms concerning population trends and employment growth rates, demands "centres of growth alternative to London," but it touches on none of the issues raised in this paper. Such statements as "a great deal depends (in plotting expansion) on the size and economic potential of the town itself and on its character" leaves to the developer and to the detailed town planner an enormous responsibility, for which he may not always be prepared, as to identifying what "character" means. Urban designers have not "succeeded to the autocratic position of earlier planners"[31]: the content of their education and the range and depth of their experience inevitably become matters of public concern.

Second, there are very special problems when, as is often the case in Europe, historical residues constitute the very core of the modern urban community. In 1964 the Council of British Archaeology produced a list of historic town centers which it believed were threatened from different quarters. This marked an important shift of emphasis from concern for individual buildings to concern for total environments. Hitherto the English Town and Country Planning Act provided only for the protection of individual buildings: the demand now was for the designation of whole areas of historic interest and the introduction of a number of pilot schemes involving an element of national subsidy. Several pilot schemes are now being evolved. In Paris, where the forms of the outer suburbs—far more than Haussmann's 19th-century boulevards—mark a sharp and disturbing break with the very characteristic, traditional Parisian sense of place, André Malraux has done an immense amount (with great imagination) to restore (the words "protect" or "preserve" in this context convey far too negative an impression) the old historic right-bank district of the Marais in the name of *"sauvegarde et mise en valeur du Paris historique."* Battles are in progress at the present time about the future Venice, as to whether its distinctive visual "identity" as a unique city can be maintained. In all these cases, opinions and interests clash, and there is need not only for expert guidance but for enlightened general argument. Answers are seldom simple, although it is clear first, that the sense of beauty itself is at stake, and second, that something more than preservation is needed: the *mise en valeur* of whole areas should be the key phrase. I agree, however, with Frederick Gutheim that "to be in the grain of a city"—an excellent phrase pointing to the core of my paper—"does not mean that there can be no innovation, that design merely projects what has been. On the contrary, the best design is frequently a reaction to historic trends rather than a continuation of them."[32]

Third, given changes in scale—and bearing in mind also that there is an element of myth in the notion of the contained city of the past—there is a need in the future to think of "place" in a far wider setting than the small local community. We can no longer say of any place like Bath what was said of it in 1793: "Bath may be said to afford a universal scope for everything that is desirable. The man of pleasure may be satisfied with amusement, the philosopher may analyse its salubrious springs, the antiquarian may pursue his researches till he wearies himself with conjecture, the man of letters will find ample repositories of genius: the poet endless subjects to exercise his wit: the painter may delineate the features of beauty; and last of all the dejected invalid may restore the shattered system of a broken constitution."[33] Bath now needs its Buchanan and an infusion of national aid. It is significant in this connection that the Council of British Archaeology and the other bodies it mobilized saw no answer to their problem of relating present to past—either economic or cultural—in purely local public action. Intense "localism," indeed, apparently paradoxically, may be an enemy to the continuing sense of place as it is expressed in distinctive form. Extending the argument into the future, since there is no point in merely complaining about scale, it may well be that the sense of place will best be strengthened in modern conditions in areas big enough to permit of the possibilities of ensuring drive, variety, visual and social contrast, interplay of subcultures, coexistence of old and new, and access to the best planning abilities. Within such areas there will continue to be changes. Many of the unplanned changes will be at least as compulsive as the planned ones—throwing up new modes and nuclei, new "places" within developing networks of transportation and communication.

Fourth, where we are free to create afresh within the spatial, economic, and cultural frameworks of our own societies, attention should be paid to the making of places, places with people. As one American architect has put it "When we are at a place we know it. If our image or perception of a specific environmental order is confused or unclear then there is no place. We don't know when we are there; we don't know where we are."[34] Or as William Blake put it less gently "to generalise is to be an idiot; to particularise is the alone distinction of merit." At this point value judgements obtrude. They can never be left out. They are part of the very texture of argument and feeling: not a kind of superimposition on technology or on the politics of adjustment. They were just as plain in the garden-city movement (which had little to do with the sense of particular "place") or in the "new towns" development in post-1945 Britain (which in the case of Cumbernauld has produced one new town with a strong sense of place) as they are in Philip Johnson's passionate plea for monumentalism (which has much to do with the sense of place). Most recently in Britain they have been expressed explicitly by Sir Donald Gibson, Director General of Research and Development at the British Ministry of Public Building and Works, in his demand for the building in Britain not of new towns but of new cities. Some of these would be deliberately located not on "neutral" sites, but in "interesting places" where topographical and visual distinctiveness would be the first component in a new sense of identity, as it has been so often in city-making in the past.[35] Considerations of this kind need to be extended from topography to sociology. The same extension is needed in the United States where schemes for urban renewal have sometimes meant the neglect of the interests of large numbers of displaced people and where within most cities it is clear that the sense of the city as a particular "place" means little to large numbers of alienated people.

Fifth, when we turn from debate to action, the institutional framework within which decisions are taken and the procedures for consultation, survey, planning, and administration need constant review. There is no finality in either framework or procedures. The issues involved in this context are primarily sociopolitical and they cannot be baulked. They could provide us with ample material for another symposium of greater length and greater intensity in which we could pool experience and compare social and administrative responses. I myself believe that in a democracy the sociopolitical issues cannot be delegated either to experts or to well-endowed agencies. "It is only in our mathematical century," Camille Sitte wrote in 1889, perhaps some years too soon, "that the process of enlarging and laying out cities has become an almost purely technical concern."[36] When we talk about places, we are talking about life, and we should never try to delegate that.

## NOTES

[1] ASA BRIGGS, *Victorian Cities,* p. 47, London, 1963.
[2] V. S. PRITCHETT, *London Perceived,* p. 4, London, 1962; *New York Proclaimed,* p. 13, 1964.
[3] BRIGGS, op. cit., p. 81. For differing contemporary views of New York, see BAYRD STILL, *Mirror for Gotham,* New York, 1956.
[4] S. E. RASMUSSEN, *Experiencing Architecture,* p. 16, Cambridge, Mass., 1959.
[5] *In* W. BAGEHOT, *Literary Essays,* vol. 1, p. 174, London, 1966.
[6] S. K. LANGER, *Feeling and Form,* New York, 1953.
[7] *In* J. JACOBS, *The Death and Life of Great American Cities,* p. 143, New York, 1963.
[8] BRIGGS, op. cit., p. 62.
[9] O. HANDLIN AND J. BURCHARD, *The Historian and the City,* p. 2, Cambridge, Mass., 1963.
[10] K. LYNCH, *The Image of the City,* p. 123, Cambridge, Mass., 1960.
[11] L. WINGO, *Cities and Space,* p. 19, Baltimore, Md., 1963.
[12] I. NAIRD, *Counter-Attack Against Subtopia,* p. 355, London, 1957.
[13] HANDLIN AND BURCHARD, op. cit., p. 1.
[14] *In* S. CHERMAYEFF AND C. ALEXANDER, *Community and Privacy,* p. 50, London, 1966.
[15] C. W. MOORE ET AL, "Towards Making Places," *Landscape,* Autumn 1962.
[16] M. M. WEBBER *in* WINGO, op. cit., p. 23. This useful book includes some fascinating differences of opinion.
[17] S. TANKEL *in* WINGO, op. cit., p. 57. For the cultural attitudes of the older working classes to their "neighborhoods" and the effects of their transfer to new housing es-

tates, see Richard Hoggart's *The Uses of Literacy,* London, 1957. Part I offers sensitive and penetrating comments.

[18] M. M. Webber *in* WINGO, op. cit., p. 25.

[19] S. MULLIN, reviewing Chermayeff and Alexander's book in *New Society,* Dec. 29, 1966.

[20] Sylvia Thrupp *in* HANDLIN AND BURCHARD, op. cit., p. 255.

[21] F. HARRISON, *Memories and Thoughts,* pp. 248–249, London, 1887.

[22] LEWIS MUMFORD, *The Culture of Cities,* p. 196, London, 1938; *The City in History,* pp. 469 ff., New York, 1961. He touched on this theme, indeed, as early as 1922 in an important essay on "The City," reprinted in *City Development, Studies in Disintegration and Renewal,* New York, 1945.

[23] CHARLES DICKENS, *American Notes for General Circulation,* 2 vols., 1842.

[24] V. S. NAIPAUL, *An Area of Darkness,* p. 205, 1964.

[25] "Birmingham in the Twentieth Century," *The Central Literary Magazine,* January 1881.

[26] B. M. Burger, *in* S. B. WARNER, *Planning for a Nation of Cities,* p. 158, Cambridge, Mass., 1966.

[27] "Naming alike" is another interesting 19th-century phenomenon. By the end of the 19th century there was a Birmingham in America as well as in England. "What the name stood for in England," proclaimed one of its pioneers, "would be a promise of what the new Birmingham would stand for in America." (M. P. CRANE, *The Life of James R. Powell,* p. 21, Birmingham, Ala., 1930). There were also at least 53 places in the world called Brighton.

[28] C. W. MOORE ET AL, op. cit.

[29] I. NAIRN, op. cit., p. 356.

[30] J. Gottman, *in* WARNER, op. cit.

[31] C. BUCHANAN, *Traffic in Towns,* p. 38, London, 1966. [Penguin ed.]

[32] F. Gutheim *in* WINGO, op. cit., p. 107.

[33] Ibid., p. 110.

[34] J. CLARKE, *A Tour through the South of England,* pp. 135 ff., London, 1793.

[35] S. van Der Ryn *in* C. W. MOORE ET AL, op. cit.

[36] In his first University of Leeds lecture as Hoffman Wood Professor of Architecture, reported in the *Yorkshire Post,* Jan. 27, 1967.

[37] C. SITTE, *City Planning According to Artistic Principles,* p. 4, London, 1965.

# THE STEWARDSHIP OF
# THE EARTH

BERTRAND DE JOUVENEL

BORN IN PARIS IN 1903, the son of Henry de Jouvenel des Ursins, Senator and Ambassador of France, Bertrand de Jouvenel des Ursins obtained degrees in science and law from the University of Paris. He has also received an honorary Doctor of Laws degree from the University of Glasgow.

Until 1939, Professor de Jouvenel was a diplomatic correspondent, international reporter, and special envoy for various journals. During this period he also wrote *L'Economie dirigée* (1928), *Vers les Etats-Unis d' Europe* (1930), *La crise du capitalisme américain* (1933), *Le réveil de l'Europe* (1938), and *D'une guerre à l'autre* (1939–41). With the advent of World War II, he served as a volunteer with the 126th Infantry Regiment but found time to write *Aprés la Défaite* (1940), *Le Blocus continental* (1942), and *L'or au temps de Charles Quint* (1943). These were followed, after the war, by *Du Pouvoir* (1945) [*On Power* (1947)], *Raisons de craindre et raisons d'espérer* (1947–48), *La dernière Année* (1947), *Problèmes de l' Angleterre socialiste* (1948) [*Problems of Socialist England* (1948)], *L'Amérique en Europe* (1948), *Ethics of Redistribution* (1951), *De La Souveraineté* (1955) [*Sovereignty* (1957)], *De la politique pure* (1963) [*The Pure Theory of Politics*], and *L'Art de la Conjecture* (1964) [*The Art of Conjecture* (1967)].

Professor de Jouvenel has lectured at the universities of Oxford, Cambridge, Manchester, Yale, and Chicago. He has taught at the University of California at Berkeley and is a professor on the faculty of Law and Economics at the University of Paris. He is editor and director of the monthly journal, *Analyse & Prevision,* director of *Etudes Futuribles,* director of *Editions S.E.D.E.I.S.,* and is a member of numerous economic commissions, including France's Commission of National Accounts, the Economic and Financial Commission of the Plan, and the group of medium-term experts of the European Economic Community. He is now chairman of a commission of the Plan on future styles of life.

HUMAN AMBITION in our day aims at settling the planets. Such a dream involves the problem of survival under environmental conditions far from those familiar to us. Landing upon the moon is but the first step: even for this, explorers must carry with them very much more than has been necessary for adventurers previously plunging into the deserts, torrid or glacial, of our Earthland. The very air, a free commodity all over our planet, becomes the most precious of products on these novel ventures, and the machinery for its regeneration is the indispensable key to exploration.

However inhospitable the moon, the planets promise to be worse. The moon is inhospitable by reason of deficiencies that can conceivably be remedied by "imports"; the planets, one hears, are far more actively inhospitable by reason of elemental forces that would buffet men out of existence.

The places to which we dispatch men carefully selected for their qualities bear no likeness to the Fortunate Islands of medieval imagination but resemble the place to which the wicked were then consigned. I do not question the capability of the human mind to meet progressively the challenge of such hostile environments. But surely many are the moments when the toughest of these future explorers will sigh for the kindness of the earth.

We see the opening of an era: it is an era of seeking beyond the confines of our atmosphere; may it be also an era of awakening to the bounties of our Earth.

As we learn what prodigies our engineers and chemists must accomplish to reproduce, in the astronauts' microcapsule, the conditions which are freely given to us in this vast capsule, our Earth with its atmosphere, is this not the occasion for a sense of wonder, and a feeling of tender respect for the abode of our kind?

The bounties of the Earth notwithstanding, it has proved possible, as we know all too well, for most of our kind in the past, and, alas, to this day, to live very miserably on this planet. Why? Because of blindness to the resources offered. We are cured of this blindness, at least in the advanced countries. Are we not still subject, however, to another blindness—lack of appreciation, lack of enjoyment? From

101

such blindness follow lack of care of our inheritance, indifference to its deterioration, failure to improve it.

We esteem ourselves masters of the Earth. But should not an owner be the husbandman of his land? Must he not tend it as he uses it? Shall he not indeed delight in its beauty as well as enjoy its fruit?

"The Lord God planted Man in a garden of delight, to dress it and to tend it" (Genesis 2:15). This I take to mean that the Earth has been given to us for our utility and enjoyment, but also entrusted to our care, that we should be its caretakers and gardeners.

A more naturalistic approach leads to the same recommendation. Through hundreds of millions of years, increasingly complex living systems—organisms—have arisen from an initial beginning as a shapeless jelly. In this great process of evolution, superiority has not meant independence. Those forms of life displaying the greater ability are dependent for their very existence upon those displaying lesser. The animal, which has locomotive ability, is a parasite on plants, and so are we, for all our achievements and pride. A mode of existence which confines us to cities where we encounter no form of life other than our own may be of bad counsel if we are to adopt a policy of ecological balance.

In a very few generations the Earth has become quite small. It was encompassed by human peregrination less than five centuries ago. In the days of Jefferson, human movement was still no faster, whether on land or sea, than it had been in classical Greece. The shrinking of the Earth began with steam and has been accelerated by the airplane, the age of which is just my own.

Now we can take pictures of our planet from outer space and have its image on our mantlepiece, even as that of our home. Shall we not therefore cherish it as our home? We have become ever more efficient slave-drivers of the forces of Nature. Should this lead us only to pridefulness, or also to a new regard for the vulnerability of the system upon which our existence depends?

Small children behave with thoughtless brutality in a garden which seems to them an expanse without limits; and because they are so small, their brutality does limited harm. But we who have grown up

102

possess such powers that we cannot afford thoughtless brutality. The time has come for us to be husbandmen of the garden.

The more we think of ourselves as masters of the Earth, the more we must be concerned with its prudent stewardship.

As I understand this stewardship, it stretches all the way from the widest to the narrowest frameworks of our lives, from recognition that the atmosphere of the planet is far the most essential of our capital assets, to recognition that what we see from our window is an important element of our welfare and education.

Animals use their environment according to the prompting of their wants, heedless of the wreck they cause and of the litter they leave. There are some few exceptions, among which Man does not figure prominently. Man is fundamentally an untidy beast; so women have ever found; against this they have strived within the home. Let me suggest that the extension of this very same striving to the planet, as our home, is a great requirement of our time.

The language we use in relation to Nature is alarming; we speak of its conquest, of its exploitation; such terms have connotations of brutality, of misuse. Of such sins we are indeed guilty, and they may well be visited upon our descendants.

Perhaps the clearest progress that Man has made is in his entrepreneurial capacity, which means his disposition to look far ahead toward the provision of future services, for the procurement of which he neatly assembles, first in his mind, and subsequently in fact, a variety of ingredients.

I have just used the expression "neatly" which seems incompatible with the previous reproach of untidiness. But the two attributes are indeed compatible. The man who is concerned with a project is extremely thoughtful and careful in the marshalling of requirements, he pays great attention to the proper joining of parts, and, in short, displays the utmost tidiness in what is relevant to the project. But he does not care about what is irrelevant to the project, and therefore behaves carelessly with respect to that.

A striking illustration is offered by strip mining in the Kentucky hills, described by John O'Callaghan in the following terms: "The

103

process consists in making a 40-foot incision around a hillside above the seam and scooping up the exposed coal. . . . The strippers, cutting with bulldozers along the seams high in the scented, tree-covered hillsides, are tossing down hundreds of tons of rocks, soil, and broken trees, which have engulfed homes and threaten to engulf more."[1]

Here we have a perfect instance of behavior which is both neat and messy. The earth cover is neatly cut out and messily dumped down. The whole operation is neat from the engineer's angle; the mess it creates in the valley is none of his concern. He has a well-defined purpose, which is to get the coal out by the most efficient means; that these should involve the brutalization of Nature and the spoiling of the environment is to him irrelevant.

It springs to our lips that this destruction instances the evils of Capitalism. Alas, the root of the trouble lies even deeper! It lies in the inspiration of the operation which has the exclusive purpose of getting out the coal at the least cost. The least-cost principle is tied up in the case of the private corporation with the profit motive, but it is just as important to the public corporation, being then tied up with the service motive.

On the 21st of October, 1966, 144 people, including 116 children, were crushed to death in the village of Aberfan, Wales, by the sudden slipping down of a mountain of rubble taken from the mine over the years. This enormous accumulation, of the order of a million tons, stood 800 feet above the village until it suddenly crashed upon it. Was the improvident accumulation of this threatening mass the product of the grasping spirit of Capitalist enterprise? Not so; in Britain the coal mines were nationalized 20 years ago; they are not run for profit. Absence of profit-motive, however, does not alter the specific obligation of actual mine-managers, which is to get the coal out at least cost. Their very zeal in the performance of that office tends to cast out of their minds the side effects, actual or potenial.[2]

What I wish to stress is that we damage our environment not only when we, as individuals, behave like uneducated brutes, but also when, as agents serving some useful social function, we conduct operations in a manner that is rational relative to that purpose but thoughtless and damaging with regard to the scene in general.

Let me again illustrate. Among the natural beauties which abound in England, none are more famous than those of the Lake District. These have been very seriously threatened, so much so that only Government intervention has saved them. Threatened by whom? By a most high-minded, public-spirited body, the municipal officers of Manchester. The urban agglomeration thirsted for water. Very properly its officers were determined to provide it. For this laudable purpose they laid plans that might have drained the lakes. Can we blame them for attending to what was their problem?

This poses a very serious question. Adam Smith rightly pointed to the division of labor as the characteristic feature of the society then in the making. Division of labor has indeed developed, not only, as he described it, in terms of the hands that perform, but also in terms of the minds that conceive and design. Our fantastic progress in problem-solving is due to a mental attitude which cuts out of the vast and complex universe those elements which are operationally relevant to our specific concern.[3] This intellectual surgery, this "Divide and Conquer" method, has served us well in the advancement of knowledge and power. This may be the key to our having achieved the Industrial Revolution and the explanation of its not having been achieved many centuries earlier by China, which then stood so far ahead of us in every aspect of civilization. That this is indeed the case is strongly suggested by Joseph Needham's admirable comparison of ancient Chinese science and technology with that of the West.[4] The great advance which the Chinese had enjoyed was overcome and reversed, Needham argues, because they were wont to think in terms of general harmony rather than to single out what was germane to a specific problem.

Such a comparison leads us to recognize what I should venture to call an intellectual toughness. The Western intellectual is apt to condemn the toughness of other social groups, but his own very thinking is tough. This is noticeable when you seek to interest one of our technologists in some foreseeable side effects of the innovation he is working on. He is apt to shrug off the intervention: "That will be someone else's problem." It is highly probable that his attitude is a condition of his success. But the more we concede the legitimacy, even the inevitability, of this attitude, the more also we must recognize that

105

our process of problem-solving is problem-generating. A simple instance is offered by the supersonic airliner, which solves the problem of faster transport but creates the problem—the extent of which is so far unknown—of the supersonic boom.

Our progress, then, is a complex of problem-solving and problem-creation. If we consider the progress achieved in a long period, we can observe that certain problems have been eagerly attended to and others left quite unattended. We can further observe that among the new problems generated by the problems solved, some have been dealt with and others not. Using these categories, what strikes us then is the *neglect of environmental problems*. This I can illustrate by citing two wholly neglected formulators of environmental concerns.

The year is 1775, we are near Besançon, attending a ceremony; the first stone of a new town is being laid. Now, explains the designer, begins a new age—the age of industry—which calls for the gathering of many workers around a factory. The whole of the mill town, he indicates, should be planned to make life pleasant by providing for the amenities and for making attractive the appearance of the proposed buildings. The building of this mill town of Chaux—which stands to this day a shining testimony to the vision of its architect, Claude-Nicolas Ledoux—was indeed a great beginning; but it was a beginning without a sequel.

In my distant youth I fostered the slogan *"Des Versailles pour le Peuple"* to denote what seemed to me a natural concern for a Democratic Civilization; that is, to give to the many the aesthetic pleasures and the educating influence of which only the few had previously understood the value. This has not occurred in the 150 years elapsed between Ledoux's effort and my outcry. What has occurred in the meantime was the abominable drabness of tenements. Why?

From the painting of Renaissance Italy there surely springs to mind the lesson that the scenery which forms the background of human existence flavors every moment of it. As soon as the artist had learned to detach figures from the wall where they had been stuck posterlike in Byzantine art, he opened up vistas behind these figures. The background might be a perspective of architecture, as in the works of Carpaccio; of nature, as in those of Giorgione; or a blending of both, such as preferred by Raphael. More subtly it would be a glimpsing of nature through an architectural framework, as in Perugino's art. Imagine rubbing out the backgrounds of these painter's works: you will see that most of the magic would be lost.

Did such paintings reflect a concern of the mighty for a seemly decor of life, or did they foster it? Surely both. While medieval society was concerned with bringing beauty to places of worship, the more man-oriented society arising from the Renaissance was concerned with the frame of its daily life. One would expect that, with the dawn of a more philanthropic view of life, a concern with the human setting might have been more generalized. Was it? Unfortunately, it was not so. The rich of the 19th century apparently thought of "hands" as devoid of any sensitivity, possessed of no eyes capable of enjoying beauty or suffering from ugliness. This may be due to the rise of a new class itself insensitive to loveliness, preoccupied with power and pridefulness; that which Veblen has described.

Let us now move to another pioneer, Charles Fourier. Concern for the disfavored countries of the world is no novelty: it was displayed by Fourier 160 years ago, in 1808. It seemed to him that the great handicap under which these countries suffered was a matter of climate, and that climatic improvement should be sought—an improvement for which he rested his hopes upon the systematic control of vegetation.

Neither Fourier's suggestion nor Ledoux's actual start have been followed up.

I am quite incompetent to say whether modern science could contrive any improvement of the climate in the disadvantaged countries. I am quite sure, however, that the negative cannot be proved. I understand, indeed, that the prevention of hurricanes is not an unmanageable problem. Hurricane Betsy, hitting a rich country, caused havoc that was measurable financially. I gather that the insurers alone were called upon to meet obligations of well over 80 million dollars. If one thinks of such disasters striking countries which lack the same ability to duplicate assets, one feels that it would be a great boon to have a defense force to dispel these destroyers at their very inception. Just how much of the world's research-and-development is being directed to investigation of such possibilities? I gather also from experts that it is not too difficult to divert rainfall. Now if one thinks of the floods that inundated Northern Italy—where two months' rainfall fell in two days—one is moved to ask whether some of this precipitation might not have been diverted to the sea if the state of the science were somewhat more advanced; i.e., if it had been somewhat more encouraged. It did not, in any case, require any scientific breakthrough to avoid the denuding of the hills which is said to have had so much to do with the floods that wrought havoc in Florence. To put it bluntly, these are not the sort of problems to which the bulk of our science and technology is addressed.

Ignorant as I am in this realm, I do not know just what the currents of heat spewed into the atmosphere by our centers of industry and population do to the movements of air. I regret this lack of information, but I regret even more that nobody else seems to be very much informed about it. Our atmosphere has only lately—and thanks to the mishaps of Los Angeles—become a subject of interest. From Los Angeles came Professor Neiburger's warning about the gradual piling up in our atmosphere of noxious products.[5] The atmosphere is, after all, not unlimited in extent, and if the refuse we send into it is not broken down, it may in time cause changes in surface conditions. This biological hazard may be uncertain and far removed. As against it, however, we have the clear, present, and growing unpleasantness of our environment. But here we come up against the difficulty that the defacing of nature, as it entails no financially measurable injury to persons, is an uncounted loss with no standing in our national accounts.

Those of us whose active life has spanned the years from 1929 to 1967 are conscious that the national store of plant and equipment we enjoy today is far superior to that existing in 1929, be it in the United States or in my country, France. If I may evoke personal memories, in the early years of the Great Depression we had to fight the quite fantastic belief that that great social disaster was due to what was then called "overinvestment." We had to plead that the way out was *more* investment, and we did our best through our lifetimes to introduce or invigorate the feeling that each generation owes it to its successors to

108

hand down a much richer national store of plant and equipment than it received.

We know that in the allocation of resources each year a large share must be allotted to the upkeep and improvement of plant, be it private (e.g., factories) or public (e.g., roads, schools, etc.). We should regard it as ridiculously shortsighted to care only for the accumulation of inventories and short-lived equipment and to disregard the plant. Yet we display this very shortsightedness when we neglect to care for the upkeep and improvement of our basic plant, nature. This natural plant is an inheritance which we hand down greatly deteriorated. Why have we been so careless?

Because the productive services of nature are free, the enjoyments nature provides are free, and therefore nature does not figure under capital assets in our view of things. Of this oversight I can offer a striking example. In our carefully designed input-output tables for the French economy, water does not figure as an input of the steel industry. This omission is quite justified in an economic table, water being but an infinitesimal item in the costs of the industry. But what this goes to show is that an economic view, in which things are seen in terms of financial costs, leads us to forget nature, and therefore to neglect what should be done, on the one hand, to preserve and improve it as a resource and, on the other, to preserve it as a source of enjoyment.

I have sometimes wondered whether, to redress the errors into which we are led by our way of thinking, we should not restore to rivers the status of persons, which pertained to them in pagan times. That this could well promote the efficient and farsighted use of resources has been demonstrated by my good friend Gilbert Tournier. President of the Compagnie Nationale du Rhône, he has been responsible for the most ample series of dams constructed in my country, which harness the forces of our most powerful rivers. This prince of engineers is also the author of entrancing films which chant the glory of the "deity Rhône." Let me hasten to add that he is a most devout Catholic; nobody in my country deems it at all strange that this Christian engineer, turning a part of God's creation to man's use,

109

should express his respect for it in words, pictures, and treatment imbued with a reverence for nature.

I may be criticized for having intermingled in this paper concern for the potential dangers of a thoughtless handling of nature with an interest in the boon of an aesthetically pleasing environment.

I make no apologies for this intermingling. These two considerations are but different aspects of one subject. Surely what we are concerned about is the flowering of the "plant Man." Having ever used this expression of the poet Alfieri, I am especially pleased that an American commission, led by my friend Daniel Bell, should take as its theme the development of the human potential.

The flowering of the plant Man is greatly assisted by environmental conditions, which continuously flavor daily existence and educate our taste. For the fulfilment of these conditions, it is necessary that we regard it as a goal to place Man in a garden of delight. And this will mean both a wise handling of the whole system of natural resources in general and a specific styling of the places where men live or work, or through which they travel daily.

It will also mean overcoming certain practical difficulties. The values relative to the general husbandry of resources do not at present figure in the operational calculus of agencies attending to specific wants. Nor can we expect a great deal from the ultimate power of the consumer because of the great difficulty of manifesting aesthetic preferences with respect to the environment by way of the market-place. Market behavior cannot afford us any evaluation of the importance people attach to a seemly landscape, since most people have no possibility of gaining access to such a landscape.

No matter whether his qualifications be high or low, a man needs to be employed and must live within reach of his place of employment. Moreover, his wife must shop and often herself be employed and his children must be sent to school. Thus there are quite a number of constraints upon the family's location; these determine the area within which the family must settle and within which its choice of residence must be made. In most countries, obtaining living space of any kind is a problem and no choice is possible; in others, the choice is very restricted. The family takes what home it can get, regardless of setting. Generally it has no opportunity to manifest its preference for an aesthetic landscape.

We could have a market measure of the value placed upon the seemliness of the landscape only if people had a choice of equally convenient dwellings with different aesthetic qualities. While we lack any such measure, we can observe in Paris that the apartments which have been carved out of the Palais-Royal and look upon its enclosed garden are, notwithstanding their lack of elevators, priced far beyond others that are their equivalents in space but are devoid of aesthetic appeal.

Indeed, if you peruse a list of lodgings for rent or sale, you will find emphasis laid upon the view and upon its character (e.g., "view of Notre-Dame"). But it is not only in money that people are willing to pay for the aesthetic quality of the setting. They will also pay in fatigue. The cost may take the form of climbing up a staircase, in a long uncomfortable journey to work, in the inconvenience of shopping, etc.

It would be simple to contrast the migration of the American social elite to new suburbs and that of the French to the oldest parts of Paris or to ancient houses and farms around Paris. The motivation is, however, quite the same; it is the search of an aesthetically pleasing setting. It is our misfortune in France that we can turn only to what was done in the past in order to satisfy this urge; but no doubt this will change. The question of interest here, however, is not whether seemly surroundings shall be contrived for a few, as they are in some American suburbs, but whether they shall be contrived for the many and how this can be done.

It seems to me that the main object of a discussion bearing upon man's environment should be to find out the reasons for the miscarriage of the opportunities we are given, which are certainly no less than those of which the builders of an Italian city in the Renaissance availed themselves. Why does one shudder at the thought that as much housing as exists in France at present will be built there within the next 30 years? Why does one not think that the beauty of the country will enormously benefit therefrom, as it did from the construction boom which occurred after the Wars of Religion—that is, from the beginning of the 17th century onward?

Given this great building effort, what are the impediments to the provision of an enchanting framework for the many? Thinking in terms of my own country, I see chiefly three. First, an architect is much hindered when he is commissioned to provide only the dwellings in an urban agglomeration while responsibility for the schools, hospitals, etc. is given to others. A condition of harmony is that the design of the whole community be in the same hands (I recognize that there are people more expert than I who urge that the effort to accommodate to what has been done by another affords inspiration, but I submit that the gap may be too large to bridge.)

The second point is cost. I hear all the architects concerned with housing projects complain about cost constraints. Cost constraints are the great excuse offered by our public jerry-builders. It does seem to me that a campaign of public education stressing the harm wrought by parsimony would do much to redress this difficulty. As an economist I see no case for keeping the cost of housing within the inhabitants' present capacity to pay. If you build so that rent (or staggered payments) corresponds to the present income of the occupant, you build in a manner not consonant with his future income or that of future occupants. Thus, the dwelling may soon have to be pulled down to make way for a better. Cheap building is associated with rapid obsolescence, itself a cause of high cost. If you build for a long term, social utility is better served. Of course, financial devices will have to be found to distribute the burden over time so that less of it falls to the first occupant, more to his successors. In short, the idea of a rapid writeoff, much of which is bunched at the beginning, such as developed in the case of industrial equipment, should be inverted in the case of housing.

This principle recognizes that we build living quarters for a long time. This is a key consideration. The idea is very current that, as our society is characterized by change, housing projects should be regarded as camps to be pitched for use overnight and folded up on the morrow—except that overnight represents, say, 15 years. In my opinion, this is a mistaken policy. A society characterized by rapid change is a society that changes its instruments rapidly, but living quarters are not in the category of instruments.

Our cities today reflect the momentous change in the 19th century when the age-old use of light tools by individual workers was superseded by the service of heavy machinery by clusters of workers. The machines were important and well housed; not so the men. There sprang up the deplorable agglomerations we all know so well, which can best be designated, in Orwellian style, as un-cities—human colonies lacking every one of those amenities and exercising none of those influences that in the past justified the identification of the words "city" and "civilization." They were no more than the servants' quarters appended to the palaces of machines. Such subordination of housing to plant has no justification in our day. It is, moreover, 19th-century thinking to imagine that we must live increasingly huddled in and around the big cities. Every augmentation of the cities lends greater credibility to this conception and leads to the continuance of the phenomenon; yet the more the cities grow the closer they approach their death from congestion. We paradoxically cling to the expression of distance in terms of miles rather than minutes, and we still think in terms of transport rather than communication. Hence we crowd into the cities and their outskirts for the sake of a supposed convenience. And we pile city upon city. It seems strange to many Americans that the French equivalent of Cambridge (Mass.), Detroit, and Washington should all be heaped together in Paris. No doubt New York, however, offers similar unnecessary conglomeration. It is a prescription for constriction. One of the great problems with which modern civilization must deal in the course of the coming generation is the urban bottleneck. The race between congestion and engineering devices to relieve that congestion is increasingly costly and will prove to be a losing game. The large city has outlived its civilizing purpose; it will go the way of the saber-toothed tiger.

It is fashionable to speculate upon the changes that may be brought about by a "New Age of Leisure." Let me stress that, even as things stand today, the job, including the trip to work, absorbs only some 10 percent of the time of all members of society. Whenever I say this, it causes surprise, but it can easily be verified. Allot 2,200 hours per year to work including the trip to work, note that this affects but about 42 percent of the population, set this total against the total of hours lived by all; it comes out at about 10 percent. Most of the remaining 90 percent is spent in the home or neighborhood. Say that paid vacations away from home are going to cut into this ever more deeply, and that these involve the whole group; even so you can count on 80 percent of the time lived to be spent at home or in the neighborhood.

The importance of the amenities available in the neighborhood is thus evident. The houses in which we live should look upon a pleasing scene of playgrounds for the children, recreational facilities for teen-agers and adults, promenades for the elderly, landscaping through which children can safely wend their way to school. The tunnels through which income-earners travel to work and return should be pleasantly screened. Presumably for some time we must still think of roads for that purpose, though underground railways would, of course, be more progressive. When such railways are generally available, shelters should be provided in which cars could be stored out of sight; they are efficient instruments only when the purpose of movement is individualized. Reflecting the place education should have in the life of a family, homes should cluster around the schools and playgrounds, and it is to the potential capacity of the schools and playgrounds that the community must be adjusted in size if we are to have true cities. And it is around "places to live in" that work places must be sited.

The point I wish to make is that technological change determines what is feasible but not what is pleasant. Whether you live in 1768 or 1968, a pleasant room, a pleasant view, a pleasant walk, a handsome place of meeting are much the same. What is changed is not the desirable but—and this most fortunately—our ability to procure it for an ever widening percentage of the population. Our achievements in that direction would be much greater than they are if we were less muddled in our thinking. It is absurd to regard the increase in our technological capacities other than as a great boon; if people suffer from sorry or monstrous living conditions, it is because we have not made the right use of our technological opportunities. At the same

114

time it is also absurd to regard technological progress as determining what is to be enjoyed. Technology is here to serve; it is, or should be, the handmaiden of amenity.

Architects are often criticized for not making sufficient use of the new means which technology makes available to them. I am incompetent to judge of the relevance of this criticism. But I would formulate and vigorously urge another. For my own taste, architects are far too preoccupied with keeping up with the Joneses of engineering. Engineers have achieved wondrous progress in providing us with means, but it is not for them to tell us that these means are the amenities with which we must make do. If we let them, they shall lead us in the direction opposite to what makes life pleasant.

Let me cite another example. I cross the Atlantic faster in an aircraft than in a steamship. This does not imply that I am more comfortable in the aircraft; it is the other way around. The astronauts go where man has never been before; this does not imply that they are more comfortable in their capsule than I am in my study; it is again very much the other way around. Now if the architect draws inspiration from a rocket capsule, he is apt to build something more impressive to the eye than pleasant for everyday life.

The engineer and the architect are in utterly different lines of business; one is concerned with enlarging our possibilities, the other with utilizing these possibilities to extend the framework of the good life. What the good life is does not change with technology. The engineer and the architect are meant here to symbolize two mental attitudes each of which is valid in its time and place. It seems reasonable to feel that where the bulk of the population lives very poorly, efficiency should be stressed, while as abundance develops, amenity should become the more important. Puzzlingly enough, the enhancement of the pleasantness of life seems by no means to keep pace with our growing productivity. In our age of efficiency, those properly concerned with the provision of amenities are so bankrupt of ideas that they turn to the imitation of the engineers.

Surely the architect lacks no indications of the qualities of the physical setting that contribute to the good life. First, he can find such indications in the testimony of the civilization of the past. He can

115

observe what kind of physical settings the better-off have always contrived for themselves, noting their concern for landscape, which was certainly far more pronounced, even, in Asian than in European societies. (See what Needham has to say on the subject in his great work, *Science and Civilization in China.*) Secondly, he can observe what tourists seek; on the one hand ancient cities that testify to the skill of earlier architects in designing a humane environment; on the other, natural environments—"unspoiled," as the advertisements put it.

To sum up what I have to say: men have not so changed that the pleasurable is changed. What *has* changed is the opportunity to procure the pleasurable for the many.

Recently I visited Warsaw for the first time since I was with the Polish army in the first days of the last war. I was immensely impressed by the rebuilding of the old town and the restoration of the 17th and 18th-century buildings—not only the public buildings, but even the private houses—to their pristine condition and indeed beyond that. This fantastic achievement was undertaken at a time of utter misery, when Poland had suffered immense destruction. This was a heroic effort. Seeking explanations for the priority given the task, I received a variety of answers, all of which contained this common part; beauty is a public good and a formative influence for good.

In our far richer countries, can we not afford such a public good; do we not need a beneficent influence?

One of the most promising utterances of our times is the White House message of February 8, 1965. It contains in its exordium this remarkable statement: "The increasing tempo of urbanization and growth is already depriving many Americans of the right to live in decent surroundings."

The idea here put forward in the form of a "right to live in decent surroundings" is of the utmost importance. Obviously there can be no such right without the counterpart of a responsibility to contribute to the decency of the surroundings. The man who enjoys the use of a noisy toy like the outboard motor commits an indecency just as much as the industrialist who contaminates the water—indeed, he is more guilty because he affords no service as a counterpart.

116

The quality of our surroundings can be achieved, maintained, and enhanced only if people individually are made aware that the behavior that impairs them is indecent behavior. No such awareness is as yet widespread. Cain, after murdering his brother said: "I am not my brother's keeper." Similarly, we protest, tacitly or otherwise, that we are not nature's keeper, and we are heedless of the injuries we inflict upon our surroundings.

We can and we must spell out public policies for the control of all those forms of pollution with which we are debasing our environment and for the creation of harmonious cities, but we shall not achieve very impressive results unless education at the very earliest stage breathes into our conscience reverence for the earth's bounty, on which we depend, and regard for beauty as Man's only lasting achievement.

Surely the United States as the richest country of our world, should take the lead. When Italy held this position, in the late Middle Ages and during the Renaissance, it gave the world what is still our richest patrimony. Is it not time for her heirs to emulate her?

## NOTES

[1] *Manchester Guardian Weekly,* July 10, 1965.
[2] This view, which I first expressed in a February 1967 lecture, has since been confirmed by the Report of the British Tribunal of Inquiry, issued in July: "Tips are the discards of the coal-mining industry. Constituted of industrially-rejected materials, hitherto they have been largely banished from thought." *Report of the Tribunal Appointed to Inquire into the Disaster at Aberfan.* H.L. 316, H.C. 553, H.M. Stationery Office.
[3] This has been well brought out by MASANAO TODA and EMIR H. SHUFORD, JR. in their paper "Utility, Induced Utilities, and Small Worlds," *in Behavioral Science,* vol. 10, no. 3.
[4] JOSEPH NEEDHAM, *Science and Civilization in China.* The volumes of this masterly work have been brought out in succession by the Cambridge University Press since 1954.
[5] MORRIS NEIBURGER, "Diffusion and Air Pollution." *In, Bulletin of the American Meteorological Society,* vol. 46, no. 3, March 1965.

# PASTORAL IDEALS AND CITY TROUBLES

LEO MARX

DR. LEO MARX brings to this volume a discussion of the interrelationships between American literature and man's outlook on his environment. His essays and reviews have appeared in America's leading literary journals and his lengthier published works include an annotated edition of Samuel Clemens' *Adventures of Huckleberry Finn,* introductions to reprints of numerous American classics, and his 1964 *The Machine in the Garden: Technology and the Pastoral Ideal in America.*

A professor of English and American Studies at Amherst College since 1958, Dr. Marx has twice been a Guggenheim Fellow (1961–62, 1965–66) and was the Fulbright Lecturer at the University of Nottingham, England, in 1956–57, and at the University of Rennes, France, in 1965–66. After receiving his S.B. from Harvard College in 1941, Dr. Marx served four years with the U.S. Navy. He then returned to Harvard to accept a Teaching Fellowship (1946–49) and to work on his Ph.D., which he received from Harvard in 1950. From 1950–57 he was a member of the Department of English at the University of Minnesota.

Dr. Marx is a member of the Modern Language Association and the American Studies Association.

> She told him about her childhood on a farm and of her love for
> animals, about country sounds and country smells and of how
> fresh and clean everything in the country is. She said that he
> ought to live there and that if he did, he would find that all his
> troubles were city troubles.

THE WOMAN whose opinions are being reported here is
Betty, the robust, beautiful heroine of Nathanael West's macabre fable
of modern American life, *Miss Lonelyhearts*. She is offering them to
the protagonist, the writer of an advice-to-the-lovelorn column, Miss
Lonelyhearts himself, who is neurotically obsessed with the anguish
of his correspondents. And he momentarily assents, as many of us
would, to Betty's plausible argument. She exaggerates, to be sure, yet
who would deny that a great many of our troubles *are* city troubles?
What does give us pause, however, is the notion that we can cope
with them by retreating to the country. How shall we take this familiar
idea? We know that it is deeply implanted in American culture, and
especially in our literary culture. We know that American writers,
from the beginning of a distinct national literature, have been fascinated by the theme of withdrawal from a complex, relatively "advanced" civilization to a simpler, more natural environment. This
movement in space typically has served to represent a movement of
mind and spirit—a quest for a new and happier way of life. And even
in the 20th century, when the theme might be thought to have lost its
relevance, it has in fact retained its hold upon the imagination of many
of our leading writers. Why? What does it signify? What bearing can it
possibly have upon the problems of our urbanized society? My aim
here is to answer these questions, and to suggest some ways in which
the answers may be useful to those who plan the development of our
physical environment.

But as a student of American culture, and one who has been
concerned with the interplay between literary and extra-literary experience, I recognize that most attempts to trace the mundane consequences or implications of imaginative writing have been unsatisfactory. The crux of the difficulty is the need to make connections
between two kinds of discourse. In poetry and fiction the controlling
context is imagistic and metaphoric, and when we attempt to translate

121

its meaning into everyday, practical language we all too often flatten the intricate, multidimensional structure of image, thought, and feeling; by reducing literary language to merely logical, discursive statements, we lose touch with precisely that affective power which is, after all, the distinctive property of literature—its reason for being.[1] To name this difficulty, however, is to suggest why the present enterprise could be worthwhile. Because imaginative literature remains one of our most delicate and accurate means of joining ideas with emotions, public with private experience, I believe that it can provide insights into the relations between mind and environment which are unavailable elsewhere. I want to show that the literary landscape, properly understood, could help us in planning the future of the actual landscape. I do not propose, of course, that literary works can be made to yield a blueprint or, for that matter, any specific, tangible features of a physical plan. But I do believe that they can help us sort out, clarify and reorder the principles which guide (or should guide) the planners.

No one needs to be reminded that imaginative writing, especially in the modern era, is a storehouse of ideas and emotions that men have attached to the landscape. In the American consciousness, as D. H. Lawrence observed long ago, the spirit of place is particularly strong.[2] I want to begin, therefore, with an ideal type of a familiar symbolic landscape—one that recurs everywhere in our native literature. This terrain characteristically has three sectors: a community (village, town, or city); a partly developed middle ground, neither urban nor wild; and a wilderness. But this imaginary countryside does not serve our writers merely as a backdrop or setting. In the best known American fables—I am thinking, for example, of Thoreau's *Walden,* Melville's *Moby-Dick* and Mark Twain's *Huckleberry Finn*—the symbolic landscape is inseparable from the action or narrative structure, which may be divided into three movements: the retreat, the exploration of nature, and the return.[3]

First, then, the retreat. The action begins with the hero-narrator's withdrawal from a relatively complex, organized community from which he is alienated. Here life seems to be dominated by an oppressively mechanistic system of value, a preoccupation with the routine means of existence and an obliviousness of its meaning or purpose. Here, Thoreau says, men have become the tools of their tools. Unable to relate his inward experience to his environment, the narrator retreats in the direction of nature.

In the second, or central, movement he explores the possibilities of a simpler, more harmonious, way of life. At some point, invariably, there is an idyllic interlude when the beauty of the visible world inspires him with a sense of relatedness to the invisible order of the universe. During this episode, which can only be described as a moment of religious exaltation, he enjoys an unusual feeling of peace and harmony, free of anxiety, guilt, and conflict. But the possibilities of a life beyond the borders of ordinary society prove to be limited, and two characteristic kinds of episode help to define those limits.

In one, which may be called the interrupted idyll, the peace and harmony of the retreat into the middle landscape is shattered by the sudden, often violent intrusion of a machine, or of a force or person closely associated, in the figurative design, with the new industrial power. (Recall the scene in which the shriek of the locomotive destroys Thoreau's revery at Walden Pond; or when Ahab's violent declaration of purpose, which he associates with mechanized power, follows Ishmael's pantheistic masthead dream; or the decisive moment when the steamboat smashes into the raft in *Huckleberry Finn*.) The second characteristic limiting episode occurs when the narrator's retreat carries him close to or into untouched, untrammeled nature, and though his exposure to the wilderness often proves to be a spiritual tonic, evoking an exhilarating sense of psychic freedom, it also arouses his fear. For he soon comes to recognize that an unchecked recoil from civilization may destroy him—either in the sense of extinguishing his uniquely human traits or in the quite literal sense of killing him. He discovers, in short, that there are two hostile forces which impinge, from opposite sides of the symbolic landscape, upon the gardenlike scene of his retreat: one is the expanding power of civilization, and the other is the menacing anarchy of wild nature.

These insights lead, however indirectly, to the third and final phase of the action: the return. Having discovered the limited possibilities of withdrawal, above all its transience, the narrator now returns, or seems to be on the point of returning, to society. But the significance of this movement, which is also the ending of the work, is clouded by ambiguity. Has the hero been redeemed? Is he prepared to take up, once again, the common life? What is he able to bring back, as it were, from his exploration of the natural environment? Though he apparently acknowledges that society is inescapable, he usually remains a forlorn and lonely figure. Our most admired American fables seldom, if ever, depict a satisfying, wholehearted return, and in the closing sentences of one of them—*Huckleberry Finn*—the protagonist already has begun a new retreat, as if to suggest an unending cycle of withdrawal and return.

So much, then, for the design of the symbolic landscape. I propose to show that it is an embodiment of a more or less coherent view of life, a conception of the relations between imagination and reality, which may be called a peculiarly American version of romantic pastoralism. Before attempting to describe the viewpoint and its contemporary implications, let me briefly consider its specifically pastoral, its distinctively American, and its romantic components.

The "psychic root" of this thematic design, perhaps of all literary pastoralism, is the impulse to retreat from a complex society in search of happiness and virtue.[4] In Western literature the theme can be traced to the work of Theocritus and Virgil, but in fact we all know it at first hand. It is the familiar urge, in the face of civilization's growing complexity and power, to "get away"—to leave a complex world (traditionally associated with the royal court and city) and begin a new life in a simpler environment (traditionally associated with the actual rural landscape.) The pastoral element of the design, then, lends expression to this centrifugal impulse; it turns upon the contrast between two styles of life, one sophisticated and the other simple, one identified with a relatively "advanced" society, the other with a life "closer to nature." The continuing appeal of pastoralism evidently derives from the universality of the conflict represented by the two physical environments, and if there is a single device which may be considered a constant feature of the mode, it is the symbolic landscape that has been used to figure forth that conflict from Virgil's time to that of Robert Frost, Ernest Hemingway and William Faulkner.

124

To appreciate the special affinity between the pastoral mode and the American consciousness, we have only to recall the symbolic topography invented by Virgil. We all remember Arcadia, the ideal site of harmony, beauty, and material sufficiency that chiefly engages Virgil's attention. But we tend to forget the extent to which this earthly paradise derived its charm from the two contrasting kinds of terrain upon its borders. In the first eclogue Virgil insists upon the encroaching presence both of Rome—locus of imperial power, authority, and repression—and of the bare rocks and marshland that epitomize unimproved, inhospitable, infertile, wild nature. Pastoralism may be regarded as an ecological literary mode, its purpose being to mediate between the claims of these two conflicting yet inescapable human environments: one associated with man's biological origins, the other a product of technological change and sociocultural evolution. When the pastoral ideal is pictured as a middle landscape located between the extremes of wildness and overcivilization, it is easy to see why it lent itself, beginning in the Age of Discovery, to interpretations of life in the New World. Here, in place of an imaginary Arcadia, was the utopian promise of the new colonies, with the old world to the east, realm of sophistication, power, and history, and the whole reach of the North American wilderness to the west. It is not surprising, under the circumstances, that the transit of Europeans to America often was conceived, like the good shepherd's retreat to an ideal, green pasture, as a symbolic movement toward a new, simpler, and happier way of life.

The crucial distinction, then, between American and traditional versions of pastoral, is the new realism that was imparted to the ideal by the new world situation. Before the Renaissance, poets had seldom if ever thought of Arcadia as anything but a dreamland. But in Shakespeare's time the symbolic landscape which had for so long been considered a mere poetic figure suddenly acquired a real geographic location. Now the pastoral ideal was taken seriously, with a novel literalness, as a social and political possibility, and its temporal location was shifted from the golden past to the utopian future. In America, by Jefferson's time, it had acquired political as well as geographical reality. When the authors of the Declaration of Independence rephrased John Locke's enumeration of the rights for whose protection government is instituted, replacing his "life, liberty and property" with "life, liberty and the pursuit of happiness," they in effect transferred the ancient pastoral dream of human possibilities from its conventional literary context to an actual political context. No wonder that the enemies of the third President of the United States called him a poet and dreamer! In formulating the goals of the Republic, Jefferson subordinated material well-being, national wealth, and power, to what nowadays would be called the general "quality of life."

That the American public responded favorably to the pastoral idiom of the Jeffersonians seems beyond dispute. During the 19th century the image of a green garden, a rural society of peace and contentment, became a dominant emblem of national aspirations. In the general culture the image of the garden served to blend the ideals derived from literary pastoralism and from Christianity. Only the most astute grasped the contradiction between the kind of society that Americans *said* they wanted and the kind they actually were creating. While the stock rhetoric affirmed a desire for a serene, contemplative life of pastoral felicity, the nation's industrial achievements were demonstrating to all the world its tacit commitment to the most rapid possible rate of technological progress, and to an unlimited buildup of wealth and power. This is the conflict of value dramatized by the interrupted idyll, the episode in which a machine suddenly destroys the tranquillity of an asylum in nature.

Before this time, however, the attitudes born of international romanticism also had been assimilated to the native version of the pastoral design. To elucidate the complicated and obscure relations between the romantic vision and the pastoral mode is beyond the scope of my subject. Suffice it to say, right here, that under the influence of the romantics the pastoral retreat into nature took on a far more explicitly metaphysical, quasireligious significance. By Wordsworth's time the natural landscape had become a repository for those ultimate values formerly attributed to the Christian deity. As Emerson put it, nature (which he usually represented by lanscape images), had become for his generation "the present expositor of the divine mind." At the same

126

time in the "high culture," the machine was becoming a dominant symbol for the impersonal, squalid, and inhumane world of the new industrialism, so that the movement in the direction of nature now could be depicted as a melodramatic withdrawal from a cold, mechanized city into a warm, living, spiritually nurturing countryside. In the romantic era native pastoralism acquired new vitalistic sanctions. If the retreat to the countryside made possible a simpler, more harmonious worldly existence, it was because it provided closer access to divine sources of order, meaning, and purpose.

So much, then, for the classic, American version of the pastoral design. That it engaged the attention of our writers in a period when a vast population was moving into a prehistoric landscape hardly is surprising. But it is more difficult to account for its continuing hold upon the literary imagination in the 20th century. Again and again, in the work of writers like Frost, Fitzgerald, Hemingway, and Faulkner (to name only a few well-known examples), we find a similar preoccupation with the pastoral impulse, that is, with a movement away from urban society toward nature as the outward expression of a search for happiness, order, and meaning. Yet anyone familiar with the work of these writers would agree, I believe, that they are not sentimentalists; we cannot imagine them seriously entertaining the illusion, cherished by Nathanael West's Betty, that we can solve our city troubles by moving to the country. Their work does not, in other words, encourage us to believe that the recovery of a rural style of life is a genuine alternative to life in our intricately organized, urban, industrial society. But for what purpose, then, do they continue to employ the pastoral design? Why does it engage the attention of so many of our best writers and, presumably, the audience which admires their work? What significance, in short, does the design have?

To answer the question, I will consider a few examples from the work of Robert Frost and Ernest Hemingway.

Of all modern American writers, Robert Frost belongs most directly in the line from Virgil and the romantic pastoralism of Wordsworth and Emerson. It is significant that he placed, as the first poem in the

127

*Complete Poems*[5] a brief and deceptively slight invitational lyric, "The Pasture." There he invites us to leave the house of everyday life and move out toward nature.

> I'm going out to clean the pasture spring;
> I'll only stop to rake the leaves away
> (And wait to watch the water clear, I may):
> I sha'n't be gone long.—You come too.
>
> I'm going out to fetch the little calf
> That's standing by the mother. It's so young
> It totters when she licks it with her tongue.
> I sha'n't be gone long.—You come too.

Like most of Frost's work, the poem may be taken in two ways, either in the plainest sense, for the pleasure of reference, or for its extended meaning. In this case we are also being invited into a poetic world, an ideal pasture where the writer will clear a channel to a hidden source of renewal and creativity. Raking away the clutter of dead leaves and nurturing the just born calf are images that suggest how much—and how little—he expects of the retreat.

The landscape sketched here is the symbolic landscape of Frost's memorable lyrics.[6] As in earlier versions of the pastoral design, this topography is divided into three sectors: a community, a middle terrain or pasture, and beyond that the dark woods and desert places. When Frost occasionally looks directly at organized power, he too is likely to represent it by technological imagery (as in "A Brook in the City" or "The Egg and the Machine"), but the typical Frost lyric turns upon a moment after the speaker already has turned away from the urban-industrial environment. The poet's subject is retreat, and in the opening line of "Directive" he captures the root impulse of native pastoralism: "Back out of all this now too much for us." How many modern American novels and poems begin with variants of this statement! The theme is retreat—both what it promises and what it threatens, and it carries the speaker into a middle ground—for Frost it is likely to be a meadow with a brook at its center—where the water wells up from a savage source, offering the hope that we might "Drink and be whole again beyond confusion." But withdrawal into nature has specific limits in space and time, and Frost is careful to insist, always, that it must end with a return to the common life. "I sha'n't be gone long."

By now it should be evident that the pastoral motif as it is used by Frost is almost wholly drained of the literal meaning it had acquired in the Jeffersonian political tradition. Here the movement outward from society toward nature has little to do with the practical superiority of rural ways, and in a poem like "New Hampshire" Frost ends by mocking that idea. The concluding lines, where the speaker faces a choice between being "a prude afraid of nature" or a "puke," that is, between a prudish New England rustic or a New York (Freudian) alec, he says:

> Well, if I have to choose one or the other,
> I choose to be a plain New Hampshire farmer
> With an income in cash of say a thousand
> (From say a publisher in New York City).
> It's restful to arrive at a decision,
> And restful just to think about New Hampshire.
> At present I am living in Vermont.[7]

And in a letter to William S. Braithwaite,[8] Frost made clear his skeptical attitude toward sentimental pastoralism.

> I kept a farm, so to speak, for nearly ten years but less as a farmer than as a fugitive from the world that seemed to me to "disallow me." It was all instinctive, but I can see now that I went away to save myself and fix myself before I measured my strength against all creation. I was never really out of the world for good and all.

The purpose of Frost's retreat, in short, is not social or political but rather psychological or metaphysical. Its value is inward. What impels the speaker is a yearning for an indefinable value, order, meaning—a sense of relatedness to that Wordsworthian "something" that is unavailable in the social environment. Following the romantics, Frost is tempted by the notion that natural facts, properly perceived, can be made to yield a surrogate for the moral or metaphysical coherence

129

formerly expected from Christian revelation. And so, again and again, in poems like "The Most of It" or "Mowing," he seizes upon a particular natural fact, suggesting the tantalizing possibility that he may be able to wrest from it a moral or transcendent meaning. In "Mowing" the speaker is working in a soundless pasture beside the wood, when it occurs to him that his relation with nature, figured by the whispering sound of the scythe, can be captured in a statement. "What was it it whispered?" he asks, but in the end he characteristically retreats from that invasion of the realm beyond the visible, where Nature is an embodiment of ultimate value, to a mediating middle ground: "The fact *is* the sweetest dream that labor knows."

Not only is the "content" of Frost's poetry controlled by the pastoral design, but his explanation of the creative process, and of the function of poetry, conforms to the same pattern. The inception of a poem is an impulse similar to the retreat, or what Freud might have called an enactment of the pleasure principle. "It begins in delight," Frost says, "and ends in wisdom. The figure is the same as for love." As he describes it, there is a similar reaching out for gratification, a similar arrest of the centrifugal motion, checked in this case by the requirements of form, and then a denouement comparable to the hero's return:

> It begins in delight, it inclines to the impulse, it assumes direction with the first line laid down, it runs a course of lucky events, and ends in a clarification of life—not necessarily a great clarification, such as sects and cults are founded on, but in a momentary stay against confusion.[9]

With Frost, then, the pastoral design is more than a convenient device for structuring a work of art. It figures the rhythm of consciousness itself; it is a landscape of mind. Moreover, Frost's popularity—and he is beyond question the modern American poet with authentic gifts who has the largest audience—would seem to argue the universal appeal of the design. His most popular poem, which has been subjected to endless critical explication, reprinted in mass circulation magazines, and repeatedly anthologized, is "Stopping by Woods on a Snowy Evening." It would de difficult to imagine a more complete statement

130

of our theme, and familiar as the lines are, it is useful to reconsider them with the pastoral design in mind.

> Whose woods these are I think I know
> His house is in the village though;
> He will not see me stopping here
> To watch his woods fill up with snow.

The complex institutional world has been left behind, and though we are made to feel how it impinges on the countryside, in the property owner's invisible presence, the speaker's attention is drawn to the landscape. The falling snow obliterates details, harmonizes the scene, and provides a receptive field for his meditation. (As in "Directive": "Back in a time made simple by loss of detail.") Yet his withdrawal is far from complete.

> My little horse must think it queer
> To stop without a farmhouse near
> Between the woods and frozen lake
> The darkest evening of the year.
>
> He gives his harness bells a shake
> To ask if there is some mistake.
> The only other sound's the sweep
> Of easy wind and downy flake.

Now the sense of being in the precarious middle, having to mediate the claims of two environments, becomes acute. The horse, trained to a workaday routine, would pull the speaker back to the daily round. But he is transfixed by the serenity and beauty in the sphere of Not-Man, and the enticing, barely audible whisper of the snow, like the sound of the scythe in "Mowing," suggests some obscure fulfillment or possible transcendence. The temptation to keep going is strong. The poem ends:

> The woods are lovely, dark and deep,
> But I have promises to keep,
> And miles to go before I sleep,
> And miles to go before I sleep.[10]

131

In spite of the lovely woods, with all that they imply of soothing release, the speaker turns away, as if aware that to continue his retreat is to court the ultimate simplification—a total merging into dark otherness, a deathlike loss of self. The repetition of the final line underscores the precariousness of this resolution, but in the end he has turned back to the obligations of the common life.

Turning now to the work of Ernest Hemingway, we often find a strikingly similar moral landscape. Organized society is identified with organized violence, often with a brutal war, with mechanical, meaningless killing. And the action originates in something like the pastoral impulse to get away; the hero has been wounded, physically or psychically or both, and he opts out—declares a separate peace—retreating from the impersonal cruelty toward a simpler life in a natural setting. The retreat may take the form of an African safari, a fishing trip in Michigan or Spain, but its true object, as in Emerson, Thoreau, or Frost, is psychic and moral renewal. But let me consider a specific example.

"Big Two-Hearted River," the final story in Hemingway's first book, *In Our Time,* has had a strange history.[11] At first many readers, including some who were intrigued by it, thought the story was pointless. Once F. Scott Fitzgerald and Dean Gauss taunted Hemingway for "having written a story in which nothing happens."

"Big Two-Hearted River" is an account of a two-day fishing trip that Nick Adams takes in Michigan. In the course of the story Nick leaves the train that has brought him to the country, hikes overland to a meadow where he pitches his tent, eats supper, and goes to sleep; the next day he goes fishing, catches some fish, and decides not to fish in a swamp. That's all. He meets no one, and there is no significant action. The whole tale is told in simple, declarative sentences, constructed with a fastidious attention to detail and in a seemingly calculated monotonous rhythm. Here is an example:

> There was no underbrush in the island of pine trees. The trunks of the trees went straight up or slanted toward each other. The trunks were straight and brown without branches. The branches were high above. Some interlocked to make a solid shadow on the brown forest floor. Around the grove of trees was

a bare space. It was brown and soft underfoot as Nick walked
on it.

Since its publication, in 1925, a number of critics—notably Edmund Wilson, Malcolm Cowley and Philip Young—have uncovered
certain of the story's unstated themes. They have noticed that it belongs to a chronological sequence of Nick Adams stories in the book,
which has a degree of thematic unity. Nick has suffered a traumatic
wound in the war, and now he has come back to Michigan to recuper-
ate. On careful inspection, it becomes evident that the central action
lies beneath the surface, in Nick's mind, and that the numbed, almost
lobotomized prose is an index of his effort to repress his panicky
emotions.

But the implications of "Big Two-Hearted River" become even
more evident when we examine its symbolic landscape. Here is the
way the story begins:

> The train went on up the track out of sight, around one of the
> hills of burnt timber. Nick sat down on the bundle of canvas and
> bedding the baggage man had pitched out of the door of the
> baggage car. There was no town, nothing but the rails and
> the burned-over country. The thirteen saloons that had lined the
> one street of Seney had not left a trace. The foundations of the
> Mansion House hotel stuck up above the ground. The stone was
> chipped and split by the fire. It was all that was left of the town
> of Seney. Even the surface had been burned off the ground.

The great world from which Nick has withdrawn is represented only
by the train, moving out of sight, and by the unexplained fire that has
obliterated this outpost of civilization. The surrounding country is a
burned out wasteland. For a time, Nick walks over blackened earth
with no green vegetation; even the grasshoppers have turned black.
The idea that preoccupies him is getting away. "He felt he had left
everything behind, the need for thinking, the need to write, other
needs. It was all back of him." Or, in Frost's words, "Back out of all
this now too much for us." Later he reaches the place where the fire
ended, and the country turns green. He walks along the river in the hot
sun. When he finally selects a spot to make camp, it is a meadow on

133

the shore of the river, and on the other side there is a dark swamp. The train and the burned out town and war-decimated Europe are behind him. Like Thoreau at Walden, his aim is to reduce life to its simplest elements. He cooks his dinner, makes his bed, and gets ready for sleep.

> Nick was happy as he crawled inside the tent. He had not been unhappy all day. This was different though. Now things were done. It had been a hard trip. He was very tired. That was done. He had made his camp. He was settled. Nothing could touch him. It was a good place to camp. He was there, in the good place. He was in his home where he had made it.

Nick's camp is a psychological middle landscape, and the next day, when he goes fishing, his mind starts to work. But he cannot stand too much emotion. When he loses a big fish he becomes overexcited, feels sick, and decides not to "rush his sensations." Throughout the detailed account of the fishing, Hemingway reminds us several times of the swamp across the river. Its presence makes Nick uneasy. Toward the end of the story it becomes his preoccupation, like the dark woods that transfix the speaker of Frost's poem.

> He did not feel like going on into the swamp. He looked down the river. A big cedar slanted all the way across the stream. Beyond that the river went into the swamp.
> Nick did not want to go in there now. He felt a reaction against deep wading with the water deepening up under his armpits, to hook big trout in places impossible to land them. In the swamp the banks were bare, the big cedars came together overhead, the sun did not come through, except in patches; in the fast deep water, in the half light, the fishing would be tragic. In the swamp fishing was a tragic adventure. Nick did want it. He did not want to go down the stream any further today.

And then, after Nick cleans his fish, and washes them, the story ends abruptly and, as many readers have testified, enigmatically.

> Nick stood up on the log, holding his rod, the landing net hanging heavy, then stepped into the water and splashed ashore. He climbed the bank and cut up into the woods, toward the high ground. He was going back to camp. He looked back. The river

just showed through the trees. There were plenty of days coming when he could fish the swamp.

And miles to go before I sleep! What is striking here, apart from the similarity to Frost's version of the design, is the close correlation between the external landscape and the pattern of Nick's inner life—the structure of his feelings. First, the burned-over land, identified with machines and war, and with Nick's anxious sense of threatening, repressive, wounding forces; then the camp in the meadow, a good safe place midway between the world of collective imperatives and raw nature, represented by the third sector of the landscape, the swamp identified with darker, impulse-ridden, unknown life that is both attractive and frightening. Nature in Hemingway's world is at once benign and menacing—it is, like the river, two-hearted. Variations of this design recur elsewhere in his work, as they do in the work of other gifted American writers of our time. But here the story will suffice as a representative embodiment of a peculiarly American version of postindustrial romantic pastoralism.

With these examples from the work of Frost and Hemingway in view, it should be evident that the pastoral design does not embody an unqualified affirmation of the initial retreat toward nature. The movement in the direction of a simple, preindustrial setting does not reach an alternative, in any literal sense, to the complex world we inhabit. What it does offer, however, is a symbolic structure of thought and feeling, a landscape of mind in which the movement in physical space corresponds to a movement in consciousness. The literary topography is built, in other words, on a subjective model. The succession of contrasting spatial images (town, meadow, swamp) is a vocabulary for expressing a sequence of feelings—feelings which we ordinarily would regard as irreconcilable. A typical starting point is our ambivalent attitude toward the urban-industrial environment. We are simultaneously repelled and captivated by it; we may feel a strong impulse to escape from it, but we recognize that it is finally inescapable. By deploying these contradictory feelings in literary space the pastoral design enables us to sort them out, and to impose a degree of order

135

upon them. To indicate how this happens, I shall review the tripartite structure of the design: the retreat, the exploration of the limits of nature, and the return.

The retreat from the complex world has both a negative and a positive aspect. The negative aspect is escapist. It expresses a revulsion against the more unpleasant features of the urban-industrial landscape: the ugliness, the noise, the poisoned air, the chaotic overabundance of stimuli, the symptoms of social disorganization, and the general impression of incoherence and individual powerlessness. Since Carlyle's time this environment often has been represented in literature by the image of a vast machine. As Lewis Mumford explained recently, the word "machine" may be used to represent the dominant forces in the world today.

> Most of the creative forces in our time have been canalized into the Machine, a systematic organization of scientific discovery and technical invention that, under the pressure of excessive pecuniary gains and exorbitant political power, has transformed the entire existence of the Western World. The insensate dynamism of this mechanical organization *with no goals but its own ceaseless expansion and inflation,* has broken down the continuities of history.[12]

Whether or not it accurately represents the state of the "Western World" in our time, the image of the Machine as an emblem for a system with "no goals but its own ceaseless expansion and inflation" does express an attitude toward industrial society that permeates modern literature. It implies that the course of contemporary history is largely, perhaps irresistibly, determined by the course of technological development. And however much we may disapprove of this fatalistic idea, it does *seem* to be confirmed by the fact that when technical skill makes possible a flight to the moon, the building of an H-bomb or a supersonic jet, our society seems invariably to follow the lead of technology.[13] Given a world dominated by such a machine, in any case, the pastoral impulse to withdraw (or to "drop out," in the idiom of today's radical youth), is an impulse to recapture a human situation as it might be imagined to exist beyond, or to have existed anterior to, our intricate technological order. The withdrawal of the pastoral hero

136

in effect repudiates the assumption of Western culture that man is or can be wholly distinct from nature, and that the environment exists chiefly as a source of raw material for the satisfaction of our unique needs. At the outset, accordingly, the hero does seem to deny any possibility of locating worthy purpose, meaning, or value within the collective existence of which the machine is our cardinal symbol.

The positive aspect of the retreat, on the other hand, may be described as a tribute to the pleasure principle. It expresses a desire to achieve felicity through a simplification of living that restores priority to basic instinctual gratifications. It is a search for precisely those qualities of life which our urban environment allegedly fails to satisfy. It would be useful, therefore, as a way of understanding the shortcomings of urbanism, to make a careful study of the satisfactions that writers of pastoral continue to identify with retreat to the natural landscape. I shall return to that proposal. But the point here is that the impulse to escape from our complex environment may prove to be regressive or progressive, depending upon what happens during the next stage: the exploration of nature.

The first thing to be said about the "return to nature" in our sophisticated pastoralism is that it avoids, or at least masks, the conventional romantic claim for the superiority of a rural or wilderness life-style. If the retreat can be salutary, it is not because it provides access to a mysterious, divine, or absolute principle inherent in the natural landscape. Our best writers are in remarkable agreement on this elusive metaphysical issue. Accordingly, they do not provide much comfort for those who would have us deal with city troubles by refurbishing preindustrial institutions. In other words, they recognize the irreversibility of history. But this is not to deny that they present the symbolic return to "nature" as a source of real satisfactions. Their work indicates that it can be just that. Again and again they show us that withdrawal from society in the direction of nature makes possible moments of emotional release and integration, a recovery of psychic equilibrium comparable to the release of repressed feelings in dreams or psychotherapy.[14] This fact, to which the record of Western religion and literature abundantly testifies, imparts a degree of authenticity to the idea of a valuable "return to nature." At the same time, our

137

sophisticated writers of pastoral are virtually unanimous in their emphasis upon the limited value of such withdrawals from the world. Retreat is useful only if temporary. It does not, cannot, satisfy the hero's longing for a permanent alternative to our social environment. What it does provide, in Frost's well-known phrase, is a "momentary stay against confusion." If unchecked, however, the pastoral impulse can lead to disaster. It leads the protagonist into the dark woods, or that swamp of instinct and uncontrolled feeling where, as Hemingway's hero senses, the fishing will be tragic.

What requires emphasis, then, is that while the first stage may seem to sanction the impulse to escape the machine of modern history, the second stage discloses the necessarily individualistic, transient character of the satisfactions that such an escape provides. Contrary to the connotations usually attached to the word, pastoralism reveals the inadequacy of the retreat to nature as a way of solving social and political problems. (The fate of William Faulkner's pastoral hero, Ike McCaslin, is perhaps our most eloquent testimony on this point.) Thus the recurrent episode of the interrupted idyll has served to convey our writers' sense of disenchantment, however inchoate, with the promise of individual redemption that our literary culture took over from the radical antinomian strain in native protestantism. The retreat to nature represents moments of integration but, as Melville warned, "what plays the mischief with the truth is that some men will insist upon the universal application of a temporary feeling or opinion."

Hence the return. In the end, however equivocal the denouement may seem, the pastoral figure characteristically has turned back toward the world defined by the machine. Having discovered that the retreat can provide only a "momentary stay," he seems to recognize that his true home is, after all, society. If the endings of our pastoral fables generally are unsatisfactory, if they seem to place the protagonist in equivocal, self-contradictory postures, it is largely because of the seemingly insoluble dilemma in which he has been put. How can he carry back into our complex social life the renewed sense of possibility and coherence that the pastoral interlude has given him? None of our writers has been able to find a satisfactory answer to this question.

At the outset I suggested that our imaginative literature, and particularly those works which embody the pastoral design, might be of some use—at least as a source of guiding principles—to those who plan the development of the physical environment. Yet there is a paradox here, for the significance of the design, as we have seen, is primarily subjective. It refers chiefly to the inner, not the external, landscape. The topographical imagery in our 20th-century pastoral fables must be understood as a metaphoric vehicle for a landscape of consciousness. It would be a serious mistake, however, to conclude that the design therefore is irrelevant to the problems of the actual landscape. On the contrary, literary criticism insists that a powerful figurative relationship of this kind is never merely decorative or illustrative. It is not a one-way channel of meaning. If our writers consistently employ a pattern of landscape imagery, and if readers understand and lend assent to it—and, to repeat, the works which embody the pastoral design do seem to have a special appeal for a contemporary audience—then we must assume that the vehicle (in this case, the entire topographical design) is an indispensable feature of the total aesthetic result. So far as the design is convincing, the landscape imagery contributes to that conviction. Aesthetic success confers a kind of validity upon the pattern. What valid principles, then, can planners derive from the view of life inherent in this body of literature?

The most obvious inference is that more attention be paid to the subjective and in large measure traditional, aesthetic, or symbolic significance that our culture attaches to images of the external landscape—urban, rural and wild. (On first looking into the literature of planning, the cultural historian cannot help being impressed by the lack of allusion to the centuries-old accretion of meaning that clings to our dominant topographical images.) The continuing hold of pastoralism upon the literary imagination in this urban-industrial age is but one measure of the power of such images. A specific measure, already mentioned, is that we undertake a thorough, precise, analytic inventory of the satisfactions that men have derived, or have claimed to derive, from various features of the landscape. Such a survey ultimately would require the collaboration, in addition to planners and literary scholars, of art historians, urban and rural sociologists, and

139

psychologists. One aim of the inventory would be to sort out the kinds of satisfaction, real and illusory, that are associated with the pastoral retreat. Decisive here is the sense of repose, renewal, and sensual gratification identified with withdrawal from the city to a more natural environment. We know that some of these pleasurable feelings derive as much from what is missing as from what is actually present in the extra-urban setting. In the literary retreat, the pastoral figure's mind is released from the nagging responsibilities of a complex social life, the flood of conflicting stimuli, and the painful omnipresence of history itself. Some of his satisfaction, however, actually derives from the natural landscape, either from its specific physical attributes (the fresh air, the greenness, the color of flowers, etc.), or from its psychological and associative attributes. A natural setting, if only because it is less cluttered with man-made objects, provides a more hospitable field for the projection of his feelings. It thereby enhances, if only momentarily, his sense of his own power and importance. But a vital element here is the residuum of teleological modes of thought—the tendency to identify the seeming orderliness of the natural landscape with the hypothetical design and purpose of the cosmos. Whether these ideas are objectively "true" or not, they do in some measure control our responses to the physical environment, and planners might profitably use more information about them.

Another principle suggested by literary pastoralism is the importance of diversity in physical settings—the need to preserve the distinctness of the three spheres of our environment: the city, the rural countryside, and the wilderness. Our literature supports the idea that each of these performs an important role in our psychic economy, and that quite apart from nostalgia, sentiment, or any narrow measures of utility, either economic or recreational, each offers indispensable satisfactions. Hence the prospect of the disappearance of any one of them, or of the irrevocable blurring of the boundaries between them, as in the spread of suburbia, would be an intolerable loss. The literary pastoral emphasizes the value of contrast as a mental resource, and seems to endorse the views of those ecologists who define the relation between the urban and extra-urban environments as a form of symbiosis.

Our pastoralism would therefore seem to confirm the view, advanced by Paul Goodman and others, that our society requires rural as well as urban reconstruction. Indeed, urban renewal without rural renewal is self-defeating, if only because rural decay is driving an impossibly large population into our cities. To make our small towns and vast countryside economically viable and culturally interesting is an indispensable aspect of solving the urban problem. Besides, the countryside should be made available to our city dwellers, and not merely a select few, as a necessary retreat from the nerve-racking demands of our complex civilization. Here again we see the relevance of the symbiotic relation that the pastoral design tacitly establishes between the contrasting environments. In Western society the wealthy and aristocratic always have appreciated the advantages of periodic retreats from the world, of moral and physical holidays from complexity. Today, in the United States, when only a small fraction of the population can be classified as rural, enjoyment of the land itself is denied to most of the people. What is needed is not the extension of suburbia or the proliferation of commercial resorts, but the invention of means whereby city dwellers can temporarily enjoy the pleasures of an alternative way of life. To make such facilities available to a much larger segment of our population would seem to be a legitimate goal for planners in an affluent, democratic society.

My final suggestion brings us back to the realistic implications of the third stage of the pastoral design: the return. Our literary pastoralists, surprisingly enough, reinforce the inescapable lesson of common sense, namely, that the mainstream of contemporary history is to be found in the urban-industrial environment. If many people feel the urge to retreat, it is in some measure an effort to invest their lives with a sense of order and meaning that is lacking in the world of the machine. The curious tendency to find more significance in the seemingly haphazard dispersal of trees, animals, and hills than in the relatively deliberate patterning of streets, buildings, and parks, cannot be wholly attributed to the actual physical character of the two settings. The flight to suburbia, which might after all be described as a debased and doomed version of the pastoral retreat, is in part at least a gesture of revulsion at the chaos, contradiction and nonmeaning that

141

we associate with our cities. It is, by the same token, an effort some-how to recapture certain social and political attributes of smaller communities.

In arguing for the importance of the social and political as well as psychological motives for the effort to escape the city, I do not mean to discount the importance of "real" physical discomfort, ethnic preju-dices, and sheer ugliness. But there is reason to believe that the almost universal preference for the suburban "country" over the city (and however foolish the idea may seem, the commuter on his way to Levittown does say that he is on his way to the "country"), also derives from the symbolic significance of the two settings. That is why it would be useful to learn more about the values that men attach to various forms of pastoral retreat, and to distinguish between those aspects of rural or wilderness living which are capable of fulfillment, and those which are illusory. For it is possible that our planners could find ways to provide some of those satisfactions within the city. They could accomplish this purpose both in the traditional manner, by reproducing certain physical conditions of rural life (parks, play-grounds, open spaces), but also by taking into consideration the need for social and political surrogates for rural and small town institu-tions.[15] Our literary pastoralism suggests that physical planning with-out political (to use the word in its broadest sense) planning is futile. What I am saying, in short, is that today the planner finds himself in a position analogous to that of the pastoral figure at the conclusion of an American fable. His problem is to find ways of creating, within the urban environment, that sense of belonging to an orderly pattern of life which has for so long been associated with the relatively unspoiled, natural landscape.

## NOTES

[1] A relevant example of this reductive method is Morton and Lucia White's book, *The Intellectual Versus the City* (1962). In effect the book is an attack upon the great American writers—indeed, upon the entire intellectual community—from Jefferson's time to that of Frank Lloyd Wright, for idealizing rural and other preindustrial ways of life and thereby creating what the Whites call an "antiurban roar." I would not deny that an antiurban bias is to be found in our literature, but I would contend that the Whites, by neglecting the conventional, metaphoric character of the urban-rural

contrast, its long history in Western thought, miss the subtle ways in which that bias often is qualified, and most important, they miss its deeper meaning. For the apparent animus usually is directed not against the city itself, i.e., the city as an actual physical environment, but rather against the system of value which the city, within a specific historical and cultural context, has come to represent. The model for this distinction is the metaphor: it is a distinction between the city as a *vehicle* or *secondary subject* (which it so often is for the literary imagination) and the city as the *primary subject*.

[2] *Studies in Classic American Literature* (1923).

[3] In the section that follows I summarize, in simplified form, material developed in greater detail in *The Machine in the Garden: Technology and the Pastoral Ideal in America* (1964).

[4] RENATO POGGIOLO, "The Oaten Flute," *Harvard Library Bulletin,* vol. XI, pp. 147–148, 1957. I am paraphrasing his definition.

[5] *Complete Poems of Robert Frost.* Copyright 1923, 1939 (c) 1967 by Holt, Rinehart and Winston, Inc. Copyright 1951 by Robert Frost. Reprinted by permission of Holt, Rinehart and Winston, Inc.

[6] I have in mind a group of the well-known short poems such as "Mowing," "The Oven Bird," "The Last Moving," "A Time to Talk," "The Tuft of Flowers," "A Brook in the City," "The Need of Being Versed in Country Things," "Spring Pools," "Desert Places," "Design," "The Most of It," and probably the most detailed and complex version of the design, "Directive."

[7] *Complete Poems of Robert Frost.* Copyright 1923, 1939 (c) 1967 by Holt, Rinehart and Winston, Inc. Copyright 1951 by Robert Frost. Reprinted by permission of Holt, Rinehart and Winston, Inc.

[8] L. THOMPSON, editor, *Selected Letters,* p. 158. Letter of March 22, 1915.

[9] "The Figure a Poem Makes," *in* COMPLETE POEMS OF ROBERT FROST. Copyright 1923, 1939 (c) 1967 by Holt, Rinehart and Winston, Inc. Copyright 1951 by Robert Frost. Reprinted by permission of Holt, Rinehart and Winston, Inc.

[10] *Complete Poems of Robert Frost.* Copyright 1923, 1939 (c) 1967 by Holt, Rinehart and Winston, Inc. Copyright 1951 by Robert Frost. Reprinted by permission of Holt, Rinehart and Winston, Inc.

[11] ERNEST HEMINGWAY, "Big Two-Hearted River," *in In Our Time.* Quoted herein by permission of the publisher, Charles Scribner's Sons.

[12] "Constancy and Change," *The New Yorker,* p. 162, March 6, 1965. My italics.

[13] The seemingly universal appeal of this theme, and especially the tendency to regard Western culture as technologically determined, is nowhere more tellingly revealed than in the notorious 1965 statement of the Chinese Minister of Defence, Marshall Lin Piao, in which he defined the present world power struggle as in essence a conflict between the big cities of the West and the revolutionary spirit of the people of the Asian, African, and Latin American countryside. "Taking the entire globe," he said, "if North America and Western Europe can be called the 'cities of the world,' then Asia, Africa and Latin America constitute the 'rural areas of the world.' " And, most interesting in the present context, his argument turns upon the association of the superior inner resources ("courage and spirit of sacrifice") of the revolutionists with their rural lives, and the relative weakness of Westerners with their urban, industrial environment. "The spiritual atom bomb that the revolutionary people possess is a far more powerful and useful weapon than the physical atom bomb." And the current spectacle of huge American bombers attacking a peasant nation in Southeast Asia may well seem to lend credence to this melodramatic image of world conflict. *New York Times,* p. 2, Sept. 4, 1965.

[14] There is a striking analogy between the symbolic landscape that recurs in our modern pastoral fables and the theory of ego autonomy held by certain Freudian psychiatrists, notably Anna Freud, Erik Erikson, Heinz Hartmann, and David Rapaport. Running through this literature is a tacit spatial metaphor, in which the ego appears as a psychic middle ground between the claims of the unconscious id and external (social) reality. To maintain the health of the ego is to maintain a precarious equi-

librium, and in Rapaport's formulation, which is comparable to the idea implicit in the examples I have cited from Frost and Hemingway, when the ego achieves maximum autonomy from one side, it risks increasing impairment from the other side. Experiments in sensory deprivation have shown that when the subject is given virtually total autonomy from the external environment, for example, he quickly becomes vulnerable to inward, instinctual drives. Similarly, when Nick Adams cuts himself off from the social environment identified with war, fire, and machines, he becomes prey to attack from his inner drives identified with the swamp. For a concise example, see David Rapaport's "The Theory of Ego Autonomy: a Generalization," *in Bulletin of the Menninger Clinic,* vol. 22, pp. 13–35, 1958.

[15] For a convincing account of the degree to which the loss of certain features of community determines attitudes toward urbanization, see Maurice. R. Stein, *The Eclipse of Community: an Interpretation of American Studies* (1960).

# WHY WE WANT OUR CITIES UGLY

PHILIP JOHNSON

A PAST DIRECTOR of the Department of Architecture and Design of the Museum of Modern Art, and a trustee since 1958, Philip Johnson is one of America's leading architects. His recent contributions to the American scene include the East Wing and Sculpture Court of the Museum of Modern Art; the New York State Theatre, Lincoln Center, in New York City; and the Glass House in New Canaan, Conn. He was a co-architect of the Seagram Building in New York City.

Born and raised in Cleveland, Ohio, Philip Johnson came east to college and has stayed and worked primarily on the East Coast ever since. Soon after his graduation from Harvard in 1930, he co-authored *The International Style, Architecture since 1922*. His other major publication, *Mies van der Rohe*, was published in 1947. Mr. Johnson is also the subject of two publications: *Philip Johnson*, by John M. Jacobus, Jr. (1962); and *Philip Johnson Architecture, 1949–1965*.

I HAVE READ for a decade now the countless wails of protest against our urban life. The complaints are all familiar to you. All do-gooders, including myself, agree on the general horror of it all. We are righteously against air pollution, water pollution. We are against poverty, ghettos, elevated super highways. We are for planning. We are for waterfront development. We are for parks, green spaces, Greenwich-Village-type neighborhoods. In sum, we are for mother-hood and against sin.

It is safe to assume that everyone is in hand-wringing agreement. And further, we all know many of the causes of our manifold troubles: the taxation system that is tilted in favor of speculation by private persons and against public planning; the built-in confusion of our myriad local governments; the almost total paralysis of our city gov-ernments in the field of planning; the unfair Federal tax system that returns only dribbles of dollars to the city; the racial prejudice, the unfair zoning; the automobile; population explosion—what more!

But what I should like to discuss is how this great mess in our environment could possibly have happened to us. We seem to be able to do some things well. We got rich, did we not? We shall get to the moon, we can fight wars, we can make automobiles. In other words, we do pretty much whatever we want to. Why can't we live in good cities?

It can only be that we do not wish to. Why, then, do we not want good cities—beautiful cities? That is my question. What sort of values have we that we should end up in helpless ugliness? No one *wants* or *wills* ugliness. But we obviously want things compatible with ugliness more than we want beauty which is not compatible with ugliness.

Now I do not say that everybody does not want beauty. Everyone does. But everyone seems to like other things more. It is my thesis that we shall not get cities designed closer to our hearts' desire until the values of people change. Unless our *"Weltanschauung,"* the color of the particular lenses we use to view the world, the presuppositions, the beliefs, the mystique we live by change first, we shall surely go from bad to worse. If I am right, we face a dismal future. Popular faiths change slowly, slowly.

It is hard to talk about values. Even the words I use to describe

147

others' values betray my own bias, my own *parti pris*. Yet we must try, for there are some values that help build beautiful places and some that do not. Utilitarians of the 18th-century variety, Puritans of the 17th were inimical, for instance, to glorious spending for beauty. Militarism, imperialism, royalism, patriotism, religion—whatever their other effects—are favorable for great building. So are glory, pomp, festival, nobility, ceremony, finery, magnificence. Science, knowledge, progress, cost control, rationalism, and technology are all, to say the least, neutral as to building. If I stated that they were actually inimical I would, I think, be nearer right, but in the present ambiance I dare not put myself so much in opposition to accepted ideas.

In my extreme moments I even talk against words. Words tend to become tools of knowledge, as distinct from love, and tend to need more words, tend to increase interest in the values of the description of things and not in the things themselves. Words multiply and feed on themselves. Words are for the mind, not the eye. Perhaps ours is not a poetic age. Words lend themselves to rationalization, to explainable situations, clarifiable situations, and when so employed deny us the mysterious communication by the eye, the ennoblement that comes from visions or from mere vision. Words then help the quantifiable and reinforce our preference for the quantifiable.

But these thoughts occur only at night or in despair. How can a sane man be against material progress and scientific knowledge? He cannot. I cite these contradictions mainly to sharpen the problem. How, with our present values, which have made us the most powerful civilization that history has known, are we going to proceed to the next step of transvaluing these values sufficiently to make our environment great?

The values of materialism, private enterprise, prevail today. We are the children of Adam Smith. God, glory, beauty—the intangibles in life—take second place. Classical economics emphasizes by its very nature what is quantifiable. If you can make a statistic about something, it exists. If a thing is not a number, it cannot exist. Nobility, honor, beauty have no numbers. Negro education has a number, so have calories and the consumption of gasoline. It is an interesting subnote on our attitude toward the values of the past that Falstaff's denigration of the word "honor" which could raise eyebrows in a culture like Shakespeare's where honor was a definite and achievable trait, today arouses sympathy. Falstaff, you remember, asks, "Can honor mend a broken leg? No. Honor is a word." In other words, what use is honor? So beauty, including the beauty of cities, is a word. What use is it? It does nothing for business; it costs money and money does have a use. Even a do-gooder would have to say, better to spend money for *more* housing rather than more *beautiful* housing.

"It costs money" is a terrible indictment in current terms. There is something reprehensible, something guilt-inducing about spending. Spending is respectable only if a proper return is envisaged. "It costs money to make money" is fine. "It costs money" is not.

The concept of private enterprise being more important than public enterprise is a peculiarly American version of Adam Smith. In the case of many European cities, the city owns its own land. Here, increased land values, though resulting from community undertakings—streets, sewers, parks—are considered a part of the legitimate area of private profit. Land speculation makes money, does it not? Even public expenditure must be good business. The Eisenhower road program, the largest construction program ever undertaken in history, very carefully had a measurable use: to benefit the truckers, increase travel, and sell automobiles. It paid.

In addition, roads are a milestone of materialist progress. And progress is another of our fixed ideas. It usually connotes material progress, quantitative progress: more cars, more airplanes, greater GNP, fewer cases of VD, and what not. Progress is never ethical or aesthetic. Nobility and beauty, alas, do not progress. That the Eisenhower roads are not things of beauty (God knows) is not considered counter-progressive. "Why are they not beautiful?" we might ask. Our leaders would answer, "What has beauty to do with it? Why do you ask such a question?" Compare the funds available for highway-beautification with the funds available for highway-construction.

Business and economics are "good" words. "Business" is a serious expression in Americanese. Being "businesslike" is good. Being artistic is a little long-haired. Being long-haired is being beatnik. Being beatnik is LSD and all that. And that, as we all know, is against the

**149**

law. So—applying the principle to our environment—we must run our cities on a sound business basis, which interpreted means sound business profits for the private developer and bankrupt breakdowns of all kinds for the public sector. Someone someday, I hope, will be called on to comment that it does not seem a very businesslike way to run a city. Why, for example, should private landowners on Staten Island walk off with a windfall of four billion dollars as a result of the Verrazzano bridge, while the city itself reaps none of this harvest?

As John Kenneth Galbraith has written, the only way to run a city for the people is to disregard false economies, to rise to a higher efficiency and economy and to build, no matter what the cost, a city that people will love to look at, a beautiful city. In that sentence, my friends, Mr. Galbraith (and I) have transgressed some of the finest taboos of our culture. I wonder if even Mr. Galbraith has any hopes for the future. I have none.

I confess to a sneaking sympathy for some of our "black" thinkers of a hundred years ago, with their gloomy prophecies. Henry Adams wrote, "My belief is that science is to wreck us, and that we are like monkeys monkeying with a loaded shell; we don't in the least know or care where our practically infinite energies come from or will bring us to."[1] Kierkegaard was more outspoken. He dared to call science, the sacred cow of our century, "that increasing mass of drivel."

Whether the causes are science-worship or reason-worship, a progress-worship or what, it is interesting to note that no culture in history has built fewer great public architectural masterpieces. The story of medieval Siena brilliantly outlined by my colleague, Professor Braunfels, is the exact opposite of ours. The Sienese had the Officio del Ornato to watch over their civic beauty. Beauty was a day-to-day care.

We obviously do not care. The Sienese pattern of thought—that the city was a simulacrum of the Heavenly City—is totally foreign to our system of values.

What culture has built so little? Some of the American Indian cultures? Certainly not the Mound Builders of Ohio or the Cliff Dwellers of Arizona. Maybe the Huns or the Mongols. But were they cultures? We know many building cultures that had no writings, or at least none that has come down to us. But I know of no literate cultures

150

which built no monuments. Two of my favorite cities come to mind—
Teotihuacan in Mexico and Fatehpur Sikri in India. I cannot tell
you what impelled their builders to build places of such beauty, what
the wellspring of desire was in their hearts. In the one case there is no
writing remaining. All who might have spoken for the culture are long
since dead. Teotihuacan lasted a thousand years, but left no written
records—just the beautiful causeway, the pyramids bigger than
Egypt's, the majestic public scale of the civic center. Only these remain for our wonder.

Fatehpur Sikri was built with incredible speed by Akbar the Great
as a palace town and was deserted 30 years later. Constructed of the
finest red sandstone, it is as perfect today as in the 16th century when
it was erected.

What made these people build such beauty? It could not have been
alone in the mind or heart of a ruler. For one man—even Akbar—to
impose an ideal on a whole people, even in a slave society, would not
have been possible. No, some urge was present that we lack today.

It is illuminating to recall the history of the past 150 years of public
civic building in our country. The story tells in its way the development of the *Weltanschauung* we now seem to have. The salient fact is
that Adam Smith's classical economics idea did not catch on quickly
and, to begin with, we built, on strange pretexts, noble and monumental buildings for less than useful purposes. I use, you note, a "bad"
word for this—*monumentality*—by which I mean buildings built primarily—not solely, necessarily, but primarily—for purposes other
than mere usefulness.

Thomas Jefferson, an 18th-century gentleman, considered architecture important for his young country. He and the best architects he
could find built monuments whenever they could. University architecture, for example, got a start at Charlottesville, Va., and among
educational institutions of its size, the University of Virginia has no
successor, for all our progress and our prosperity. Jefferson's attitude
was right.

Jefferson was not, of course, a New England Puritan. The Puritans
were, alas, in favor of usefulness. Their faith was iconoclastic, antihe-
donist. By no accident were their buildings simple. Their harsh theol-

151

ogy fitted only too well the rise of business. Max Weber's Protestant Ethic has made the connection firm. The degree to which the Puritanical streak in the American culture is responsible for our indifference to or suspicion of beauty is hard to measure but it fits all too well. Jefferson worked on the nation's capital. The city of Washington was formed and planned by monumentalists. L'Enfant's was a grand, not a practical, plan.

After such a good beginning, we start downhill. The great plan of Washington was never consummated. The Mall, which was intended as a Champs Elysées—a thoroughfare—became instead the backyard of official Washington and we have slums on the only ceremonial avenue we have left: Pennsylvania. It was only because of Daniel Burnham, a man of vision of the 90s that we managed to get the railroad tracks removed from the Mall. Practical men took over, and public buildings came under the control of the careful GSA— the-most-square-feet-for-the-dollar Government Services Administration—or the nonarchitect Architect of the Capitol, who builds expensively enough, in all conscience, but even uglier buildings than GSA.

Washington's great era did not, however, end altogether with the Federal period. After the Civil War the flush of victory brought about a renewed desire for monumentality in the capital. For a time, one hundred years ago, we built on a Gargantuan scale. The State-War-Navy Building, constructed under President Grant, was the largest office building in the world and, though not great architecture, has presence and great and costly elegance of materials—materials that today we simply would not spend enough to buy. The old Pension Building, on Fifth and F Streets, built in 1885, though ordinary outside, has the greatest room—I can truly say the only *great* room—in the nation's capital, used indeed up to the time of Taft for inaugural balls. It has come on evil days. The Great Hall is now filled with desks. No more need for grand balls. Burnham's great hall, Union Station, which was finished in 1908, is now hauntingly deserted. It is a sad era for Washington. The Rayburn Building has neither great rooms nor the appearance of greatness.

And look at our memorials and war monuments! The closer we come to the present, the fewer they are. George Washington has

152

perhaps the finest memorial of any hero in history. Even the assassinated President Garfield had the grandest, tallest structure in Cleveland for his tomb. Woodrow Wilson—surely one of the outstanding Presidents—has none. The dissension over the proposed memorial to Franklin D. Roosevelt, the perennial suggestions that we honor his memory with scholarships or trees, indicates that we have lost the sense of monumentality, or are no longer capable of the pride—vaunting, if you like—that expresses itself in monuments.

As for war memorials, we have most of all for the Civil War, fewer for the Spanish-American war, fewer still for World War I and none for World War II—except a statuary group that is a replica of a photograph. We do not live well today with memorials.

The story of Washington's monumental building is duplicated in New York. The heyday once again was the 70s, when Frederick Law Olmsted built his Central Park and his Prospect Park. Since then the city has doubled in size again and again, but parks have become vest-pocket editions. Today we simply could not afford Central Park. We can only helplessly ask: how could our forefathers?

Again, like Washington, New York came through the period of a railroad age. The great robber barons of the early century, though private citizens, had the visions of grand dukes. They built for glory. There are no entrances to any city in the world that could have vied with our Pennsylvania and Grand Central stations. In nice round figures, the Pennsylvania would cost in today's dollars 600 million. But in those days the railroads had the money and were not afraid to spend it. There was then no moral prohibition against spending. When, in 1931, the next generation's turn came for grandeur, the inhibitions of thrift and utilitarianism were beginning to be felt. Yet Rockefeller Center, though far from a gesture of profligate expenditure, like the railroad stations, made history by pulling together into architectural unity the dull, heterogeneous, conventional New York gridiron while opening it up to space, giving the visitor a sense both of splendor and of place. Again, 600 million dollars had made its mark in New York.

Today, when our generation's turn has come to build grandly in New York, what do we do? We tear down the great Pennsylvania

153

Station gateway to the city to build a money-making facility. Then we build our little Lincoln Center, a small addition indeed to the city-scape.

Philadelphia has torn itself down, but the rebuilding consists of green-glass business blocks built by private speculation, and super highways built by insensitive highway departments. Ditto New Haven. The spirit of grandeur is not in us. Our practical age has no place for great building. Statistically, perhaps, we build greatly. We build so many housing units, factories, business blocks, and what-have-you. These are—oh, so obviously!—not of a cultural or public impact. There are no new great man-created spaces or monuments in these United States.

Why do we not build great cities? Why do we spend billions building roads but nothing in cities for the roads to end up in? We subsidize—pitifully enough—housing, but we do not subsidize the great amenities of the city that make housing meaningful. Planners today refer to themselves as "housers." Is nothing more important? Or are our housers despairing of ever getting more? Will there never be anything more?

And let no one ask the stupid question, "Where is the money coming from?" Seventy billion a year to defend our country comes from somewhere. Moon travel is not cheap. Our greatest authority on spending these days is certainly Secretary of Defense McNamara. He said only last February, "Building or rebuilding our cities is not a question of money. We can afford to defend our country and *at the same time* rebuild it beautifully. The question is one of the *will* of the American people."[2]

An apt (but odd) illustration of two approaches to city-rebuilding occurs in divided Berlin, the one representing businesslike practicability, the other glory and monumentality. I am sure we all know which half of Berlin we would rather live in. Yet if one half demonstrates what is sacrificed in an approach concerned only with monumentality and the interests of a tyranny, the other advertises what is missing when efficiency, mobility, and profits-as-before (or as never before) reign supreme.

In 1945 the Russians were feeling their oats. Victory was heady in

Berlin. So with no regard for the functional needs of the inhabitants, they built for glory. Stalinallée was to have been a beaux arts dream. Towers, preposterously wide avenues, *rond-points,* and the rest. It never was completed and the architecture is quite ugly. And it is falling down slightly. Like a Potemkin village, only dismal slums lie behind. Yet it has a wild impressiveness. Someone (Stalin?) cared to express something with city planning, dared to make a statement. "A builder was here" one feels. The other monument of East Berlin is the great Soviet cemetery, The Garden of Remembrance, where full-grown trees were planted in the suburb of Treptow, where granite walls and marble steps were installed, where a magnificent processional unfolds in the visitor's path, where green grass is meticulously mown. As a Westerner I came away with the feeling that the Russians had suffered and that they cared to honor the sacrifices of their sons.

Turn to West Berlin. There are no grand cemeteries, there are no trees—only the small saplings in the Tiergarten. There are no *allées,* no avenues, no architecture at all. The atmosphere is hygienic. The rubble is cleared. Streets are clean. New buildings are growing up. What of urban design? What of that pride that we connect with President Kennedy's visit? Nowhere! The keynote is return to the status quo. The first job was to build roads à la Americaine, super highways with clover-leaves and underpasses, to take care of the automobiles to come. (As in America, public money for highways seems easy to get.) The most obvious feature to the visitor is the selling off of the land as usual to the developers along the same stupid streets that were there before Berlin was leveled. No new ideas, no new solutions. And needless to say, no glorious monuments to symbolize a reborn city. Nothing to mark for our eyes the horror and the glory of a beleaguered city.

Thus are the old decaying imperialist values converted to the newer technological values of the world in which we live.

Our American imperialist period of pride ended with the private competition of a couple of railroad buccaneers, the European period with the death of Stalin. When are we going to conceive a new set of values? If we don't, we may sanitize our towns, we may tear them down like Philadelphia and New Haven. We may change them to

155

towns with super highways like the ones that keep us in New York from our waterfront and will soon cut Washington into separate spheres, strangling the Kennedy Center as they go in hopeless tangles of spaghetti. Our cities will only grow drearier. There is nothing unsanitary about Queens or The Bronx. But neither is there any glory. We can clean our air, we can clean our water. London has cleaned its air. On the continent even the industrial Ruhr river has been sterilized. The technicians can see to these things. We might even redeem our transportation system. Montreal, Toronto, San Francisco have made a beginning.

This is all possible. We shall perhaps also learn to save our old buildings, to plant little trees along the roads. But what of the city? In New York they are building what they call a civic center. It is composed of spaghetti and crowned with public buildings that are designed—camouflaged really—as imitations of commercial skyscrapers. No one has the power, the money, the authority, or—what is sadder—the passion to recharge the city. Much less the vision that Frank Lloyd Wright always preached, to build a new capital in the center of our country.

Our passions in this country seem bound up with money. They are never for a moment unreckoning of cost. The only public passion transcending that preoccupation is war. At war we leave our counting rooms and go all out.

Just as William James tried to find a moral equivalent for war, we might search for some equivalent, too—an equivalent to War, Imperialism, Religion, Glory, Pride—to enable us to build our cities, to create for our homes gardens of delight (to use Bertrand de Jouvenel's charming phrase). We have no Louis XIV. We have no Pope Julius, no Akbar the Great. We no longer have our robber barons and their type of pride. We want no Stalin. Army generals today, unlike General M. C. Meigs who designed and built the grand old Pension Building in Washington, no longer have the authority or the wish to execute heroic gestures in masonry. We can rebuild our cities, but where will the passion come from? Not from the planners, not from Congress. Everything will be cheap—cheap and, it may be hoped, clean. But cities must be great.

156

Nor can we look to have greatness thrust upon us. India, when the British conquered it, was given by their rulers a brand new capital city, New Delhi, which in 1911 was so great that it serves today as the capital of a vastly more populous India and will be adequate for generations to come. Alas, England is not about to conquer us. Whence then the inspiration?

This is a real need, for monumentality has its uses. Louis XIV and XV planned the Paris we know with enlargements by Napoleons I and III. But the Paris we know is a lot more useful than if it had grown functionalistically. De Jouvenel points out the usefulness—even the money-profit kind of usefulness—of the Palais Royal in Paris. But, alas, just look at Paris outside the central city! Olmsted may have been a Tammany man, most of the money for Central Park may have been drained into the pockets of politicos, but Central Park is invaluable today. The robber barons may have stolen the West, but they built our stations and they put the railroads underground. That is more than our highway commissioners do with their works. It is cheaper to elevate the highways and the public be damned. Commodore Vanderbilt was more sensitive to the public weal than our public servants are today.

Monumentality is strangely functional. Olmsted's park works even better now than when he planned it. Vanderbilt's Grand Central is still adequate after 50 years, whereas Kennedy Airport was obsolete 10 years after it was built. No monumentality. When again will someone in authority (even if it be for the wrong reasons) declare "Let us have an entry to our country that will say, as the Statue of Liberty says to the ocean liners, 'Welcome to the States'?" That could mean an airport many times greater, many times bigger than any little group we have designed. And then in 10 years the airport might still be functional. When we think where our puny practicability has put us, we can only hope for grandeur.

It has already been proven on a small scale. Example: school libraries, to serve their purpose, have to be monuments to show off learning—as Jefferson so clearly understood. But Jefferson, alas, has been followed by "modern" architecture and "modern" library standards. The reading room has disappeared, everything has been made

157

cheap. The result: no feeling of pride in work, no relation of students to university, the relative standing of books diminished. And worse, no way to find your way around the building. Today, librarians are beginning to react, to appreciate the functional results of a more monumental approach. Monumental rooms help circulation and orientation—as well as pride. Another example: the railroad station. Compare the old Grand Central with the *new* Pennsylvania Station in New York, which is nothing but a subway terminus beneath a palace of entertainment. No comment is necessary.

Must we therefore invent monumentality to make our cities work? Patriotism, Nobility, Grandeur, Beauty, Glory are no longer any use. Perhaps we can call what needs to be done a war, like the War on Poverty. We might PR ourselves into a War on Ugliness.

Perhaps one way is to pick a great organization like General Motors and put it in charge of the cities. Tell it, "Now look, turn your aims around. You now want to build great cities, not make automobiles. As in World War II, when you served public ends so efficiently and built no pleasure cars, adapt your incredible know-how, your great management abilities to this new task. Do it efficiently and beautifully. Here is 100 billion or so for the first two years. Give us an accounting when you have used it up. We shall leave you alone until then. After that we'll see." Is this not Secretary McNamara's way with Boeing or General Dynamics? Is this not the way with the Saturn project? The Government pays the bill. We citizens go to the moon. But we do not ask General Motors to rebuild our cities. We would rather go to the moon. That is our substitute for monumentality.

The desire for monumentality might be said to be one of the primordial urges, like sex and food. Unfortunately, it is difficult to satisfy on an individual basis. It lies more or less within the power of each of us whether we shall eat or go hungry, have a mate or do without. Unfortunately, the average citizen cannot put up his own Arc de Triomphe. Yet surely we reveal our latent urge for monumentality in our addiction to status, beautiful clothes, gourmet meals, private swimming pools and other things we cannot afford, and pilgrimages to places of beauty—especially to beautiful old European cities; we pay hundreds and millions in precious foreign exchange every year to visit them. The urge for monumentality, like other urges, will, if repressed, find vent one way or another—and surely it could take a more desirable form than a devotion to ostentatious, over-sized motorcars that crowd one another off the streets. Is not going to the moon itself a status event dressed up as science? Surely the basis of it is pride, maybe pride only in beating the Russians, but pride. If only the Russians would build some beautiful cities, so we could take pride in building more beautiful ones! Or, while we are dreaming, if only it were to some great organization's interest to promote city-building, so our great Madison Avenue industry could be brought into high gear to tickle our pride. Alas, our promotional methods do not serve to stimulate society to outdo itself but serve only to impel consumers to buy bras, cosmetics, alcohol, automobiles.

Yet it is true that the urge to monumentality lurks in all of us, ready to betray itself in the unlikeliest ways. Has monumentality ever had a greater victory over functionalism than the spike-heel shoe? High heels are uncomfortable, destructive, expensive, dangerous. Functional, practical, in other words, they are not. Prideful status-seeking emotional monumentality has, in this case, beaten down common sense. In this battle I am on the side of common sense, and delighted that the spike heel is gone. On the other hand, women's fashions in which rationality and functionalism are thrown to the winds in favor of the splendid, preposterous gesture, may afford a clue to the type of pride that could be turned to making a beautiful environment.

There are signs, dimly on the horizon, that this pride can be on its way. The pride of the Bronfman family that built the Seagram Building, the pride of a town that builds a great museum of the arts, for example. And there is the monument that is by far the greatest of our sad times, the rebuilding of the capital of New York State. Governor Rockefeller, in the great tradition of Rockefeller Center, is out to outdo the monumental capital of Brazil at Brasilia, to create a modern city center for the pride of New Yorkers. This modest billion dollar beginning at Albany just might be the appetite-whetting hors d'oeuvre that could cause a moon-going type of craze for rebuilding our environment. It is sure that "practical" palliatives, "good" housing, clean slum-clearance projects will never start us off; a monumentally rebuilt capital city just might.

A final quote from Bertrand de Jouvenel's paper: "When Italy [was the richest country] in the late Middle Ages and during the Renaissance, it gave the world what is still our richest patrimony. Is it not time for her heirs to emulate her?"

## NOTES

[1] Letter of August 1902 to his brother, Brooks Adams.
[2] Personal conversation with permission to quote.

# HUMAN NEEDS AND INHUMAN CITIES

EDWARD T. HALL

EDWARD T. HALL is Professor of Anthropology in the College of Arts and Sciences and Professor of Organization Theory in the School of Business at Northwestern University. He is in his seventh year of continuing research on man's perception of space in the United States and abroad. His most recent book, *The Hidden Dimension* (1966), deals with proxemics—man's use of space.

Born in Webster Grove, Mo., in 1914, Dr. Hall received his A.B. from the University of Denver and his Ph.D. from Columbia University. After service in World War II, he conducted fieldwork in Micronesia. For five years he served as Director of the State Department's Point IV Training Program where he trained Americans for service overseas. He has taught at the University of Denver, Bennington College, the Harvard Business School, and the Illinois Institute of Technology.

A consultant to the Government, private foundations, and business, Dr. Hall is a Fellow of the American Anthropological Association. He is also a lecturer and the author of *The Silent Language* (1959), *The Hidden Dimension,* and numerous articles in professional journals.

THE UNITED STATES today finds itself in the midst of four interrelated crises. The first is political and is particularly critical overseas in Vietnam. The second concerns the macroecological system as defined by Barbara Ward in *Spaceship Earth*. The third crisis is the population explosion, and the fourth is the urban crisis. Additional subcrises which are byproducts of our rapid economic growth complicate the distressing state of the culturally deprived in "the other America." I think history may show that, in spite of the urgency and the seriousness of our political-military involvement in Vietnam, the last three crises will require our greatest expenditure of energy and wisdom, and a far greater concentration of total effort than that demanded in this war. From my own point of view, I find it impossible to separate these three crises: ecological-systems, population explosion, and urban deterioration. All of them bear directly on the topic of this symposium.

One does not shape and maintain the physical environment independent of the spatial experience which may range from the most intimate—like the physical touching of bodies—to reveries of future excursions to lakes and mountain streams. The sense of crowding—or its obverse—is so subtle and so complex that I am continually amazed by some newly-identified facet of the subject. I was once discussing spatial needs with a psychiatric colleague, and he pointed out the relationship of unused distant space to one's immediate feelings about life in the city. He phrased it as follows: "If I were to hear that the people of the United States no longer had access to our national parks—the forests and the mountains and the great outdoors—even though I might never visit them again, my anxiety rate would be very considerably increased. The important thing is to know that they are there and available." When someone says that his anxiety rate has risen, this is only another way of saying that he is under stress and that his adrenals are working overtime. There are, of course, a great many individuals who, having lived all of their lives in cities, have no conscious need for open space and, in fact, may even be quite threatened by the outdoors. There is great danger, however, in allowing a large segment of our population to grow up without ever experiencing the complex relationships that make up ecological systems: we could

163

develop a citizenry so uninformed as to permit the destruction of its own biotope. I'm not certain that we have not already done so. As recently as five years ago, it was difficult to interest people in the significance of John Calhoun's work with rats or John Christian's studies of the consequences of animal crowding. Today, one can hardly pick up a newspaper without reading about a new study on the effects of crowding. This recent preoccupation with crowding is symptomatic of our times, and our growing awareness of its consequences is extremely encouraging. There is also an increased awareness of the fact that each species inhabits its own biotope, and that each biotope constitutes part of a complex of interrelated ecosystems. All too many Americans, however, still demand specific answers to specific problems. In considering the human environment we are not dealing with the kind of phenomena in which one can identify specifics. Rather, we are dealing with systems that require a holistic approach, a point made repeatedly and elegantly by René Dubos. The ethological evidence is overwhelming: as populations build up, so does stress. Eventually, the animals' capacity to withstand stress begins to diminish, and the population collapses for a variety of reasons.[1]

Man has confounded the issue considerably and in a number of different ways. Not only has he produced a variety of extensions—like automobiles and factories—but his evolution is now primarily *by means* of his extensions. Man has conditioned himself to respond in quite different ways to the environmental pressures of crowding. In a sense, people of different ethnic groups respond differently to crowding because they perceive space differently. Man, as a culture-producing and culture internalizing organism, has created a number of different types of biotopes for himself. There is no standard way of measuring spatial adequacy for man. What is crowded to an Englishman would be impossibly controlled or understimulating to an Arab. Because of such cultural differences, it is necessary to introduce an added dimension that will make it possible to equate space needs of different cultures according to some sort of self-anchoring scale. We have this instrument in the various theories of sensory deprivation and information overload. Man can suffer from both, and an excess of either can destroy him.[2] An adequate environment balances sensory

164

inputs and provides a mix that is congenial as well as consistent with man's culturally conditioned needs. This principle applies to housing standards for our own socioeconomic groups in the United States. I mention this by way of introduction because the hidden structure of culture is one of the most consistently ignored features of our 20th-century life.

What are we facing today in our cities? In the summer of 1966, Joseph Alsop devoted three columns to cities. In his first column he wrote: "The problem of the cities, in the form it is now assuming, is the most urgent, the most difficult, and the most frightening American domestic problem that has emerged in all the years of this country's history since the Civil War."[3] In a recent *Fortune* article, Edmund Faltermayer states: "Two things are common to all the great cities: an exciting and beautifully designed downtown section, and a large middle-class population living close to the central core. Most American cities fail miserably on both counts. Only New York, Chicago, and San Francisco can even make claims to greatness."[4] Elsewhere I have stated: "the implosion of the world population's into cities everywhere is creating a series of destructive behavioral sinks more lethal than the hydrogen bomb. Man is faced with a chain reaction and practically no knowledge of the structure and the cultural atoms producing it."[5] The current urban crisis is sufficiently acute that its seriousness is widely recognized by laymen and specialist alike.

In the last thirty years, the character of our major cities in the United States has changed radically.[6] Our cities have been bombed by urban renewal in as devastating a way—and just as effectively—as though they had been bombed by an outside enemy. The difference is that if the bombing had come from an enemy, we would have recognized the crisis and would have done something about it. As it is, there is no coherent program for our cities. People are moved about, neighborhoods destroyed, whole viable social groups disrupted, and the fabric of life disintegrated—all in the name of progress. Fried's and Gleicher's studies of the Boston West End are particularly relevant.[7] For the first time we have documentation on an impressive scale of what happens when the members of a dominant ethnic group and class look at the biotope of another group and fail to see its structure.

165

Seeing no structure, they then proceed to destroy. The same thing has happened in many other American cities.

Lewis Mumford accustomed us to thinking of the city as a process. He showed the city as the focus of the activities that make up what we have come to know as civilization. It is not too farfetched to think of a society as a living organism. Using a physiological analog, the city can be compared to various parts of the nervous system. If we were, therefore, to perceive in a human body the wild and uncontrolled growth of cells in the central nervous system or in an important ganglion of nerves controlling the functions, we would know that there was a serious crisis and act accordingly. In considering the plight of our cities, I do not detect signs of the kind of urgent action that the symptoms warrant. In fact, Vice President Humphrey observed recently that if the war in Vietnam were to end tomorrow he questioned whether the United States was prepared to spend the released billions on the urban environment.[8]

In our economic development programs overseas, we recognize that there is very little that can be done about underdeveloped countries until a large, stable, middle class has been established. These countries that have been recipients of so much foreign aid are by and large characterized by a massive, undereducated, underskilled working or peasant class. Our own major cities are now taking on many of the population characteristics of the so-called underdeveloped countries. As the poor move into cities and the middle-class flees to the suburbs, the situation in the cities becomes increasingly unstable. Cities today are principally for the very rich and the very poor.

In New York City, traffic is at a standstill because we cannot bring ourselves to do the obvious: discourage private vehicles from entering Manhattan by imposing high tolls, and restrict the time when trucks can use the streets. A recent issue of *Newsweek* was devoted to the incredible difficulty that Americans experience getting around this country.[9] A city that is impossible to get out of without going through the added tension of traffic jams has a higher stress factor than one with decent, pleasant public transportation. There is an added element of the irrational here for, as Alsop says in the columns referred to above, we are willing to spend billions upon billions for freeways and expressways that pour automobiles into our cities, and virtually nothing for schools. Yet our schools represent one of the single most important features of our environment: people will make all kinds of sacrifices to move into an area where there are good schools, and almost nothing will hold them in an area where the schools are inferior.

When Europeans first settled North America, man was presented with an entire continent rich in resources. He had the tools, the know-how, and the energy to exploit it. No such situation has ever existed before, nor will it exist again on our planet. In the four generations since the Civil War, when this country was forming itself, we acquired some very bad habits which permitted every man to do as he pleased. Now we have suddenly run out of frontier, and we have produced an economy which, like a chain reaction, is self-sustaining. Our prosperity could ruin us, not because it is bad to be prosperous, but simply because we don't know how to plan for the added dwellings, automobiles, boats, and airplanes. Nor have we learned how to dispose of the resulting pollutants, or how to design the spaces for the masses of people that are moving in and out of our cities each day.

In the United States we allow individuals to do virtually anything: pollute the lakes, contaminate the atmosphere, build a high-rise next door that makes our own living space uninhabitable because it shuts off the view, create walled-in slums in public housing high-rise, transform a potential recreation area on a lake into a run-down industrial waste, plow up the countryside, bulldoze trees, and build thousands of identical prefabricated bungalows in open country. Peter Blake in his book, *God's Own Junkyard,* has documented this aspect of our anarchic and anomic approach to planning. I have discovered (to my sorrow) that in building a house, plumbers and electricians often make important decisions overruling the owner and the architect: they change walls with abandon, run pipes where they should never be, and arrange interior spaces at will. Similarly, important decisions on the national scene are often made by officials, both public and private, who have little or no knowledge of the consequences of their actions.

If our historical traditions have been no help to us in the face of our

167

environmental crisis, the state of present day knowledge about man also leaves much to be desired. We need to learn much more about man's basic nature and his requirements as a biological organism. Also lacking is basic data on what constitutes optimum conditions for man's social and cultural development. In recent years I have been conducting research on one aspect of man's requirements: his spatial needs. In the course of my work on proxemics—man's perception and use of space—I've observed that man shares with lower life forms certain basic needs for territory. Each man has around him an invisible series of space bubbles that expand and contract, depending upon his emotional state, his culture, his activities, and his status in the social system. People of different ethnic origins need different kinds of spaces, for there are those who like to touch and those who do not. There are those who want to be auditorially involved with everybody else (like the Italians), and those who depend upon architecture to screen them from the rest of the world (like the Germans). A more detailed description of cross cultural differences in the perception and use of space can be found in my book on proxemics, *The Hidden Dimension.*

In addition to ethnic differences in spatial requirements there are differences in people's tolerance for change and mobility within their own culture. Studying the effects of urban renewal on slum dwellers, I've found evidence that indicates that very poor uneducated people have a much lower tolerance for being displaced than people of the middle class. Even a move across the street can be traumatic because it alters the pattern of social relationships. This is one of many reasons why the "Instant Rehab" experiments in New York are of great importance. These experiments involve a procedure for stripping the interior of an old building down to the brick or masonry wall, cutting a large hole in the roof and lowering a core of preassembled utility systems through the roof. Using this technique, trained crews of workmen have completely rehabilitated a small building in less than two days. For this short period, the building's occupants can be moved to a hotel and then moved back to their old home with no disruption of their relationships with friends and neighbors.

For several years I have been investigating the relationship of the

168

working class urbanite to his environment. It is a widely known fact that high-rise public housing has not been popular with high-rise occupants, particularly those families who have recently come to the city from rural areas. My studies indicate that the high-rise not only structures relationships between the occupants in specific ways, but it removes many of the challenges and the reasons for neighborhood organizations that, in turn, perform important social functions. The high-rise has proved to be a new source of anomie in ghetto life.

To further complicate the problem of providing adequate public housing for our urban populations, Glazer and Moynihan have documented the long suspected fact that the United States is not the melting pot that we once believed it to be. Ethnicity is much more tenacious than had originally been supposed. Yet, nowhere do I find evidence that plans for public housing recognize the existence of different needs for different ethnic groups. Recent growing concern about air pollution and water pollution, sparked by newspaper and TV publicity, has helped alert the country to these dangers. Hopefully we will soon have national pollution controls. Another grave danger, but one that is not widely understood, is the very real danger we face from overcrowding in our urban centers.

It seems obvious to say that our total environment must be protected and enhanced by the establishment of national and local planning authorities using the best available professional advisors. Two key disciplines needed for successful environmental planning are architecture and city planning. Unfortunately, neither discipline is presently prepared for this responsibility. The education of architects and planners is, with few exceptions, extraordinarily limited. Conspicuously absent from their curricula are the social sciences and humanities, to say nothing of ecology. Training in even rudimentary research procedures is rare. In the last seven years, I have addressed at least three thousand architects, published in the principal architectural journals, taught architecture students, and interviewed dozens of architects. In all this time I have failed to find a single instance of a systematic recording of feedback from users which could later be incorporated in the program or design phase of a new building. All over the United States, rooms have been getting steadily smaller,

**169**

ceilings lower, walls more transparent to sound, views cut off, and what do we know about the consequences? What hard data is there? What feedback from users? Every year the Government spends millions for building, yet nowhere is there a requirement for impartial reporting on the degree to which these buildings serve the needs of their occupants. For example, FHA requirements for housing, promulgated with the best of intentions, bear little or no relation to man's sense of crowding and often place a straitjacket on all but the most pedestrian designers. Even the Pueblo Indians in New Mexico, if they are to qualify for FHA loans, must choose from among FHA designs (White man's designs). Pueblo designs do not meet FHA standards, yet they are vastly more suited to the needs of the Indians than any design produced by FHA.

The professions of architecture and city planning suffer from serious deficiencies which must be corrected if this nation is to plan intelligently to improve the total environment. I refer to: first, the widespread practice of architects and planners to pay close attention to a narrow reference group (other architects), awarding prizes on the basis of two-dimensional representations of structures often *before they are built!* Few designers see *people* in their projects, only prizes from other architects and planners. Second, there is a failure to get feedback on the consequences of their design decisions. Third, there are no plans for making available the results of studies that could be used in plans for future building: there is no clearinghouse for architectural programs or designs by geographic area, class, or ethnic group. The result is that even when architects and planners want such data they have virtually no way of finding it.

The extreme seriousness of our environmental crisis demands immediate and total response from this nation with the full participation of business, Government, and universities. By and large our universities have failed to become involved in environmental problems until very recently, and most of them are still only peripherally involved. It is no wonder that students all over the country are setting up their own underground colleges to meet today's problems. I would suggest that the university, as we know it, should be stood on its head.

It is not enough to set up centers for "urban studies," which are usually only a sop to the urban crisis and a means to tap Government and foundation funds. Instead, the entire university should be *involved* in the urban process.

In recent years I have had the good fortune to work with design students. As a group they are the most responsive students I have ever taught. If they are properly trained, they question the basic design of virtually everything. They examine the processes at work in a given activity and they question assumptions endlessly. Because they are already trained to look for new ideas and new solutions, I have found that I can train these students in half the time required for liberal arts students. Tómas Maldonado has suggested that design education be integrated into the university curriculum on a level with the divisions of physical science, behavioral science, and the humanities. This idea should certainly be tried. I can think of nothing more important than teaching young people about environmental design, using data from such disciplines as ecology, psychology, and anthropology. Particular attention should be focused on research into man's spatial requirements. I am confident that such research and training would produce students who could discover better answers to man's needs than are currently being provided.

In addition to training and research programs, I would hope that some of our universities would begin to produce some working models of man's biotope. These would enable us to make accelerated studies of the total environment including our cities. At the moment we have no working model for the city.

In closing I would like to stress the importance of considering this small planet as an entire ecological system. This concept is basic to any planning for the improvement of our environment. We can regard our cities either as disaster areas beyond remedial action or as opportunities to learn more about man and his relationships to his environment. If we choose the latter course we will find that most of our urban problems merely reflect basic inadequacies in our total environment; inadequacies which will have to be remedied if man is going to persist on this planet.

## NOTES

[1] This process has been described in detail by JOHN CHRISTIAN (The Pathology of Overpopulation; *Military Medicine,* no. 7, pp. 571–603, July 1963) and V. C. WYNNE-EDWARDS (Self-regulatory Systems in Populations of Animals; *Science,* vol. 147, pp. 1543–1548, March 1965: *Animal Dispersion in Relation to Social Behavior,* New York, 1962). Highly relevant here is the work of Wilhelm Schäfer, director of the Frankfort Natural History Museum. Schäfer's 1956 monograph, *Der Kritische Raum und die Kritische Situation in der Tierischen Sozietät* (*Critical Room and Critical Situations in Animal Societies*), deals with the added dimension of pollution and how it has been handled in the past on simpler organizational levels. Schäfer's point is that as population builds up, a critical situation is reached when a population contaminates its environment with its own waste products. If this crisis is not solved, the population dies rapidly and the process is irreversible. Each solution to a crisis has in it the seeds of new crises because solutions permit larger and larger concentrations of organisms, hence greater volume of pollutants which, in turn, demands more drastic solutions.

[2] In a paper presented at the 133d annual convention of the American Association for the Advancement of Science in Washington, D.C., on Dec. 27, 1966, A. S. Welch and B. L. Welch reported that small laboratory animals went into a stupor when crowded (overstimulated). The specific agent was an overabundance of three chemicals—norepinephrine, dopamine, and serotinin—which carry messages across the synapses separating nerve cells in the brain. See also: A. S. WELCH AND B. L. WELCH, Differential Effect of Chronic Grouping and Isolation on the Metabolism of Brain Biogenic Amines, *The ASB Bulletin,* vol. 13, no. 2, p. 48 (April 1966); B. L. WELCH, Psychophysical Responses to the Mean Level of Environmental Stimulation: a Theory of Environmental Integration, Symposium on Medical Aspects of Stress in the Military Climate, Washington, D.C., April 1964 (sponsored by Walter Reed Army Institute of Research).

[3] JOSEPH ALSOP, Matter of Fact, *The Washington Post,* Aug. 1, 3, and 5, 1966.

[4] EDMUND K. FALTERMAYER, What it takes to make great cities, *Fortune,* vol. LXXV, pp. 118–123, 146–151, January 1967.

[5] EDWARD T. HALL, *The Hidden Dimension,* Garden City, N.Y., 1966. See, in particular, chap. XII, p. 155.

[6] This has been extensively reported on by: CHARLES ABRAMS, *The City is the Frontier,* New York, 1965; CONSTANTINOS A. DOXIADIS, *Urban Renewal and the Future of the American City,* 1966; *Architecture in Transition,* New York, 1963; MARC FRIED, Grieving for a lost home, *in* Leonard J. Duhl's *The Urban Condition,* New York, 1963; HERBERT GANS, *The Urban Villagers,* Cambridge, Mass., 1960; NATHAN GLAZER AND DANIEL P. MOYNIHAN, *Beyond the Melting Pot,* Cambridge, Mass., 1963; VICTOR GRUEN, *The Heart of Our Cities,* New York, 1964; E. H. GUTKIND, *The Twilight of Cities,* New York, 1962; JANE JACOBS, *The Death and Life of Great American Cities,* New York, 1961; BARBARA WARD, The Menace of Urban Explosion, *The Listener,* vol. 70, no. 1807, pp. 785–787, November 14, 1963 (BBC, London).

[7] MARC FRIED AND PEGGY GLEICHER, Some Sources of Residential Satisfaction in an Urban Slum, *Journal of the American Institute of Planners,* vol. 27, 1961.

[8] JAMES RESTON, Washington: The State of the Union, *New York Times,* January 8, 1967.

[9] The Agony of Getting Anywhere, *Newsweek,* vol. 69, no. 2, pp. 43–48 (January 9, 1967).

# SCIENCE AND THE CITY

ROBERT C. WOOD

ROBERT C. WOOD took office as Under-Secretary in the Department of Housing and Urban Development on January 18, 1966. For more than a decade prior to that, Dr. Wood was on the faculty of the Political Science Department of the Massachusetts Institute of Technology. He was also, in 1965, a member of the Advisory Board of the National Capital Transportation Agency.

Dr. Wood is a member of the American Academy of Arts and Sciences, the American Society for Public Administration, and the American Political Science Association. While attending Princeton University, where he received his A.B. in 1946, he was elected to Phi Beta Kappa.

Born in St. Louis, Mo., in 1923, Dr. Wood spent his early life in Jacksonville, Fla. Following his service with the 76th Infantry during World War II, he attended Harvard University where he received his Master of Public Administration in 1947, an MA in 1948, and a Ph.D. in 1950. From 1949–51 he was the Associate Director of the Legislative Reference Bureau of the State of Florida. In 1951 he joined the U.S. Bureau of the Budget as a management organization expert in the field of housing. In 1954 he accepted an invitation to become a member of the faculty of M.I.T.

Dr. Wood is the author of *Suburbia, Its People and Their Politics* (1958), *Metropolis Against Itself* (1959), *1400 Governments, the Political Economy of the New York Region* (1960), and is the co-author of *School Men and Politics* (1962), and *Government and Politics of the U.S.* (1965).

EVER SINCE the beginning of the Industrial Revolution, science has been associated with industrial advance. It is responsible for many developments that make urban life possible. Consequently it seems odd that in discussions of cities and their ills science is so often made the chief culprit. Perhaps, given the historical roots of most urban experts, this is inevitable. In any case, I should like to focus here on the *positive* potential of science in urban affairs, a potential which has increased steadily and dramatically.

My subject is one that my friends in the Defense Department might call "the city-science interface"—that still-largely unexplored frontier along which modern concepts of science and technology can encounter the problems of urban growth and urban living. In this encounter, I believe, lies the possibility of effective modification of the urban environment in response both to increased understanding of the forces which shape it and to the goals of the community and the nation. A heightened awareness and clarification of these goals should be both the starting point and the result of this most urgent endeavor.

My topic is not current urban policy and program (I shall take a brief vacation from these), but rather some basic postulates and assumptions out of which policy arises.

Let me make clear at the onset that I am talking particularly about the urban experience in the United States. American cities, towns, and suburbs are the principal area of my professional concern and personal experience. Urban development everywhere, however, has shown many common patterns and stresses. And the techniques of analysis which I will be discussing are certainly widely adaptable.

As the theme of this symposium implies, certainly both our national challenge and that of other nations has become not only the protection and development of our natural environment, but the restoration and molding of our artificial environment to meet the needs of man. The new "conservation" turns more often on the creative and effective utilization of space, not on preserving its primeval status.

The environment of almost everyone in the years to come will be a large urban complex: an intense matrix of physical and social structures within which we will be in daily confrontation with hundreds of other human beings. Everyone knows by now that atoms that are friendly when far enough apart become fearsomely explosive when enough of them are so compressed and arranged that a stray cat called a neutron can start a chain reaction among them. We know that people, too, generate energy from togetherness, although almost nothing is known about their "critical mass."

A distinguished scientist, Walter Rosenblith, has described the city as a combination of physics and biology, and he has observed that the constraints of both disciplines still operate when it comes to social organization. The first constraint of science—as well as its strength—lies in a tie to reality, to what can be observed, measured, or deduced in a repeated and predictable fashion.

In assessing our urban condition, we can profit greatly from a precise approach and scientific techniques. If we appraise our situation as carefully as possible, and approach its shortcomings in a rational manner, we can turn the power of science and technology to the humane purposes which we share. This, in any case, is the simple thesis I wish to put before you. Parenthetically, we are starting pretty much from scratch in this effort. Urban research and development are remarkably new additions to the postwar R & D "explosion."

The line of departure is a brief review of the nature of the so-called urban "crisis" and the conjunction of demographic, political, and technical factors which make the improvement of our urban environment at this time both possible and necessary. Next, the emphasis falls on certain useful concepts borrowed from the physical sciences and their relevance to this improvement. Finally, some features of our metropolitan political structure will be highlighted—features which will partly determine whether and how these changes will come about.

You are all familiar with the melancholy tenor of the analyses of our urban scene during the past fifteen years. Our general domestic incompetence has been indicted by a series of impressionistic writers, operating on the whole from extraordinarily narrow empirical bases.

In the 1950's, the emphasis was on the just-blooming suburbs. The popular sociology painted a dark view of unhappy gray-flanneled conformists manipulated by the persuaders of Madison Avenue. More serious observers—Riesman, Whyte, Keats, Mills, Mumford, Lyne—

176

granting important difference in social emphasis, agreed that the post-war generation's social pattern was distressingly undifferentiated and that its criteria of land use were both deplorably inefficient and taste-less. Optimists thought they detected the beginning of a return to the city, a general forsaking of crabgrass and backyard barbecues.

More recently, a similarly impressionistic indictment has been fo-cused on the central city. Its chronic fevers—decay, poverty, ugliness, despair—are viewed with fresh alarm. Its temperature is measured on a thermometer that runs only from critically ill to hopelessly mori-bund. We are being urged to desperate and radical measures.

Some commentators are increasingly skeptical of relying on govern-ment as an instrument of change in urban affairs. They would put as much responsibility as possible back in the private sector. They would cut back Federal aid programs in favor of block grants to State and local governments, and direct transfers of income to poor families.

These indictments have a strong emotional appeal. They speak to our personal encounters with junkyards and honky-tonk commercial strips, with repetitious suburban developments and abrasive urban slums. They speak to our impatience with the complexity and sluggish-ness of federal administrative machinery. They speak to our nostalgia for the towns and cities of our childhood.

Emotion, personal observation and nostalgia are not, however, the most reliable guides for policy and action. It is from the facts, the realities of our environment, that we must begin. It is in the most careful and systematic analysis that the opportunity lies for under-standing and change. The tools now available for this analysis are so advanced that they threaten to render a whole generation of social scientists—myself included—obsolete. But challenges to personal careers ought not to impede general progress.

The studies and information that are available suggest that the urban obituaries are exaggerated, that our present metropolitan struc-ture operates tolerably well and that its problems are neither mysteri-ous nor unmanageable. The problems of the spread-city involve trans-porting, educating, and employing people. They involve maintaining and extending the services and facilities necessary to a modern com-munity. They involve finding ways to ascertain the community will and make it effective. Above all, they involve improving the life of the residents of the city.

These problems are not easy to resolve but they certainly are susceptible to rational solutions, and we live in a singularly suitable time in which to begin on them. This is a critical period in urban affairs, not because our cities are on the brink of death, but because the decisions and actions of the next few years will make a genuine difference in their entire life pattern.

Several factors give us at this time a unique opportunity to master the urban environment:

First, this is—relatively speaking—a "pause period" in urban population growth. We have a few years, perhaps three or so, in which experimentation and fresh patterns of development are possible—until the children of World War II's baby boom reach the stage of family formation and submerge us once again in the waves of demand for housing and facilities which characterized the period from 1945 to 1947.

Secondly, the public spotlight has finally turned to urban affairs. The press, television, State legislatures, professional and civic organizations have shown sustained concern with urban issues, and these are high on the public agenda.

Third (partly as a result of this new attention), we have flexible new legislative tools with which to work. I refer particularly to the model-cities, metropolitan-development, and new-communities provisions of the Housing Act passed in November of 1966.

Fourth, our technical capability is enormous and increasing. In the effort to understand and modify our environment, we have at our disposal a tool chest any magician would envy: advanced computers, materials research, information systems, simulation theory, and communications engineering. These developments will continue to have profound effects on our environment. They can, however, be made the servant of our values and not their master.

The convergence of these four factors—the pause in urban growth, sustained public interest, and new technical and legislative tools— makes the immediate improvement of our environment possible. Such improvement is also necessary.

It is necessary not because our suburbs are untenable or our cities moribund. It is necessary, first of all, because simple equity demands that our unprecedented national prosperity be made to touch the lives of the poor. The present residents of our urban ghettos are *not* worse off than their predecessors, the tired refugees from European poverty. In most cases, they live better.

Better, however, is not enough. As the Midwestern enunciation on radio has tended, in the past few decades, to become the standard of American speech, so our comfortable middle-class world of television is becoming the standard of our expectations and our image of the good life. The poor, trapped in our cities, are made aware daily and graphically of the gap that separates them from this life. As our sullen summers of discontent have testified, rising expectations have a boiling point.

Immediate improvement is necessary, secondly, because the present "pause period" will be followed by an indefinite period of rapid rise in urban population. The human flood will tend to course down existing streambeds. Its speed and volume will make the establishment of new patterns and directions increasingly difficult.

Finally, the great promise of our present capability has its own moral imperative. If we have the chance to raise the quality of the urban environment, if we have the chance to recapture the historic options offered by urban life, we have a certain obligation to try and do just that.

Our national mode has always tended toward a pragmatic approach to social issues. The multiplication of our information-processing capabilities means that our pragmatism in urban affairs can be based on increasingly realistic assessments and predictions. Until the last decade or so, decision-making for the city was largely a matter of seats-of-pants judgment, of political intuition. With the use of computers and mathematical models, these decisions can now be made on the basis of thousands of units of actual data.

If we can proceed from a rational, problem-solving stance, urban problems can be undertaken in the classic scientific manner. The phenomena are identifiable, alternative approaches can be found, testing and experimentation are not impossible.

179

Postwar developments in computer and communications technology have revolutionized research in both the biological and physical sciences. Except in isolated instances, these technologies have not yet been exploited in dealing with urban problems. It takes only sixteen minutes from the time a soldier is injured in the jungles of Viet Nam until he is under anesthesia in a modern operating room, and yet the ambulances in our cities still crawl and howl their way through rush hour traffic.

Developing urban technology is not, however, our first or most difficult task. The task is not even getting more money, although proper research—as we all know—is expensive. As we move to make use of our considerable capacity for modifying our environment, the great need is for rigorous analysis: analysis of what the shortcomings of that environment are and how they relate to one another; analysis of what we are trying to accomplish and what the obstacles are to doing so. We need to use people trained in many disciplines to confront these obstacles in fresh ways. We need to make our goals clear, to explore their implications, to be willing to take risks.

The modern garb of this kind of rigorous and rational endeavor is "systems analysis" or a "systems approach." Being fashionable, these terms are used in as many ways as there are shades of blonde in a chorus line. This faddishness, however, should not negate their utility. The systems concept is important because it is a technique for dealing manageably with very complicated problems; for getting a handle on reality.

Two hundred years ago, King Stanislaus of Poland described science as "nothing but good sense and sound reason." The same might be said of systems analysis. When we talk about applying systems analysis to metropolitan planning, we are not trying to add another layer of academic sophistry to an already jargon-laden process. We are describing a way to make planning work by relating it to what is really happening, by making it realistic and precise. When we talk about viewing the city as a system, we are not trying to hasten the arrival of 1984, we are emphasizing the intricate but not indecipherable relationships among all the institutions and processes making up a modern urban center.

A city can be seen as a total network of internal systems—systems for assuring people's health, mobility, and cleanliness, fighting fires, enforcing laws, providing shelter, educating children, and so forth. One enthusiast for this approach, architect John Eberhard, suggests[1] dividing a city's sub-systems between "hardware" and "software," analogous to the usual distinctions between the nuts and bolts of a computer and its programs. He compares a city's hardware systems to those of the human body:

—the metabolic system—"the network which provides for the ingestion each day of hugh quantities of water, supplies, food, and fuel and the consequent production of waste in the form of sewage, garbage, trash, and air pollutants;"

—the cardio-vascular system—"the horizontal and vertical paths of movement and the objects which move along them, like subways and trains, highways and automobiles, sidewalks, stairways, and people;"

—the nervous system—"the information-communication network of the city which makes it possible for its many parts to keep in touch, for it to be (at least potentially) managed as an entity, or for signals to be emitted at the proper time in order for the other systems to remain under control;"

—the enclosure system—"the combination of skeletal . . . subsystems . . . which surround the hollow places of the city in which the life of the city goes on."

The "software" of the city could be similarly grouped, he suggests, around the economic, the political, the educational, and the life-support systems.

The usefulness of this or any other list lies not in the categories chosen but in the degree to which they facilitate analysis and fresh insight. The techniques of systems analysis offers certain special contributions to urban problem-solving. These include the following: first, the emphasis on considering total processes rather than individual units; second, the emphasis on the relationships, the "intersections," between various processes; third, the emphasis on the use of models and/or field experiments to examine the effect of changes at different intersections or at different points in a given system; fourth, the emphasis on an interdisciplinary approach, on communication not only

181

among various engineering specialties, but among engineers, planners, biologists, psychologists, politicians, and anyone else who can contribute to understanding how the system works; and fifth, the emphasis on identifying goals and balancing them off against other goals as possible courses of action.

For examples of how these techniques might be applied to aspects of our urban environment, I will rely on the report of the Woods Hole summer study on Science and Urban Development. Sponsored jointly by the Department of Housing and Urban Development and the President's Office of Science and Technology, this six-week study was a fruitful preliminary exercise in gathering together gifted men and women from many disciplines to examine the contributions which systematic research and applied technology might bring to certain important urban problems.

The participants decided to divide their explorations into five areas providing a sampling of the city's systems: new housing, rehabilitation, transportation, environmental engineering, and health services. Here are a few of the avenues they identified for further study:

*New Housing:* This panel discussed the use of models as an aid to determining the optimum size, composition, location, and spacing of nuclei or enclaves of new housing within the inner city. They pointed to the use of operations research to generate alternatives in the distribution of population density, both for single cities and the nation. They urged that we learn how to design our cities and our homes with a view to the replacement of their components as these become obsolete. They recommended a computer-simulation of the housing market as being well within the limits of current computer technology. Most importantly, they saw the question of new housing as being inseparable from that of the entire manmade environment.

*Rehabilitation:* This panel considered not only the rehabilitation of housing but of whole cities. In meeting the costs of improving substandard dwellings, they suggested the possibility of finding—on a cost-benefit basis—the optimum mixture of three approaches: lowering housing costs, raising levels of income, and subsidizing to close the gap remaining. They identified a great many possible "hardware" innovations: vertical shopping centers, improved systems of security,

182

improved flow of traffic and access to dwelling units by means of moving belts for the transport of pedestrians, outdoor and indoor elevator systems. They emphasized the possibility of thorough study of the direct and indirect costs of antiquated housing and neighborhood facilities, which could be compared to the cost of making them adequate.

*Health Services:* This panel, like the others, began with a sense of the intimate relationship of health services to the full scope of human services—including education, welfare, recreation—and to urban development programs as a whole. Its members focused on the problem of the *delivery* of health and other services to people living in urban communities, on the need for new techniques and organizational patterns such as neighborhood service-centers, closely integrated with comprehensive health-care centers which would provide a complete community program of preventive, diagnostic, and curative services. Their concerns included enhancing the humaneness of services as well as their availability. They recommended also the application of management science, computer technology, and the latest automated medical techniques for mass-health screening, monitoring of patients, laboratory procedures, record keeping, and communication.

*Environmental Engineering:* The panel concerned with this field urged immediate interdepartmental efforts to review and coordinate Federal policies and programs relating to water supply, sanitary sewerage, storm drainage, solid-waste disposal, and air pollution. It suggested the establishment of a demonstration-project area in which all transportation would be by vehicles not producing exhaust, and a tax on solid waste which would stimulate research by private industry on methods of eliminating excessive packaging materials and on replacement of disposable with reusable items. They were concerned not only with a wide variety of research possibilities—such as pneumatic tubes for trash-disposal in multifamily dwellings—but with the lack of coordination and with the political constraints which restrict the use of research results.

*Transportation:* This panel showed the possibility of finding fresh answers to the old transportation problems by bringing to them two new technologies—electronic semiconductors (transistors that, in

183

computers, make possible inexpensive as well as high-speed processing of data) and highly reliable mechanical devices. They described a whole series of possible "add-ons" to buses and trains—dynamic scheduling keyed to requirements, curbside ticket-dispensers, job jitneys—as well as more futuristic devices such as automated highways. They were very concerned with the ties between transportation and job opportunities and between transportation and city design.

Such a rapid review does injustice to the scope and number of challenging ideas which came out of the Woods Hole study. This sampling, however, suggests the ways in which an interdisciplinary, systems-oriented approach can help us to move in new directions. The summer study was only a beginning, and the panelists were unanimous in their conviction that urban institutes or other devices for furthering systematic urban studies were essential. They also noted repeatedly the need for innovation in management and institutions, as being at once more difficult and more important than technological innovation.

To dwell on the need for careful, rational approaches to urban problems is not to suggest that they will produce magic solutions. The gains from systems analysis—as from most scientific research—are usually small increments: small savings in time, money, effort, and human anguish; gradual improvements in comfort, efficiency, equity, elegance. These gains, however, can bring immediate benefits to people who live in our "frantic file cabinet(s) of human hopes," our towns and cities.

The systems approach to the city, like any other, must ultimately turn on this question of satisfying human hopes and human needs. A community cannot solve its problems without knowing what its goals are. But the goals of any community are varied and complicated, overlapping and even contradictory.

Through the possibility of predicting the results of alternative courses of action, the use of mathematical models and computers offers a way of evaluating our goals as well as our means. In effect this permits us to predict the future and thus, to some degree, control it.

No foreseeable increase in the GNP is going to make it unnecessary for the nation and for local communities to set priorities, to make hard choices among various desirable alternatives. In this process, our predictive capability—particularly in the form of "cost-effectiveness"—can be extremely useful. To interject "cost-effectiveness" into a discussion of the quality of man's existence may automatically qualify me as a Philistine. It certainly arouses visions of uprooting rose bushes to plant carrots.

Cost effectiveness, however, does not mean that efficiency and economy need take precedence over other values: it is simply a way of making choices more deliberate by making their implications clear.

To fail to use our predictive capability may leave our environment, in the words of Max Ways, "an archipelago of successes glittering in a swamp of unintended consequences." By coupling it with our operational technical capability we can serve and preserve humanistic values, if we choose to do so.

In studying the case of basic research in science, economist Carl Kaysen concluded that continued Federal support was essential. Private industry could not be expected to provide—and, in fact, did not provide—an adequate flow of financial support. The gains of basic research are, from the company's point of view, too unpredictable and too hard to keep for its exclusive use. Since the "pay-off" benefits the entire community, expenditures on basic science, Kaysen points out, should properly be regarded as "social overhead," as "capital investments in the stock of knowledge."

If this is true in the electronic and chemical industries, it is equally the case in urban affairs—in the areas of housing, safety, education, social sciences, and transportation.

Individual communities and companies with imagination can bring innovation to the solution of man's immediate urban problems. Systematic research of the kind we have been discussing almost certainly will require national efforts, using both Federal and private capabilities.

As a nation we are just beginning to deal with major questions of urban strategy; the optimum size of cities, how to distribute people within them, the balance and location of new communities. These require not only research but the assessment and balancing of national goals.

In the process of appraisal, analysis, and problem solving which I

185

have advocated lies the possibility for intelligent modification of the urban environment. This is also a strong argument for public action in the broadest sense.

The strategy of the Department of Housing and Urban Development and the Administration is based on the premise that government can contribute meaningfully within appropriate limits to the achievement of our common goals: revitalizing our cities, bringing greater coherence to our patterns of metropolitan development, developing new urban patterns, encouraging innovation and experimentation.

In the long run, however, if we are to change our urban environment, we shall need to know not only more about the forces which shape it, but more about the way community decisions are made.

If the tools of modern science make modification of our environment possible, and the demands of the times make it desirable or even necessary, it must be said that the realities of local decision making make all changes highly adventurous.

In the spread-city, which at least quantitatively will establish the dominant urban pattern of the future, crucial powers are divided functionally: zoning boards, school districts, water and sewer districts, have a good deal of autonomy which they exercise over wide geographical areas. Individual suburbs often have little influence over the decisions—such as the location of highways—which most affect their development.

In this setting, change is a subtle and complicated process. Local government must rely for its cohesion on communication rather than formal structure. New alliances must be formed—through education and persuasion—for coping with a changing spectrum of common problems. The Federal government must find new mechanisms for making a national consensus felt.

Urban issues will always be in a real sense "political." As Leonard Fein of the Massachusetts Institute of Technology observed, "the political problem is always how to spend the scarce resources of the society, whether to build roads or schools, airports or hospitals, jails, or gardens. These are very properly matters for intense debate, and no computerized operation can ever make the final choice except as our programs specify our values."[2]

186

To emphasize the need for scientific concepts and rational analysis is not to advocate an antiseptic approach to grave human problems, to the plight of the poor or the despoiling of the environment. My own training is in the humanist tradition and I have worked with scientists for many years. My deep conviction is that the scientific and humanist approaches are not competitive but supportive, and that both are ultimately necessary. It is by the *wise* use of science that we move ahead. It is by joining the knowledge of individual behavior with sensitivity to our inevitable interdependence that we will learn to build the kind of cities that America deserves.

### NOTES

[1] JOHN EBERHARD, Technology for the City, *International Science and Technology.* September 1966. N.Y.
[2] LEONARD FEIN, Urban Challenge; Toward the Plural City, *Technology Review,* vol. 68, no. 8. 1966.

# THE CONSERVATION OF CULTURAL PROPERTY

HIROSHI DAIFUKU

As HEAD OF THE Section for the Development of the Cultural Heritage, Hiroshi Daifuku has worked with the United Nations Educational, Social, and Cultural Organization to encourage governments throughout the world to preserve their national structural heirlooms and to establish training centers for preservation technicians.

To this position, Dr. Daifuku brings a background in anthropology, archeology, and museology. Receiving his basic training from the University of Hawaii and Harvard, he was an instructor in anthropology at the University of Wisconsin while working on his doctoral dissertation (Harvard, 1951). Museum and preservation work attracted him to a curatorship at the State Historical Society Museum in Madison, Wisc., which he held from 1952–54. During that period he was also the 1953 lecturer in anthropology at Beloit College. Dr. Daifuku's museum work led him to accept a position with the UNESCO staff in Paris in 1954 as program specialist for the development of museums. This was followed, in 1962, by his promotion to program specialist for the conservation of cultural property and, in 1967, by his promotion to his present office.

Dr. Daifuku has prepared numerous reports, manuals, and articles on the conservation of cultural property and in the closely related fields of anthropology and museology.

EARLY IN HIS HISTORY man demonstrated his powers of destruction. Appearing in late Pleistocene times, *Homo sapiens* had by the end of that period contributed to the extermination of the mammoth, cave bear, woolly rhinoceros, and other species of the Old World and, having crossed the land bridge which existed in the Bering Straits, had helped mete out a similar fate to comparable game animals in the New, such as the North American mammoth, mastodon, camel, giant ground sloth, and giant bison. In spite of the fact that man during the late Pleistocene and early Holocene existed only in small numbers, dependent upon a hunting and gathering economy, he affected the ecology in other ways. For example, game drives using fire diminished forest cover in favor of grasslands with inevitable repercussions in the distribution of many species.

After the end of the Pleistocene, hunting gradually declined to a secondary human pursuit as man's way of life became pastoral and agricultural. The subsequent rise of urban societies involved the development of techniques of living in which family, kin, and tribe became less important with the rise of organizational units such as states, kingdoms, and empires. Writing and mathematics ensured that the accumulated knowledge and experience of generations would be preserved and transmitted.

In some areas the disappearance of early urban civilizations has been ascribed, in part, to the reckless overexploitation of the environment. Disappearance of forests which had been lumbered for timber or for fuel contributed to the loss of the topsoil, and the effects of erosion destroyed the ability of the land to retain moisture. Herds of domesticated grazing animals, in numbers that exceeded the carrying power of the land, were also a factor.

With the Industrial Revolution and the exploitation of new sources of energy, man's effect upon the environment increased dramatically and with deleterious consequences for many other forms of life. The number of species driven to extinction has increased constantly. Demand for living space and requirements of industry have caused marshes, forest, and grasslands to disappear and with them their associated plants and fauna. Man himself has paid a high price for the enormous advantages the Industrial Revolution has brought him. The

191

vastly increased power at his disposal, the range of tools by which it is turned to productive ends and the phenomenal acceleration of communications have improved living standards for hundreds of millions of people and greatly extended the scope of their lives. But those properties of the environment that are vital to man himself have been seriously impaired. Natural processes for the absorption of wastes have been overtaxed and the resultant pollution of the atmosphere, of riverine systems, and the sea coasts, raises the question whether man may not be poisoned by his own effluvium.

Human life, while enriched, has also been impoverished. Mass production—the manufacture of large amounts of identical items at low unit-cost—is the enemy of variety. Look-alike, built-alike office buildings, cars, homes, and appliances have become characteristic of modern communities. Newly-built areas in Tokyo, Athens, Rotterdam, Bangkok, and Los Angeles resemble one another more than they do older, neighboring communities. The use of powerful earth-moving machinery results in a standardizing of the landscape as hills are lowered and wetlands filled, while the use of powered agricultural machinery has seen the small diversified farm replaced by monotonous fields of single cash crops. The automobile with its incessant demands for increased space in the form of super highways, widened thoroughfares, and expanding parking areas dominates the urban scene and much of the countryside. While the great cities of antiquity like Paris and Rome are still characterized by the monumental architecture of the past and by fascinating historic quarters, they—as well as the urban conglomerations of the present—have given birth to vast new suburbs which are rows of similar high-rise structures, shopping centers, swimming pools, and banally landscaped lawns ill shaded by a few scraggly trees. Such changes are taking place not only in the industrialized countries but are becoming ever more conspicuous in those heretofore undeveloped.

Profiting from the deficiency in legitimate visual stimulation, entrepreneurs in many countries of the world have introduced variation into the environment by building hotels, bars, nightclubs, and so on that embody fake exotic elements with wild combinations of fraudulent objects copied from the themes of a dozen different cultures and as many periods. Intensifying the exacerbation of the nerves by ubiquitous and gaudy advertisements, these substitutes for authentic variety only aggravate our alienation from our environment, which is characteristic of modern man.

Special circumstances militate against a strong sense of the past in the United States. Except for the relatively few traces left by American Indian cultures, evidences of human habitation are barely 350 years old on the Eastern seaboard and much less as one goes farther west, until Spanish-Mexican influence is encountered. There has also been the effect of the long existence of a frontier, the importance of which was brought out by F. J. Turner in his famous work on the subject: throughout much of their history it has been characteristic of Americans to be ready to abandon their homes in search of better lands and opportunities. The result necessarily has been less attachment to a place or a community on the part of individuals and families.

Another equally important factor was the emphasis given to "Americanization" during the 19th and early 20th centuries. Immigrants and their children were placed under strong social and educational pressures to acquire American mores and ideals, to speak English, and to reject the customs of the country of their origin and any associations they might have retained with it. This led to a phenomenon rare in history—the successful assimilation within two or three generations of vast numbers of immigrants of very different backgrounds. The incidental effect of the disruption of cultural continuity of the immigrant groups has been the increase in the overall ahistoric orientation characteristic of the American people as a whole.

Techniques of mass production and of marketing in which obsolescence is built into the product (e.g., annual minor changes in body styles of automobiles) and the constant advertising extolling the new (and therefore the better) with the aim of persuading the public to purchase new items long before the old have been worn out tend to give older objects a pejorative association. While pressures toward this end have been carried to a higher pitch in the United States than elsewhere, the economics of mass production and mass marketing are increasingly subjecting the populations of the other industrially developed countries to these pressures.

193

It is axiomatic that the greatest danger to historic monuments is prosperity. Certainly, during periods of economic stagnation old buildings, historic quarters in urban centers, and historic sites and monuments may suffer from neglect. However, the landmarks of the past are not usually in danger of demolition when people are having to make do with what they have. On the other hand, during prosperity, with an expanding economy, business firms or corporations find that the quarters which they have been occupying have become cramped. Hence, decisions are made to scrap architecturally important buildings to clear sites for newer and larger structures. The price of land increases with the growth of the city and real-estate taxes go up. The older buildings of only a few stories are no longer profitable, at least in comparison with the returns to be realized from up-to-date high-rise replacements.

Another concomitant of industrial expansion is the neglect of older buildings in anticipation of future profits resulting from their eventual demolition. Such edifices may form a historically interesting complex or represent the work of outstanding architects. They may also be examples of building styles found in what had been a prosperous neighborhood, but today would be considered "run down."

Countries undergoing rapid development suffer a comparable but much more severe dissociation of past from present. For example, much of the population of the newly independent countries of West Africa still lives in small tribal groups dependent on means of livelihood—small-scale diversified farming, hunting, or pastoral nomadism—practised by their ancestors. In sharp contrast are the urban centers of the new nations which are largely European in pattern, where the language of commerce and officialdom is English or French, and where educational standards and goals are those that prevailed during the colonial period. A very wide gap exists between the largely illiterate and unskilled majority found either in the countryside or as recent arrivals in the urban scene, and the small elite found in technical and administrative positions. It is not surprising to find that, in the pursuit of material progress, much of the traditional culture is identified as "primitive" and hence rejected. For example, shrines filled with

194

carved fetishes, at times of startling power and beauty, lose their adherents and fall into ruin and their contents are stolen or sold. The old traditions suffer the same fate as their symbols, and a spread of historical rootlessness is the result.

Throughout the world the drawing power of cities is a force for such rootlessness. People desert the hinterland where they formed part of a long-established pattern amid familiar surroundings and pour into the urban centers, where life is amorphous and without antecedents. Often it is difficult to discern any gain to compensate for what is lost. In Brazil—to cite a familiar example—great numbers have left the countryside to better their lot in the city only to end in the slums—the *favellas*—still captive to their poverty and with no prospect of betterment. A similar dislocation on a wide scale—though one attended by less dire want—has been taking place in the United States. As a result of urban freeway construction, the invasion of so-called depressed neighborhoods by high-priced buildings and by other forms of urban renewal programs, socially viable neighborhoods have been destroyed and the populations scattered or reassembled in fragmented groupings. Jane Jacobs has shown that this has also led to an intensification of *anomie* and other ills attendant upon social disorganization.

Expanding economies and populations pose increasing threats to our cultural heritage. They are familiar and worldwide in scope, including:

(a) the construction of dams for irrigation, hydroelectric power or flood control;

(b) the construction of highways;

(c) the construction of pipelines and electric power lines;

(d) farming operations including deep plowing, drainage and irrigation works, and the clearing and leveling of land;

(e) urban expansion including urban renewal projects in which outstanding monuments may be spared but less important structures be removed, disrupting historic relations and the ambience of monuments or historic quarters;

(f) concomitants of the growth of industry and the technological progress of industrialized societies such as airfields, min-

195

ing and quarrying operations, and dredging of channels and harbors.[1]

The human race is threatened with the progressive loss of the artifacts in which its many-faceted history is recapitulated and the achievements of its ages-old cultural evolution represented, of that which gives a saving diversity to the daily scene and at the same time a sense of the continuity and dimensions of the human experience.

The concern of the international community represented by UNESCO over the mounting destruction of the landmarks of mankind's past led, in 1963, to the initiation of a study of the advisability of international instruments on the preservation of cultural property endangered by public and private works. The interests of the member states reflected in this decision had, in many cases, already led to the organization of national programs and services devoted to the conservation of historic sites and monuments; legislation to this end had its beginning in the 19th century. However, even countries having the largest and most competent staffs in the field could barely meet minimal needs.

That was made clear in response to a questionnaire sent by UNESCO to the member states. The questionnaire also brought out that the member states in the main agreed that what is needed to ensure the preservation of cultural property is: (1) adequate legislation; (2) adequate budgets; (3) trained staff to ensure the enforcement of the laws as well as to perform the work of restoration and preservation; (4) national services equipped to aid local bodies and private owners with technical advice and, on occasion, monetary grants; and (5) educational programs to stimulate a greater popular understanding and appreciation of the past.

Many of the member states reported that, in addition to insufficiency of staff and funds for conservation, they lacked information about new products and techniques in the field. UNESCO had already, in 1956, published a technical handbook on *The Protection of Cultural Property in the Event of Armed Conflict*. Two other handbooks: *The Conservation of Cultural Property,* on methods of treating different forms of damage (1968); and *The Restoration and Conser-*

196

*vation of Monuments* (in press), have been prepared while other comparable technical publications are being planned.

It required no questionnaire to make clear that throughout the world funds available for conservation would have to be stretched to the utmost. One means of doing so would manifestly be through the pooling of experience of specialists in the field. Being very conscious of the need for a mechanism through which this could be accomplished, UNESCO had already, in 1957, established in Rome an International Center for the Study of the Preservation and Restoration of Cultural Property through which scientific and technical information bearing on the purposes of the Center would be disseminated, research promoted, recommendations offered, and research workers and technicians in preservation and restoration trained. With 42 member states supporting it financially, the Rome Center, as it is called, has published technical papers, arranged conferences, and coordinated research among widely scattered institutions. It played an important role in the international compaign for the salvage of 20 temples (including those of Ramses II and his queen, at Abu Simbel, which would otherwise have been lost under the waters rising behind the high dam at Aswan), and is currently taking part in the reclamation of the master works of art and historic monuments damaged in the floods of 1966 in Florence and Venice.

One particularly noteworthy activity of the Rome Center carried out with the cooperation of the Faculty of Architecture of the University of Rome, and with staff members from several different countries, is a course of training for architects, art historians, and administrators responsible for the conservation of monuments and sites. Initiated in recognition of the lack of any but the skimpiest training available for architects interested in historic restoration and preservation—the result of the small number of these in any one country—the course has an international staff and student body. The first year covers principles of ancient architecture, techniques of stabilization, chemistry and physics to the extent that these are required, and comparative law. The second year is for architects working for an advanced degree by preparing plans for necessary work on an actual monument. Plans are

197

also under way at the Rome Center for a laboratory in which training will be given in methods used in the analysis of materials and in physical conservation.

Since 1965 the work of UNESCO in cultural preservation and restoration has been furthered by a consultative nongovernmental body called the International Council of Sites and Monuments (ICOMOS), supported by UNESCO and located in Paris. Among other problems on which ICOMOS is at present seeking to marshal expert opinion are those relating to the renovation of historic quarters in urban centers and to standards to be observed in cultural conservation. In this connection, it might be noted that Viollet-le-Duc, who in the past century did much to encourage the restoration of Gothic buildings and the conservation of other national monuments, and who did not hesitate to complete structures according to original plans that had not been carried out or even add new elements as he saw fit, has been merely the most prominent among a number of enthusiasts who have taken great liberties—as it would generally be considered today—with the past. The respect for historical and artistic authenticity, the need to preserve in order to understand, is not automatic, but must become a widely understood and appreciated principle.

Even before the establishment of the Rome Center, in fact since 1952, UNESCO had been providing fellowships in conservation and sending missions of experts and making grants of equipment to member states needing help. Most of the missions have been sent to help set up national programs or services or advise on the preservation of a specific monument—for example, the tomb of Kazanluk in Bulgaria, which contains the only surviving painted frescoes of Thracian origin—and have been of only a few weeks' duration. Budgetary limitations would in any case have stood in the way of further-reaching undertakings. Even the modest objectives of the missions have been apt to be defeated, at least for the time being, by lack of funds to carry out the missions' recommendations—a denouement only too typical of the experience of those concerned with the protection of antiquities.

In its fellowship program, UNESCO has had encouraging success in training specialists and in giving newly-appointed administrators in member states an opportunity to go abroad and see what their fellows in other countries are doing. The program has also run into difficulties.

In some of the newly independent countries the number of university and even of high-school graduates is narrowly limited. If the fellowship holder had been living in a nonindustrialized country where the mores and mode of life differed widely from those of the country in which his studies were carried out, it frequently was found to be impossible for him to profit from the opportunity afforded him. Language problems and the fact that his courses were designed for students of the host country, who had a much wider vocabulary and better background, created insuperable obstacles for many of the fellows. Even when a fellow was able to adapt himself and profit from his period of study the aims of the program were sometimes defeated in another way. The graduate might prefer to accept employment in the country where he was trained, or, if he returned to his own country, be dissatisfied with his status there. Finally, the training might prove too specialized or the trainee become so habituated to the use of automatic and sophisticated equipment that he refused or was unable to work efficiently using the elementary improvised equipment that was all his home country could afford.

For this reason, UNESCO has established regional training centers where working and living conditions are not dissimilar to those to which the student is accustomed. One such center, which might be considered a pilot project, has been set up in cooperation with the federal government of Nigeria in Jos for the training of museum technicians. Jos is located in the northern part of the country where the government had previously had a small museum. A laboratory, a workshop and classroom facilities, as well as a hostel, were added by the government. UNESCO has furnished an international teaching staff and technical and scientific equipment. The students follow a nine-months' course. This begins with principles of cataloging, covers the design and preparation of exhibitions, and the use of photographic techniques and tape-recording. The final two months, which include field trips, are spent on basic laboratory and workshop techniques in the conservation of cultural property. The languages of instruction are English and French and the course is unique in bringing together

199

English- and French-speaking Africans who would otherwise not get to know one another. The work is practical and the Jos Museum has profited by having its collections catalogued and its exhibitions modernized. The students do not suffer from "cultural shock" and acquire a broad basic background systematically. While some go on to Europe or to the United States for advanced training, having been "seasoned" first in Nigeria, most return to their country of origin and take up the tasks for which they are trained. The level of competence of the Nigerian staff and that of museum staffs in other African countries— Congo Republic, Ethiopia, Ghana, Mali, Niger, Senegal, Somali, Zambia—has been progressively raised.

Two other regional centers devoted to conservation were planned some time ago. One in Mexico City, having completed a trial period, will open for Latin America in 1967. The other, to begin on a trial basis in New Delhi in 1968, is to serve South Asia.

While encouragement and training in the preservation of national heirlooms may be given by the international community acting through a body like UNESCO, the necessary actual steps to that end have usually depended upon the individual nations. In most countries a low priority is given to the protection of cultural properties, not because these are not esteemed but because other needs are deemed more vital. In few countries do the requirements of defense, administration, industrial development, agricultural improvement, education, public health and sanitation leave a great deal for expenditures promising a less concrete or immediate return, even returns with a close bearing on a people's sense of its history, its conception of itself, its values and the sources of its identity and cohesion. However, when a source of income may be discovered in the legacies of the past, that is a different matter.

Monuments, sites and other cultural possessions of international repute obviously contribute much to a country's attraction to tourists. During the past decade tourism has become a primary source of badly-needed foreign exchange. Indeed, the Economic and Social Council of the United Nations, during its 36th Session (December 1963–January 1964), underlined "the importance of the role played by tourism in national economies and international trade as well as its social, educational and cultural impact and its contribution to the promotion of international goodwill and understanding." Of equal importance was its recommendation to the United Nations Development Program (UNDP) that the conservation of monuments and sites can and should be considered as part of economic development. On the basis of this recommendation projects for the conservation of cultural property can now be financed under the Technical Assistance or the Special Fund Sectors of UNDP.

A study of this aspect of the problem was undertaken by UNESCO during 1965–66, the results of which were submitted to its Executive Board.[2] The report included an analysis of financial statements from several of the member states of UNESCO summarizing their revenue from tourism as well as the results of several planning missions sent to Turkey, Iran, and Peru. One outcome was that in these countries, for the first time, representatives from the Ministries of Finance and Commerce, as well as from Departments of Public Works, Tourism, Antiquities and National Museums, met to approach the problem of conservation from an overall point of view. In two of the countries the conservation of monuments is now included in national five-year development plans and the government of the third is seriously considering a similar innovation. Now, with financial support under the United Nations Development Program having been authorized, it is possible for UNESCO to cooperate with its member states and aid them in carrying out projects in which conservation is seen not in terms of the possibility of preserving individual monuments for intangible rewards alone but as part of a nationwide program of economic investment.

Due to the rise of specialization, the environment has been treated as if it is made up of discrete parts. It is a totality, however, and the necessity to consider it as such cannot be overemphasized. Hence, economic, social, and political factors should be considered along with the countryside and the city. Many countries gained their independence during the post-World War II period, with the hope, if not the belief, that with independence there would be increased material security and freedom. Factories were constructed, dams built, new enterprises begun, without taking into account that every successful industrial plant, no matter how small, is supported by a vast and invisible pyramid including an infrastructure of trained personnel and adequate markets.

The failures which followed imposed considerable stresses upon such societies so that, in many instances, they disintegrated: the tribe and the family remain as the only meaningful social and economic units. In other words, in such countries the "nation" or the "state" exist only as a fictive ideal.

The development of cultural tourism, based upon the conservation of sites and monuments, is not a universal panacea. Nevertheless, in a surprisingly large number of cases, many developing countries could profitably make much greater use of their cultural heritage. Although much less expertise is required than for industrial development, any successful project requires an integration of economic resources which the "developed" countries take for granted. For example, it may mean a change from subsistence agriculture to the production of market fruits and vegetables for hotels and restaurants (which may later lead to exports); coastal areas long overfished have to be restored or fish-ponds developed; highways and airports are necessitated to make sites and monuments accessible, which also results in stimulating the over-all economy of the neighboring countryside; hotels (even if financed by international chains) require staffs who, in many instances, have to have the ability to read and to write (illiteracy is a widespread problem) and to understand one or more foreign languages. The long term results would be an improvement of economic standards and a gradual widening of a population possessing skills which eventually, albeit slowly, would help to lead to the development of local industries.

Increased leisure and affluence, faster and somewhat less expensive transportation plus a widespread yearning for new and different scenes—stimulated by the growing monotony and uniformity of the industrialized world—have led to an extraordinary boom in tourism in the past decade. Cuzco, Persepolis, and Katmandu, which formerly were visited only by enterprising travel-lecturers or the wealthy who were adventurously inclined, are now commonplaces on itineraries. There is every reason to believe that, barring a major war, the trend to wider travel by greater numbers will continue. It is ironical but certainly fitting that, as in the case of the African game fauna, the force chiefly responsible for the destruction of man's historic and cultural patrimony—industrial and economic development—should offer the most promising means for its succor.

We must not imagine that it is only the wish for diversion, plus growing means for satisfying that desire, that may give some part of the remnants of that patrimony a new lease on life. The concern of human beings for the fate of cultural monuments that they may never see should not be underestimated. The extent of this concern was demonstrated by the success of UNESCO's appeal on behalf of the United Arab Republic and of the Sudan for assistance in saving the Nubian temples, which 60 nations heeded. It is being shown today by the response of the world to the damage suffered by the works of art and monuments of Florence and of Venice in 1966. That peoples all across the world are awake as never before to the importance of the quality of man's entire physical background, is attested in a draft resolution now before UNESCO. Entitled "International Cooperation in the Creation of Favorable Environments," and submitted jointly by Czechoslovakia, Finland, Japan, Mexico, and Poland, it recognizes that "the creation of favorable environments—favorable from the points of view of general culture and health—should become one of the most important future tasks of all mankind." Of the totality of our environment, our cultural heritage is surely an important part.

Damage caused by natural cataclysms, warfare, or even the neglect of our cultural heritage can be explained. But, excuses are less easy to find when, for shortsighted economic reasons, monuments or historically or artistically important structures are obliterated and then forgotten. During the past thirty years, edifices of noble lineaments having associations for millions of people have been destroyed in depressing numbers. Fortunately, there are signs that a change of heart is apparently taking place. In Washington, plans for demolishing the former State-War-Navy Building were abandoned in the face of a general outcry and prospects for the preservation of the great granite period-piece have never been brighter. One of the most imposing structures built in the United States during the past century, it was

203

originally ordained by President Grant to suppress rumors that the national Capitol was to be moved to another more metropolitan city, so that its salvation is particularly fitting. In Paris, the outlook for the central district known as The Marais is also encouraging. Now run-down, grimy, its narrow streets filled with masses of trucks serving Les Halles, The Marais is a typical depressed area in a modern city. It is graced, however, by a number of beautiful historic monuments such as the hotels of Carnavalet, Soubisse, and Sully and, at its core, by the complex known as the Place des Vosges. At considerable expense it is planned to renovate the area so that many distinguished buildings (not important enough to be classified as monuments) will regain their beauty, which now is masked by scabrous walls, dingy shops, and tenementlike quarters which have been inserted into what had been the apartments and homes of the aristocracy and the well-to-do. Build-ings which have been erected since the Revolution, of styles that would clash with the atmosphere of The Marais, will be torn down and replaced by more suitable structures or by gardens, should they have preempted spaces that once were occupied by gardens. The Marais will regain its former elegance. Analogous projects, moreover, are being considered or are under way in several cities throughout the world.

Our common concern is with the quality of our environment. If the atmosphere becomes polluted, if the seas become filled with wastes carried down from rivers passing through densely populated areas, if the shoreline and the continental shelf are no longer suitable for many marine forms, if our cultural heritage is destroyed, the effects will not be limited to a single country or to the present generation. The reper-cussions will be worldwide and albeit slow in making themselves felt, will gather force and insistence. Everywhere and in all sorts of ways—biological, physical, historical, cultural—we are threatened by our excesses. It is becoming more and more evident that the world is small. Incidents, formerly thought to be isolated, now are known to have repercussions everywhere. The environment is a totality and every aspect must be considered as part of a whole. Thus if progress is to be made we must break out of narrow specializations and the resultant intellectual—and even moral—outlook of living and working in small compartments. The present generation has many responsibilities to its past, to itself, and to its posterity. The challenge that faces it must be met, for the margin of error, for irresponsibility, grows narrower every day.

## NOTES

[1] This list is based upon a 1963 study carried out by UNESCO, *The Draft Recommendation of the Preservation of Cultural Property Endangered by Public and Private Works* (UNESCO/SHC/4; Paris, 1967). The order of importance varies among the different member states.

[2] *Report by the Director-General on the Preservation of Monuments and other Cultural Property in Association with the Development of Tourism* (72EX/3; Paris, 1966).

# VALUES, PROCESS AND FORM

IAN L. McHARG

IAN L. MCHARG brings to this volume both the theoretical and the practical aspects of viewing man and his environment. On the theoretical side, he is Chairman of the Department of Landscape Architecture and Regional Planning of the University of Pennsylvania and the author of a copious quantity of articles which have been published in *Architects Journal, Architects Yearbook, Architectural Record, Landscape Architecture Quarterly,* and other leading journals in this field.

On the practical side, he is a partner in the firm of Wallace, McHarg, Roberts and Todd (formerly Wallace-McHarg Associates) of Philadelphia, Pa. He was personally responsible for the University of Pennsylvania Woodland Avenue Project, the Southwark Housing of Philadelphia, Town Center Park in Washington, D.C., and the Delaware River Park study in Philadelphia. He was also the principal investigator for the Urban Renewal Administration. Pennsylvania–New Jersey, Metropolitan Open Space Project. In conjunction with his firm, he was involved in the Lower Manhattan Plan, the Green Spring and Worthington Valley Plan of Baltimore County, the Baltimore Inner Harbor Study, the development of a Comprehensive Landscape Plan for Washington, D.C., the Midtown Wilmington Study, and I 95 between the Delaware and Raritan Rivers.

A native of Clydebank, Scotland, Mr. McHarg served from 1939–46 in the British Army, finally as a Major commanding parachute troops. He then came to America and to Harvard, where he received his BLA in 1949, MLA in 1950, and MCP in 1951.

From July 1, 1966, to July 1, 1967, he was on sabbatical leave from the University of Pennsylvania in order to write *Design With Nature* (in press) for The Conservation Foundation. He also has contributed chapters to Leonard Duhl's *The Urban Environment; The Future Environments of North America,* edited by F. Fraser Darling; *The Architect and the City,* edited by Marcus Whiffen; and *The Annals of the Academy of Political and Social Science.* Both he and his partnership contributed to *Potomac: Report on the Task Force of the Potomac.*

IT IS MY PROPOSITION THAT, to all practical purposes, western man remains obdurately pre-Copernican, believing that he bestrides the earth round which the sun, the galaxy, and the very cosmos revolve.This delusion has fueled our ignorance in time past and is directly responsible for the prodigal destruction of nature and for the encapsulating burrows that are the dysgenic city.

We must see nature and man as an evolutionary process which responds to laws, which exhibits direction, and which is subject to the final test of survival. We must learn that nature includes an intrinsic value-system in which the currency is energy and the inventory is matter and its cycles—the oceans and the hydrologic cycle, life-forms and their roles, the cooperative mechanisms which life has developed and, not least, their genetic potential. The measure of success in this process, in terms of the biosphere, is the accumulation of negentropy in physical systems and ecosystems, the evolution of apperception or consciousness, and the extension of symbioses—all of which might well be described as creation.

This can be pictured simply in a comparison between the early earth and the present planet. In the intervening billions of years the earth has been transformed and the major change has been in the increase of order. Think of the turbulence and violence of the early earth, racked by earthquakes and vulcanism, as it evolved toward equilibrium, and of the unrestrained movements of water, the dust storms of unstabilized soils, and the extreme alternations of climate unmodified by a green, meliorative vegetative cover. In this early world physical processes operated toward repose, but in the shallow bays there emerged life and a new kind of ordering was initiated. The atmosphere which could sustain life was not the least of the creations of life. Life elaborated in the seas and then colonized the earth, thus increasing the opportunities for life and for evolution. Plants and decomposers created the soils, anchored the surface of the earth, checked the movements of soil particles, modified water processes, meliorated the climate, and ordered the distribution of nutrients. Species evolved to occupy and create more habitats, more niches, each increase requiring new cooperative relationships between organisms—new roles, all of which were beneficial. In the earth's history can be seen the orderings

209

which life has accomplished: the increase to life forms, habitats and roles, symbiotic relationships, and the dynamic equilibrium in the system—the total an increase in order. This is creation.

In the early earth, the sunlight which fell upon the planet equaled the degraded energy which was radiated from it. Since the beginning of plantlife, some of the sun's energy has been entrapped by photosynthesis and employed with matter to constitute the ordered beings of plants; thence, to the animals and decomposers, and all of the orderings which they have accomplished. This energy will surely be degraded, but the entrapped energy, with matter, is manifest in all life forms past and present, and in all of the orderings which they have accomplished. Thus, creation equals the energy which has been temporarily entrapped and used with matter to accomplish all of the ordering of physical, biological, and cultural evolution. This, physicists describe as negentropy, in contrast with the inevitable degradation of energy which is described as entropy.

By this we see the world as a creative process involving all matter and all life forms in all time past and in the present. Thus, creation reveals two forms: first, the physical entrapment and ordering which is accomplished primarily by plants and by the simplest animals; and, second, apperception and the resulting ordering for which an increased capacity is observed as species rise in the phylogenetic scale. In this, man is seen to be especially endowed. This view of the world as a creative process involving all of its denizens, including man, in a cooperative enterprise, is foreign to the western tradition that insists upon the exclusive divinity of man, his independent superiority, dominion, and license to subjugate the earth. It is this man in whose image was God made. This concept of nature as a creative, interacting process in which man is involved with all other life forms is the ecological view. It is, I submit, the best approximation of the world that has been presented to us, and the indispensable approach to determining the role of man in the biosphere. It is indispensable also for investigation, not only of the adaptations which man accomplishes, but of their forms.

The place, the plants, the animals, and man, and the orderings which they have accomplished over time, are revealed in form. To understand this it is necessary to invoke all physical, biological, and cultural evolution. Form and process are indivisible aspects of a single phenomenon: being. Norbert Weiner described the world as consisting of "To Whom It May Concern" messages, but these are clothed in form. Process and fitness (which is the criterion of process) are revealed in form; form contains meaning. The artifact, tool, room, street, building, town or city, garden or region, can be examined in terms of process, manifest in form, which may be unfit, fit, or most fitting. The last of these, when made by man, is art.

The role of man is to understand nature, which is also to say man, and to intervene to enhance its creative processes. He is the prospective steward of the biosphere. The fruits of the anthropocentric view are in the improvement of the social environment, and great indeed are their values, but an encomium on social evolution is not my competence, and I leave the subject with the observation that, while Madison, Jefferson, Hamilton, and Washington might well take pride in many of our institutions, it is likely that they would recoil in horror from the face of the land of the free.

An indictment of the physical environment is too easy, for post-industrial cities are such squalid testimony to the bondage of toil and to the insensitivity of man, that the most casual examination of history reveals the modern city as a travesty of its antecedents and a denial of its role as the proudest testimony to peoples and their cultures. The city is no longer the preferred residence for the polite, the civilized, and the urbane, all of which say "city." They have fled to the illusion of the suburb, escaping the iridescent shills, neon vulgarity of the merchants, usurious slumlords, cynical polluters (household names for great corporations, not yet housebroken), crime, violence and corruption. Thus, the city is the home of the poor, who are chained to it, and the repository of dirty industry and the commuter's automobile. Give us your poor and oppressed, and we will give them Harlem and the Lower East Side, Bedford-Stuyvesant, the South Side of Chicago, and the North of Philadelphia—or, if they are very lucky, Levittown. Look at one of these habitats through the Cornell Medical School study of Midtown Manhattan, where 20 percent of a sample population was found to be indistinguishable from the patients

211

in mental institutions, and where a further 60 percent evidenced mental disease. Observe the environments of physical, mental, and social pathology. What of the countryside? Well, you may drive from the city and search for the rural landscape, but to do so you will follow the paths of those who preceded you, and many of them stayed to build. But those who did so *first* are now deeply embedded in the fabric of the city. So as you go you will transect the annular rings of the thwarted and disillusioned who are encapsulated in the city as nature endlessly eludes pursuit. You can tell when you have reached the edge of the rural scene for there are many emblems: the cadavers of old trees, piled in untidy heaps beside the magnificent machines for land despoliation, at the edge of the razed deserts; forests felled; marshes filled; farms obliterated; streams culverted; and the sweet rural scene transformed into the ticky-tacky vulgarity of the merchants creed and expression. What of the continent? Well, Lake Erie is on the verge of becoming septic, New York suffers from water shortages as the Hudson flows foully past, and the Delaware is threatened by salt water intrusion. Smog, forest fires, and mud slides have become a way of life for Los Angeles. In San Francisco, the Bay is being filled and men build upon unconsolidated sediments, the most perilous foundations in this earthquake-prone area. DDT is in arctic ice and ocean deeps, radioactive wastes rest on the Continental Shelf, the Mississippi is engorged with five cubic miles of topsoil each year, the primeval forests are all but gone, flood and drought become increasingly common, the once-deep prairie soils are thinner now and we might as well recognize that itinerant investment farming is just another extractive industry.

This is the face of our western inheritance—Judaism, Christianity, Humanism, and the Materialism which is better named Economic Determinism. The countryside, the last great cornucopia of the world's bounty, ravaged; and the city of man (God's Junkyard, or call it Bedlam) a vast demonstration of man's inhumanity to man, where existence, sustained by modern medicine and social legislation, is possible in spite of the physical environment. Yet we are the inheritors of enormous beauty, wealth, and variety. Our world is aching for the glorious cities of civilized and urbane men. Land and resources are abundant. We could build a thousand new cities in the most wonderful locations—on mountains and plains, on rocky ocean promontories, on desert and delta, by rivers and lakes, on islands and plateaus. It is within our compass to select the widest range of the most desirable lands and promulgate policies and regulations to ensure the realization of these cities, each in response to the nature of its site. We can manage the land for its health, productivity and beauty. All of these things are within the capacity of this people now. It is necessary to resolve to fulfill the American Revolution and to create the fair image that can be the land of the free and the home of the brave. But to resolve is not enough; it is also necessary that society at large understand nature as a process, having values, limiting factors, opportunities, and constraints; that creation and destruction are real; that there are criteria by which we can discern the direction and tests of evolution; and, finally, that there are formal implications revealed in the environment which affect the nature and form of human adaptations.

What inherited values have produced this plight, from which we must be released if the revolution is to be completed? Surely it is the very core of our tradition, the Judeo-Christian-Humanist view which is so unknowing of nature and of man, which has bred and sustained his simple-minded anthropocentrism and anthropomorphism. It is this obsolete view of man and nature which is the greatest impediment to our emancipation as managers of the countryside, city builders, and artists. If it requires little effort to mobilize a sweeping indictment of the physical environment which is man's creation, it takes little more to identify the source of the value system which is the culprit. Whatever the origins, the text is quite clear in Judaism, was absorbed all but unchanged into Christianity, and was inflated in Humanism to become the implicit attitude of western man to nature and the environment. Man is exclusively divine, all other creatures and things occupy lower and generally inconsequential status; man is given dominion over all creatures and things; he is enjoined to subdue the earth. Here is the best of all possible texts for him who would contemplate biocide, carelessly extirpate great realms of life, create Panama Canals, or dig Alaskan harbors with atomic demolition. Here is the appropriate injunction for the land rapist, the befouler of air and water, the uglifier, and the gratified bulldozer. Dominion and subjugation, or better call it conquest, are their creeds. It matters little that theologians point to the same source for a different text, and choose rather the image of man the steward who should dress the garden and keep it. It matters little that Buber and Heschel, Teilhard de Chardin, Weigel and Tillich retreat from the literality of the dominion and subjugation text, and insist that this is allegory. It remains the literal injunction which has been so warmly welcomed and enshrined at the core of the western view. This environment was created by the man who believes that the cosmos is a pyramid erected to support man on its pinnacle, that reality exists only because man can perceive it, that God is made in the image of man, and that the world consists solely of a dialog between men. Surely this is an infantilism which is unendurable. It is a residue from a past of inconsequence when a few puny men cried of their supremacy to an unhearing and uncaring world. One longs for a psychiatrist who can assure man that his deep seated cultural inferiority is no longer necessary or appropriate. He can now stand erect among the creatures and reveal his emancipation. His ancient vengeance and strident cries are a product of an earlier insignificance and are now obsolete. It is not really necessary to destroy nature in order to obtain God's favor or even his undivided attention. To this ancient view the past two centuries have added only materialism—an economic determinism which has merely sustained earlier views.

The face of the city and the land are the best testimony to the concept of conquest and exploitation—the merchants' creed. The Gross National Product is the proof of its success, money is its measure, convenience is its cohort, the short term is its span, and the devil take the hindmost is its morality. The economists, with some conspicuous exceptions, have become the spokesmen for the merchants' creed and in concert they ask with the most barefaced affrontery that we accommodate our values to theirs. Neither love nor compassion, health nor beauty, dignity nor freedom, grace nor delight are true unless they can be priced. If not, they are described as nonprice benefits and relegated to inconsequence, and the economic model proceeds towards its self-fulfillment—which is to say more despoliation. The major

214

criticism of this model is not that it is partial (which is conceded by its strongest advocates), but more that the features which are excluded are among the most important human values, and also the requirements for survival. If the ethics of society insist that it is man's bounden duty to subdue the earth, then it is likely that he will obtain the tools with which to accomplish this. If there is established a value system based upon exploitation of the earth, then the essential components for survival, health, and evolution are likely to be discounted, as they are. It can then come as no surprise to us that the most scabrous slum is more highly valued than the most beautiful landscape, that the most loathsome roadside stand is more highly valued than the richest farmland, and that this society should more highly prize tomato stakes than the primeval redwoods whence they come.

It is, in part, understandable why our economic value system is completely blind to the realities of the biophysical world—why it excludes from consideration, not only the most important human aspirations, but even those processes which are indispensable for survival. The origins of society and exchange began in an early world where man was a trifling inconsequence in the face of an overwhelming nature. He knew little of its operation. He bartered his surpluses of food and hides, cattle, sheep and goats; and valued such scarcities as gold, silver, myrrh and frankincense. In the intervening millennia the valuations attributed to commodities have increased in range and precision and the understanding of the operation of this limited sphere has increased dramatically. Yet, we are still unable to identify and evaluate the processes which are indispensable for survival. When you give money to a broker to invest you do so on the understanding that this man understands a process well enough to make the investment a productive one. Who are the men to whom you entrust the responsibility for ensuring a productive return on the world's investment? Surely, those who understand physical and biological processes, realize that these are creative. The man who views plants as the basis of negentropy in the world and the base of the food chain, as the source of atmospheric oxygen, fossil fuels and fibers, is a different man from one who values only economic plants, or that man who considers them as decorative but irrelevant aspects of life. The man who sees the sun as the source of life and the hydrologic cycle as its greatest work, is a different man from one who values sunlight in terms of a recreation industry, a portion of agricultural income, or from that man who can obscure sky and sunlight with air pollution, or who carelessly befouls water. The man who knows that the great recycling of matter, the return stroke in the world's cycles, is performed by the decomposer bacteria, views soils and water differently from the man who values a few bacteria in antibiotics, or he who is so unknowing of bacteria that he can blithely sterilize soils or make streams septic. That man who has no sense of the time which it has taken for the elaboration of life and symbiotic arrangements which have evolved, can carelessly extirpate creatures. That man who knows nothing of the value of the genetic pool, the greatest resource which we bring to the future, is not likely to fear radiation hazard or to value life. Clearly, it is illusory to expect the formulation of a precise value system which can include the relative value of sun, moon, stars, the changing seasons, physical processes, life forms, their roles, their symbiotic relationships, or the genetic pool. Yet, without precise evaluation, it is apparent that there will be a profound difference in attitude—indeed, a profoundly different value system—between those who understand the history of evolution and the interacting processes of the biosphere, and those who do not.

The simpler people who were our ancestors (like primitive peoples today) did not subscribe to anthropocentric views, nor did the 18th-century English landscape tradition which is the finest accomplishment of western art in the environment, and which derives from a different hypothesis. The vernacular architecture in the western tradition and the attitudes of the good farmer come from yet another source, one which has more consonance with the Orient than the West. But the views which ensured successes for the hunter and gatherer, for the vernacular farmer, and for the creation of a rich and beautiful pastoral landscape are inadequate to deal with 20th-century problems of an inordinate population growth, accelerating technology, and transformation from a rural to an urban world. We need a general theory which encompasses physical, biological, and cultural evolution; which contains an intrinsic value system; which includes criteria of

216

creativity and destruction and, not least, principles by which we can measure adaptations and their form. Surely, the minimum requirement for an attitude to nature and to man is that it approximate reality. Clearly, our traditional view does not. If one would know of these things, where else should one turn but to science. If one wishes to know of the phenomenal world, where better to ask than the natural sciences; if you would know of the interactions between organism and environment, then turn to the ecologist, for this is his competence. From the ecological view, one can conclude that by living one is united physically to the origins of life. If life originated from matter, then by living one is united with the primeval hydrogen. The earth has been the one home for all of its evolving processes and for all of its inhabitants; from hydrogen to man, it is only the bathing sunlight which changes. The planet contains our origins, our history, our milieu—it is our home. It is in this sense that ecology, derived from oikos, is the science of the home. Can we review physical and biological evolution to discern the character of these processes, their direction, the laws which obtain, the criteria for survival and success? If this can be done, there will also be revealed an intrinsic value system and the basis for form. This is the essential ingredient of an adequate view of the world: a value system which corresponds to the creative processes of the world, and both a diagnostic and constructive view of human adaptations and their form.

The evolution of the world reveals movement from more to less random, from less to more structured, from simplicity to diversity, from few to many life forms—in a word, toward greater negentropy. This can be seen in the evolution of the elements, the compounds, and of life. It is accomplished by physical processes, as in the early earth when matter liquefied and coalesced, forming the concentric cores of the planet. Vulcanism revealed the turbulence of early adaptations toward equilibrium. So, too, did the creation of the oceans. Evaporation and precipitation initiated the processes of erosion and sedimentation in which matter was physically sorted and ordered. When, from the aluminosilicate clays in the shallow bays, there emerged that novel organization, life, there developed a new agency for accomplishing ordering. The chloroplast of the plant was enabled to transmute sun-

217

light into a higher ordering, sustaining all life. The atmosphere, originally hostile to life, was adapted by life to sustain and protect it, another form of ordering. The emergence of the decomposers, bacteria and fungi, permitted the wastes of life forms—and their substance after death—to be recycled and utilized by the living, the return stroke in the cycle of matter in the biosphere. The increasing number of organisms in the oceans and on land represent negentropy in their beings and in the ordering which they accomplish. We can now see the earth as a process by which the falling sunlight is destined for entropy, but is arrested and entrapped by physical processes and creatures, and reconstituted into higher and higher levels of order as evolution proceeds. Entropy is the law and demands its price, but while all energy is destined to become degraded, physical and biological systems move to higher order—from instability towards steady-state—in sum, to more negentropy. Evolution is thus a creative process in which all physical processes and life forms participate. Creation involves the raising of matter and energy from lower to higher levels of order. Retrogression and destruction consist of reduction from the higher levels of order to entropy.

As life can only be transmitted by life, then the spore, seed, egg, and sperm contain a record of the entire history of life. The journey was shared with the worms, the coelenterates, the sponges, and, later, with the cartilaginous and bony fishes. The reptilian line is ours, the common ancestor that we share with the birds. We left this path to assume mammalian form, live births, the placenta, and suckling of the young; the long period of infantile dependence marks us. From this branching line the monotremes, marsupials, edentates, and pangolins followed their paths, and we proceeded on the primate way. Tree shrew, lemur, tarsier and anthropoid, are our lineage. We are the line of man—the raised ape, the enlarged brain, the toolmaker—he of speech and symbols, conscious of the world and of himself. It is all written on the sperm and on the egg although the brain knows little of this journey. We have been through these stages in time past and the imprint of the journey is upon us. We can look at the world and see our kin; for we are united, by living, with all life, and are from the same origins. Life has proceeded from simple to complex, although the simplest forms have not been superseded, only augmented. It has proceeded from uniform to diverse, from few to many species. Life has revealed evolution as a progression from greater to lesser entropy. In the beginning was the atom of hydrogen with one electron. Matter evolved in the cosmic cauldrons, adding electron after electron, and terminating in the heaviest and most ephemeral of elements. Simple elements conjoined as compounds, thus reaching the most complex of these as amino acids, which is to say life. Life reached unicellular form and proceeded through tissue and organ to complex organisms. There were few species in the beginning and now they are myriad; there were few roles and now they are legion. There were once large populations of few species; now there is a biosphere consisting of multitudes of communities composed of innumerable interacting species. Evolution has revealed a progression from simple to complex, from uniform to diverse, from unicellular to multicelled, from few to many species, from few to many ecosystems, and the relations between these processes have also evolved toward increased complexity.

What holds the electrons to the nucleus? The molecules in rocks, air, and water may have ten atoms, but the organic molecule may have a thousand. Where is the catalytic enzyme which locks and unlocks the molecules? The single cell is very complex indeed; what orchestrates the cytoplasm and nucleus, nucleolus, mitochondria, chromosomes, centrosomes, Golgi elements, plastids, chromoplasts, leucoplasts and, not least, chloroplasts? The lichen shows an early symbiosis at the level of the organism as the alga and the fungus unite. The plant and the decomposer enter into symbiosis to utilize energy and matter, to employ the first and recycle the latter. The animal enters the cycle, consuming the plant, to be consumed by the decomposer and thence by the plant. Each creature must adapt to the others in that concession of autonomy toward the end of survival that is symbiosis. Thus parasite and host, predator and prey, and those creatures of mutual benefit develop symbioses to ensure survival. The world works through cooperative mechanisms in which the autonomy of the individual, be it cell, organ, organism, species, or community is qualified toward the survival and evolution of higher levels of order culminating in the biosphere. Now these symbiotic relationships are beneficial to the sum of

219

organisms although clearly many of them are detrimental to individuals and species. While the prey is not pleased with the predator or the host far from enamored of the parasite or the pathogen, these are regulators of populations and the agents of death—that essential return phase in the cycle of matter, which fuels new life and evolution. Only in this sense can the predator, parasite, and pathogen be seen as important symbiotic agents, essential to the creative processes of life and evolution. If evolution has proceeded from simple to complex, this was accomplished through symbiosis. As the number of species increased, so then did the number of roles and the symbiotic arrangements between species. If stability increases as evolution proceeds, then this is the proof of increased symbiosis. If conservation of energy is essential to the diminution of entropy, then symbioses are essential to accomplish this. Perhaps it is symbiosis or, better, altruism that is the arrow of evolution.

This view of the world, creation, and evolution reveals as the principal actors, the sun, elements and compounds, the hydrologic cycle, the plant, decomposers, and the animals. Further, if the measure of creation is negentropy, then it is the smallest marine plants which perform the bulk of the world's work, which produce the oxygen of the atmosphere, the basis of the great food chains. On land it is the smallest herbs. Among the animals the same is true; it is the smallest of marine animals and the terrestrial herbivores which accomplish the greatest creative effort of raising the substance of plants to higher orders. Man has little creative role in this realm although his destructive potential is considerable. However, energy can as well be considered as information. The light which heats the body can inform the perceptive creature. When energy is so considered, then the apperception of information as meaning, and response to it, is also seen as ordering, as antientropic. Noise to the unperceptive organism, through perception becomes information from which is derived meaning. In an appraisal of the world's work of apperception, it is seen that the simpler organisms, which create the maximum negentropy, are low on the scale of apperception which increases as one rises on the evolutionary scale. Man, who had no perceptible role as a creator of negentropy, becomes prominent as a perceptive and conscious being. We have seen that

220

the evolution from the unicellular to the multicellular organism involved symbiotic relationships. Hans Selye has described intercellular
altruism as the cooperative mechanisms which make 30 billion,
billion human cells into a single integrated organism. He also has
described interpersonal altruism. Surely one must conclude that the
entire biosphere exhibits altruism. In this sense, the life forms which
now exist on earth, and the symbiotic roles which they have developed, constitute the highest ordering which life forms have yet been
able to achieve. The human organism exists as a result of the symbiotic
relationships in which cells assume different roles as blood, tissues,
and organs, integrated as a single organism. So, too, can the biosphere
be considered as a single superorganism in which the oceans and the
atmosphere, all creatures, and communities play roles analogous to
cells, tissues, and organs. That which integrates either the cell in the
organism or the organism in the biosphere is a symbiotic relationship.
In sum, these are beneficial. This then is the third measure, the third
element, after order and complexity, of the value system: the concession of some part of the autonomy of the individual in a cooperative
arrangement with other organisms which have equally qualified their
individual freedom toward the end of survival and evolution. We can
see this in the alga and fungus composing the lichen, in the complex
relationships in the forest, and in the sea. Symbiosis is the indispensable value in the survival of life forms, ecosystems, and the entire
biosphere. Man is superbly endowed to be that conscious creature who
can perceive the phenomenal world, its operation, its direction, the
roles of the creatures, and physical processes. Through his apperception, he is enabled to accomplish adaptations which are the symbioses
of man-nature. This is the promise of his apperception and consciousness. This examination of evolution reveals direction in retrospect—
that the earth and its denizens are involved in a creative process of
which negentropy is the measure. It shows that creation does have
attributes which include evolution toward complexity, diversity, stability (steady-state), increase in the number of species, and increase in
symbiosis. Survival is the first test, creation is the next; and this may be
accomplished by arresting energy, by apperception, or by symbiosis.
This reveals an intrinsic value system with a currency: energy; an

inventory which includes matter and its cycles, life forms and their roles, and cooperative mechanisms.

All of the processes which have been discussed reveal form; indeed, form and process are indivisible aspects of a single phenomenon. That which can be seen reveals process. Much of this need not be superficially visible; it may lie beneath the skin, below the level of vision, or only in invisible paths which bespeak the interactions of organisms. Yet, the place, the plants, animals, men, and their works, are revealed in form.

All of the criteria used to measure evolutionary success apply to form. Simplicity and uniformity reveal a primitive stage, while complexity and diversity are evidence of higher evolutionary forms: few elements or species as opposed to many, few interactions rather than the multitude of advanced systems. Yet, there is need for a synoptic term which can include the presence or absence of these attributes in form. For this, we can use "fitness" both in the sense that Henderson employs it, and also in Darwinian terms. Thus, the environment is fit, and can be made more fitting; the organism adapts to fit the environment. Lawrence Henderson speaks of the fitness of the environment for life in the preface to his book, *The Fitness of the Environment*.

> "Darwinian fitness is compounded of a mutual relationship between the organism and the environment. Of this, fitness of environment is quite as essential a component of the fitness which arises in the process of organic evolution; and in fundamental characteristics the actual environment is the fittest possible abode for life."

Henderson supports his proposition by elaborating on the characteristics of carbon, hydrogen, oxygen, water, and carbolic acid saying, that "No other environment consisting of primary constituents, made up of other known elements, or lacking water and carbolic acid, could possess a like number of fit characteristics, or in any manner such great fitness to promote complexity, durability, and the active metabolism and the organic mechanism we call life." The environment is fit for life and all of the manifestations which it has taken, and does take. Conversely, the surviving and successful organism is fitted to the environment. Thus, we can use fitness as a criterion of the environment, organisms and their adaptations, as revealed in form. Form can reveal past processes and help to explain present realities. Mountains show their age and composition in their form; rivers demonstrate their age and reflect the physiography of their passage; the distribution and characteristics of soils are comprehensible in terms of historical geology, and climate and hydrology. The pattern and distribution of plants respond to environmental variables represented in the foregoing considerations, while animals respond to these and to the nature of the plant communities. Man is as responsive, but he is selective; the pattern and distribution of man is likely to be comprehensible in these same terms. The term "fitness" has a higher utility than art for the simple reason that it encompasses all things—inert and living, nonhuman, and those made by man—while art is limited to the last. Moreover, it offers a longer view and more evidence. Nature has been in the business of form since the beginning, and man is only one of its products. The fact that things and creatures exist is proof of their evolutionary fitness at the time, although among them there will be those more or less fit. There will be those which are unfit and will not persist, those are the misfits; then, those which are fit; and finally, the most fitting—all revealed in form. Form is also meaningful form. Through it, process and roles are revealed, but the revelation is limited by the capacity of the observer to perceive. Arctic differs from rain forest, tundra from ocean, forest from desert, plateau from delta; each is itself because. The platypus is different from seaweed, diatom from whale, monkey from man . . . because. Negro differs from Oriental, Eskimo from Caucasoid, Mongoloid from Australoid . . . because; and all of these are manifest in form. When process is understood, differentiation and form become comprehensible. Processes are dynamic, and so coastlines advance and recede as do ice sheets, lakes are in process of filling while others form, mountains succumb to erosion and others rise. The lake becomes marsh, the estuary a delta, the prairie becomes desert, the scrub turns into forest, a volcano creates an island, while continents sink. The observation of process, through form and the response, represents the evolution of information to meaning. If evolutionary success is revealed by the existence of

223

creatures, then their fitness will be revealed in form; visible in organs, in organisms, and in communities of these. If this is so, then natural communities of plants and animals represent the most fitting adaptation to available environments. They are most fitting and will reveal this in form. Indeed, in the absence of man, these would be the inevitable expression. Thus, there is not only an appropriate ecosystem for any environment, and successional stages towards it, but such communities will reveal their fitness in their expression. This is a conclusion of enormous magnitude to those who are concerned with the land and its aspect: that there is a natural association of creatures for every environment. This could be called the intrinsic identity of the given form. If this is so, then there will be organs, organisms, and communities of special fitness, and these will, of course, be revealed in form. This might well be described as the ideal. The creation of adaptations which seek to be metaphysical symbols is, in essence, the concern with representing the ideal. Adaptation of the environment is accomplished by all physical processes and by all life. Yet, certain of these transformations are more visible than others, and some are analogous to those accomplished by man. The chambered nautilus, the bee, and the coral are all engaged in the business of using inert material to create adaptive environments. These reveal the individual, a society, or a population. Can the criteria of fitness be applied then to the artifact? We can accept that the stilt's legs, the flamingo's beak, and the mouth of the baleen whale are all splendid adaptations, and visibly so. It is no great leap to see the tennis serve, the left hook, and the jumping catch, as of the same realm as the impala's bound, the diving cormorant, or the leopard's lunge. Why then should we distinguish between the athletic gesture and the artifacts which are employed with them: the golf club, bat, glove, or tennis racquet? The instrument is only an extension of the limb. If this is so, then we can equally decide if the hammer and saw are fit, or the knife, fork and spoon. We can conclude that the tail powered jet is more fit for the air than the clawing propellors. If we can examine tools, then we can as well examine the environments for activities: the dining room for dining, the bedroom for sleeping or for loving, the house, street, village, town, or city. Are they unfit, misfit, fit, or most fitting? It appears that any natural environment will have an appropriate expression of physical processes, revealed in physiography, hydrology, soils, plants, and animals. There should then be an appropriate morphology for man-site, and this should vary with environments. There will then be a fitting-for-man environment. One would expect that as the plants and animals vary profoundly from environment to environment, this should also apply to man. One would then expect to find distinct morphologies for man-nature in each of the major physiographic regions. The house, village, town, and city should vary from desert to delta, from mountain to plain. One would expect to find certain generic unity within these regions, but marked differentiation between them. If fitness is a synoptic measure of evolutionary success, what criteria can we use to measure it? We have seen that it must meet the simplicity-complexity, uniformity-diversity, instability-stability, independence-interdependence tests. Yet, in the view of Dr. Ruth Patrick, as demonstrated by her study of aquatic systems, these may all be subsumed under two terms: ill-health and health. A movement towards simplicity, uniformity, instability, and a low number of species characterizes disease. The opposites are evidence of health. This corresponds to common usage: ill-health is unfit; fitness and health are synonymous. Thus, if we would examine the works of man and his adaptations to the countryside, perhaps the most synoptic criteria are disease and health. We can conclude that that which sustains health represents a fitting between man and the environment. We would expect that this fitness be revealed in form. This criterion might well be the most useful to examine the city of man: wherein does pathology reside? What are its corollaries in the physical and social environment? What characterizes an environment of health? What are its institutions? What is its form? Know this, and we may be able to diagnose and prescribe with an assurance which is absent today.

What conclusions can one reach from this investigation? The first is that the greatest failure of western society, and of the post-industrial period in particular, is the despoliation of the natural world and the inhibition of life which is represented by modern cities. It is apparent that this is the inevitable consequence of the values that have been our inheritance. It is clear, to me if to no one else, that these values have

225

little correspondence to reality and perpetrate an enormous delusion as to the world, its work, the importance of the roles that are performed, and, not least, the potential role of man. In this delusion the economic model is conspicuously inadequate, excluding as it does the most important human aspirations and the realities of the biophysical world. The remedy requires that the understanding of this world which now reposes in the natural sciences be absorbed into the conscious value system of society, and that we learn of the evolutionary past and the roles played by physical processes and life forms. We must learn of the criteria for creation and destruction, and of the attributes of both. We need to formulate an encompassing value system which corresponds to reality and which uses the absolute values of energy, matter, life forms, cycles, roles, and symbioses.

We can observe that there seem to be three creative roles. The first is the arresting of energy in the form of negentropy, which offers little opportunity to man. Second, is apperception and the ordering which can be accomplished through consciousness and understanding. Third, is the creation of symbiotic arrangement, for which man is superbly endowed. It can be seen that form is only a particular mode for examining process and the adaptations to the environment accomplished by process. Form can be the test used to determine processes as primitive or advanced, to ascertain if they are evolving or retrogressing. Fitness appears to have a great utility for measuring form: unfit, fit, or most fitting. When one considers the adaptations accomplished by man, they are seen to be amenable to this same criterion but, also, synoptically measurable in terms of health. Identify the environment of pathology; it is unfit, and will reveal this in form. Where is the environment of health—physical, mental, and social? This, too, should reveal its fitness in form. How can this knowledge be used to affect the quality of the environment? The first requirement is an ecological inventory in which physical processes and life forms are identified and located within ecosystems, which consist of discrete but interacting natural processes. These data should then be interpreted as a value system with intrinsic values, offering both opportunities and constraints to human use, and implications for management and the forms of human adaptations.

226

The city should be subject to the same inventory and its physical, biological, and cultural processes should be measured in terms of fitness and unfitness, health and pathology. This should become the basis for the morphology of man-nature and man-city. We must abandon the self mutilation which has been our way, reject the title of planetary disease which is so richly deserved, and abandon the value system of our inheritance which has so grossly misled us. We must see nature as process within which man exists, splendidly equipped to become the manager of the biosphere; and give form to that symbiosis which is his greatest role, man the world's steward.

# MAN AND HIS ENVIRONMENT: ADAPTATIONS AND INTERACTIONS

RENÉ DUBOS

RENÉ JULES DUBOS, Member and Professor at The Rockefeller University in New York City, was the 1966 winner of the Arches of Science Award of the Pacific Science Center. As a microbiologist and experimental pathologist, he first demonstrated the feasibility of obtaining germ-fighting drugs from microbes. Among his other scientific achievements and interests have been the development of a rapid method for growing tubercle bacilli in submerged cultures; investigations on the mechanisms of acquired immunity; the role of microorganisms in the development and functions of the gastrointestinal tract; and the biological effects of the total environment on the individual. Most recently he has become involved in the sociomedical problems of underprivileged communities, as well as those created by economic affluence in industrialized countries, with particular emphasis upon the part played by the so-called early influences—those environmental factors that impinge on the developing organism during the prenatal and early postnatal period.

For his scientific contributions, Dr. Dubos has received honorary degrees from 16 colleges and universities and 13 scientific awards, most recent among them being the 1964 American Medical Association Award. His book, *The Unseen World,* received the 1963 Phi Beta Kappa Award; *Man Adapting* received the same award in 1966; and his other works include: *The Torch of Life; The Dreams of Reason; Pasteur and Modern Science; The Mirage of Health; Biochemical Determinants of Microbial Disease; The White Plague— Tuberculosis, Man and Society; Louis Pasteur—Free Lance of Science; The Bacterial Cell;* and *Health and Disease.*

Dr. Dubos first came to The Rockefeller University in 1927 after spending three years at Rutgers University as Research Assistant and Instructor while obtaining his doctoral degree from that university. Prior to that, Dr. Dubos was a resident of France, where he was born in 1901 and where he studied at the College Chaptal and the Institut National Agronomique in Paris.

CONCERN FOR THE QUALITY of the environment first reached a conscious, rational, and coherent form probably during the second half of the 19th century. In Western Europe, then in the United States, the first phase of the Industrial Revolution had resulted in crowding, misery, accumulation of filth, appalling living and working conditions, high rates of morbidity and mortality, and ugliness in all the mushrooming industrial cities. The physical and mental decadence of the working class became intolerable to the social conscience and, furthermore, constituted a threat to the future of industrial civilization.

The social response took many forms, one of the most vigorous and original being a systematic effort to correct the evils of the physical environment. "Pure water, pure air, pure food" was the motto around which the campaign for environmental reform was initially organized. But the movement also sought to improve housing and to reintroduce in city life some of the amenities and values that had been destroyed by industrialization. Country lanes and waterways, boulevards adorned with trees and flowers, were almost as much in the minds of the 19th-century reformers as was the maintenance of sanitary conditions.

Two books stand out as expressing in practical terms the philosophy of environment that prevailed in the Western World during the late 19th century: *The Value of Health to a City,* by Max von Pettenkoffer (1873); and *Hygeia, A City of Health,* by B. W. Richardson (1876). The programs for urban planning and the specifications for housing that they offered were immensely influential in improving the health of city dwellers. Yet the message of these two books is now of only historical interest. Today's problems are different and far more intractable. The exhaustion of natural resources and erosion of the land; the chemical pollution of air and water; the high levels of noise, light, and other stimuli; the pervasive ugliness of industrial civilization; the inescapable pressures resulting from high population-densities and mechanized life; all these phenomena have become critical only during recent decades. Where our ancestors approached their problems through a creative philosophy of the environment, we are faced with situations requiring emergency action.

231

It is because we have lacked a farsighted biological and social philosophy capable of providing a basis for environmental control through technology such as might keep pace with changes in the ways of life, that we are beset by emergencies. Thus, communities are only now waking up to the danger—which could have been predicted several decades ago—created by undisciplined technology and explosive population growth. What is called "environmental improvement" really consists with us of palliative ad hoc measures to slow down the depletion of natural resources, the rape of nature, and the loss of human values. For example, the construction of great dams all over the world was prompted not by a comprehensive, integrated program of land-and-water use but by the threat of destructive floods and by the urgent need to provide more dependable and abundant water supplies. At best such programs can be regarded as social adaptive responses to acute crises.

Most human problems appear to transcend the natural sciences because they have such complex historical and social determinants. It is none the less true, however, that the approach to all problems must take into consideration man's biological needs and limitations. Plans for urban areas, public buildings, or private residences will remain largely empirical until they can be based on better knowledge of the effects of environmental factors on physical and mental health.[1] Only a few generalizations can be offered here to illustrate the extent of our ignorance of man's responses to his surroundings today.

Everyone agrees that it is desirable to control environmental pollution. But what are the pollutants of air, water, or food that are really significant? The acute effects of pollutants can be readily recognized, but what about the cumulative, delayed, and indirect effects? Does the young organism respond as does the adult? Does he develop forms of tolerance or hypersusceptibility that affect his subsequent responses? Without such knowledge, priorities in the control of environmental pollution cannot be established rationally.

Everyone agrees that all citizens should be given equal educational opportunities. But what are the critical ages for the development of mental potentialities, and for receptivity to the various kinds of stimuli? What, in this connection, are the effects of prenatal and early

232

postnatal influences on the physical, physiological, and mental characteristics of the adult? To what extent can the effects of early deprivations be corrected? And which of these effects are irreversible?

Everyone agrees that our cities must be renovated, or even rebuilt. But while technologies are available for almost any kind of scheme imagined by city planners, architects, and sociologists, who can tell how the environments so created will affect human well-being, including particularly the physical and mental development of children?

These examples show that environmental control has been considered so far almost exclusively from the point of view of technology, in ignorance of the responses that the organism makes to environmental forces and of the ultimate consequences for human welfare. Whether approached from the scientific or practical point of view, environmental improvement must take into consideration both the permissive and the formative effects of the environment and not only in the present but also in the future.

A striking illustration of the profound effects of environment on human life is provided by the differences in rate of growth under different social conditions. Japanese teenagers are now much taller than their parents and differ in behavior from their prewar counterparts not as a result of genetic changes but because the environment in Japan is very different from what it was before World War II. A similar phenomenon is observed in the Israeli kibbutz, where the children are given a diet and brought up in sanitary conditions as nearly optimum as can be devised. Early in their teens, as a result, they tower over their parents, many of whom originated in crowded and unsanitary ghettos in Central and Eastern Europe.

Not only are children strikingly taller than their parents among certain people rapidly being brought under modern influences; in western countries a trend toward earlier maturation has existed for several decades. This is evidenced by greater weights and heights of children at each year of life in such countries, and by the earlier onset of the first menstrual period. In Norway, for example, the mean age at which this occurred fell from 17 years in 1850 to 13 in 1960; similar findings have been reported from Sweden, Great Britain, the United States, and other affluent countries. Some 50 years ago, maximum stature was not being reached in general until the age of 29; commonly now it is reached at about 19 in boys and 17 in girls.

The factors responsible for these dramatic changes are not completely understood though it seems to be established that earlier puberty represents a return to pre-19th-century norms. Nor is there any knowledge of the long-range consequences of an acceleration in the rate of growth on physical health and behavioral patterns. It may turn out, for example, that the design of Japanese homes and schools and the educational patterns will be unsuited to the needs and social attitudes of the new generations. In other words, Japanese ways of life, biological and social, and perhaps the very spirit of Japanese civilization, may be profoundly altered by environmental effects, the mechanisms of which are poorly understood.

It may be useful to restate the phenomena mentioned above in the following general terms. Some unidentified factors of postwar life in Japan have brought about an acceleration of growth in children and will result in adults of larger size—probably with concomitant alterations in behavioral patterns. Such changes will certainly affect many aspects of Japanese life, architecture, and social institutions. These complex feedback relationships between man and his total environment illustrate the importance of the ecological approach in the study of human problems. In this regard, it is very gratifying to learn that Dr. Helmut Buechner, a distinguished ecologist, is in the process of developing a program of ecological research at the Smithsonian Institution.

The state of adaptedness is almost by definition an asset for biological success, since it implies that the organism is able to function effectively and to reproduce its kind under the conditions it must meet. As we shall now see, however, the concepts of adaptation developed by biologists prove insufficient when applied to human problems.

The general biologist usually defines the word "adaptation" in Darwinian terms. For him, the word implies a state of fitness to a given environment enabling the species to multiply and invade new territories. In this light, man is remarkably adapted to life in highly urbanized and industrialized societies; his populations in such societies continuously increase and spread urbanization and industrialization to

234

more and more of the earth. Granted that modern man increasingly falls victim to chronic disorders resulting from his ways of life, and that technological achievements may not contribute significantly to his happiness, these failures of modern life are of little importance from the purely biological point of view. The chronic disorders characteristic of modern civilization affect man chiefly during late adulthood after he has fulfilled his reproductive functions and after he has contributed his share to social and economic development; the problem of happiness is relevant only when attention is shifted from the purely biological aspects of life to the far more complex problems of human values. In applying the concept of adaptation to man, we must therefore use criteria different from those used in general biology.

Physiologists or psychologists give the word "adaptation" a broader meaning than that associated with Darwinian population theory, yet still fail to take into account the rich complexity of human life. To them a response is adaptive when it promotes homeostasis through metabolic, hormonal, or mental processes that tend to correct the disturbing effects of environmental forces on the body and mind. Such adaptive responses obviously contribute to the welfare of the organism at the time they occur, but unfortunately they commonly have secondary effects that are subsequently deleterious.

Scar tissue, for example, represents a successful homeostatic response at the time it is formed, since it heals wounds and helps in checking the spread of infection. But scar tissue in the liver or in the kidney is responsible for such serious diseases as cirrhosis or glomerular nephritis. Similarly, scar tissue in the lungs may seriously impede breathing; in the joints create the frozen immobility of rheumatoid arthritis. Many of man's medical problems have their origin in the biological and mental adaptive responses that allowed him earlier in life to cope with environmental threats. All too often the wisdom of the body is a shortsighted wisdom.

Man has a wide range of adaptive potentialities and therefore can survive and function under very unfavorable conditions, but practically all aspects of his life are conditioned by his experiential past. When evaluated over man's entire lifespan, the homeostatic mechanisms through which adaptation is achieved are less successful than

235

commonly assumed. Consider the consequence of adaptation to air pollution.

Ever since the beginning of the Industrial Revolution, the inhabitants of Northern Europe have been heavily exposed to many types of air pollutants produced by the incomplete combustion of coal and released in the fumes from chemical plants; such exposure is rendered even more objectionable by the inclemency of the Atlantic climate. However, the Northern Europeans have been able to adapt physiologically and culturally to the polluted air and damp cold of winter. They have come to accept almost cheerfully their dismal environment even though it appears unbearable to outsiders. Such adaptations are not peculiar to Northern Europeans; they occur in all heavily industrialized areas, where the population functions effectively despite constant exposure to irritating substances in the air. It would seem therefore that human beings can readily make an adequate adjustment to massive air pollution.

Experimental studies have shown, in fact, that animals can readily develop tolerance to a variety of air pollutants. Exposure to concentrations of pollutants that are low enough not to be lethal yet sufficient to cause symptoms elicits protective responses that enable the organism to resist higher concentrations later. The mechanisms of this tolerance are not well understood, and differ from one pollutant to another. In most cases, tolerance probably involves increased mucous secretion and other phenomena technically designated by the word "inflammation." The point is that, while the inflammatory response is protective (adaptive) at the time it occurs, it may, if continuously called into play over long periods of time, result in chronic pathological states, such as emphysema, fibrosis, and otherwise aging phenomena. It is in the light of such chronic effects that the consequences of air pollution must be judged.

The week of Thanksgiving, 1966, New York City experienced a severe episode of smog during which the concentration of several air pollutants reached extremely high levels. Yet, there was no marked increase of mortality during that period, just as there is none convincingly associated with the Los Angeles type of smog. This has led some epidemiologists to conclude that air pollution is less a medical than an aesthetic problem.

There is very little evidence, indeed, that environmental pollution constitutes a significant threat to health, if mortality and acute disease are used as the criteria of danger. But these criteria are certainly inadequate and almost irrelevant, because the most important pathological effects of pollution are extremely delayed and indirect. What matters is not so much the numbers of people that die or become acutely ill during a given episode of intense smog, as the cumulative effects of continuous exposure to low levels of pollutants. Adaptation to these low levels is bought at the cost of chronic pulmonary disease and other forms of disability in late adulthood and old age.

The delayed results of tolerance to air pollutants symbolize the indirect dangers inherent in many forms of adaptation, encompassing adaptation to toxic substances, microbial pathogens, the various forms of malnutrition, noise or other excessive stimuli, crowding or isolation, the tensions of competitive life, the disturbances of physiological cycles, and all other uncontrolled deleterious agencies typical of urbanized and technicized societies. Under normal circumstances, the modern environment rarely destroys human life, but frequently it spoils its later years.

To view with disquiet the emission of poisons into our environment is not to favor the creation of a hothouse atmosphere in which man will be protected from all discomfort. There was some factual basis for the concept of the healthy happy savage popularized by Rousseau and his contemporaries. The 17th- and 18th-century explorers had discovered a few peoples—Polynesians, Amerindians, or Eskimos for example—that had lived for long periods in restricted areas almost isolated from the rest of the world. As a result of the relative stability of their surroundings and ways of life, these populations had achieved a high degree of adaptive fitness to their physical, biological, and social milieu; they were spared many of the trials and tribulations inevitably associated with the more dynamic European life. But such isolated and stable human groups represented arrested civilizations.

While modern technology has not made man the "master" or the

237

"conqueror" of his environment, despite what we hear, it has enabled him to take shelter from it and thus avoid its effects. In fact, man's ability to cope biologically with environmental stresses appears to decrease with advances in technological civilization. Man now demands that his dwellings, offices, and factories, be cooled during the summer as well as heated during the winter. His eating, working, and playing habits are becoming so standardized throughout the year that his physiological life has fewer and fewer degrees of freedom. Admittedly, modern man can reach into outer space and the depth of the oceans, but to do it he must maintain around himself a terrestrial atmosphere and a Mediterranean climate. Whatever he undertakes, he seems always to long for a semitropical Arcadia where all his physical demands will be so unfailingly anticipated that he will be unconscious of them. Wherever he goes, he tries to duplicate the conditions under which *Homo sapiens* emerged and acquired his biological needs.

We must realize that man innovates and thus fully expresses his "humanness" by responding creatively—even though often painfully —to stimuli and challenges. Societies or social groups that have managed to escape from the world into a pleasure garden have achieved little else and generally have not been permitted to enjoy it for long.

The diversity of civilizations originates from the multifarious responses made by human groups to environmental stimuli. This versatility of response, in turn, is a consequence of the wide range of potentialities in human beings. Persons differ, of course, by reason of their genetic constitution; except for identical twins, no two individual persons are genetically alike. But contrary to popular belief, genes do not determine the traits of a person; they merely govern his responses to the life experiences out of which the personality is built. Recent studies suggest, furthermore, that many different factors can affect the activity of the genes, and thus influence the phenotypic expression of the total organism. Through complex and indirect mechanisms only now being recognized, environmental stimuli determine which parts of the genetic endowment are repressed and which parts are activated at any given time. And these stimuli range from nutrition to education, from the topography of the land to religious background. The acci-

238

dents of experience differ from person to person and give to each an experiential uniqueness, so that each person is as much the product of his experience as of his genetic endowment. Human beings perceive the world, and respond to it, not through the whole spectrum of their potentialities, but only through the areas of this spectrum that have been made functional by environmental stimulation. In other words, life experiences determine what parts of the genetic endowment are converted into functional attributes.

One can surmise also that mankind is still undergoing biological (Darwinian) evolution as a consequence of the adaptive responses that individual persons and social groups make to environmental stimuli. In fact, evolutionary changes have been established for certain biochemical characteristics that are readily measured, such as those of red blood cells. More importantly, Darwinian changes may also affect mental characteristics. For example, higher population-densities may favor the selective reproduction of the human types best suited to regimentation; or again, the greater variety and intensity of certain stimuli characteristic of complex societies may enhance the development of the brain cortex and of intelligence. There is no doubt, however, that sociocultural evolution is now far more important than genetic evolution. It is changing human life at an accelerated rate, independently of any changes in the biological nature of man.

Whatever the conditions of early and adult life, each person has a wide range of untapped innate potentialities. Whether physical or mental, these potentialities can become expressed only to the extent that surroundings and the way of life are favorable. Society thus plays a large role in the unfolding and development of man's nature.

One can take it for granted that latent potentialities have a better chance to become actualized when the social environment is sufficiently diversified to provide a variety of stimulating experiences, especially for the young. As more persons find the opportunity to express more completely their biological endowment, society becomes richer and civilizations continue to unfold. By contrast, if the surroundings and ways of life are highly stereotyped, the only components of man's nature that flourish are those adapted to the narrow range of prevailing conditions.

239

Man has been highly successful as a biological species because he is adaptable. He can hunt or farm, be a meat-eater or a vegetarian, live in the mountains or by the seashore, be a loner or a team member, function in a democratic or totalitarian state. History shows, on the other hand, that societies which were once efficient because highly specialized rapidly collapsed when conditions changed. A highly specialized society is rarely adaptable. Cultural homogenization and social regimentation resulting from the creeping monotony of technological culture, standardized patterns of education, and mass communication will make it progressively more difficult to exploit fully the biological richness of our species and may constitute a threat to the survival of civilization. We must shun uniformity of surroundings as much as conformity in behavior and strive to create diversified environments. This may result in some loss of efficiency, but the more important goal is to provide the many kinds of soil that will permit the germination of the seeds now dormant in man's nature. Diversity of social environment constitutes a crucial aspect of functionalism, whether in the planning of cities, the design of dwellings, or the management of life.

The influences experienced during the very early phases of human development, including the intra-uterine phase, deserve special emphasis here because they profoundly affect the physical, physiological, and behavioral characteristics of the adult. Observations in man and experiments with animals leave no doubt that the environmental insults to which the organism is subjected during the formative periods of its development have consequences that persist throughout its life. Often, indeed, the effects of such early influences appear irreversible. Hence the need for precise observations and searching experimental studies of the effects of external conditions on the fetus, the newborn, and the child.

Much has been learned of the effects of biological and social deprivation during development, but hardly anything of the delayed and indirect consequences of early exposure to the conditions prevailing in affluent societies. This is not surprising. Until very recently, the populations of urban and industrial centers were being constantly replenished and renewed biologically by large numbers of immigrants from

240

rural areas and from primitive countries. This biological transfusion will soon come to an end. If present trends continue, most people in this country will be born, develop, live, and reproduce within the confines of urban agglomerations under conditions of biological abundance. Yet there is no empirical information or scientific knowledge to enable us to predict the long-range consequences of man's adaptations to urban, technicized life.

The experiences of early life are of particular importance because the human body and especially the brain are incompletely differentiated at the time of birth and develop as the infant responds to environmental stimuli. Anatomic structures, physiological attributes, and behavioral patterns are thus molded by the surroundings and the conditions of life during childhood; furthermore, the effects of such early influences commonly persist throughout life. For example, a child brought up in Rome is constantly exposed to the sights, sounds, and smells characteristic of this beautiful city; his development is conditioned by the stimuli derived from palaces, churches, and parks. He may not be aware of the responses aroused in him by these repeated experiences, but they become part of his biological makeup and render him lastingly different from what he would have become had he developed in London, Paris, or New York. Although I have spent almost two-thirds of my life in the United States, my tastes, attitudes, and responses are still conditioned by the biological remembrance of the stimuli that shaped my physical and mental being while I grew up in a small French village and later in Paris. Truly, the child is father to the man.

Since human life is forever being altered by social and technological innovations, a positive philosophy of the environment must take a long-range view instead of being dedicated to ad hoc projects focused on the correction of immediate evils. An effort should be made to foresee changes in order that social mechanisms be developed for rapid adaptation to them. In this sense, environmental control cannot be dissociated from social planning and forecasting. And, as we have seen, the most important effects of the environment are probably those which are slow in developing and therefore not readily detectable.

241

Scientists can best contribute to a wise environmental control by developing techniques for prediction of long-range biological and mental responses.

Basic to such a study should be the recognition that man can achieve some form of adjustment to even highly objectionable conditions under which, as in the case of adjustment to polluted air, the ultimate ill effects may long be masked.

As we may observe, man can learn to accept treeless avenues, starless skies, tasteless food—a life without the fragrance of flowers, the song of birds, the intoxication of spring days, or the excitement of autumn. Loss of these amenities has no obvious detrimental effects on his physical well-being or on his ability to perform effectively on the economic scene. Increasingly, in fact, most of his professional life is spent in denatured dwellings, offices, and industrial plants. Schools are even being built underground for the reason that the upkeep of rooms will thereby be facilitated and the pupils be less distracted!!

Little if anything, however, is known of the effect on man of such drastic elimination of the natural stimuli under which he has evolved as a biological being. Air, water, soil, fire are not only chemical mixtures and physical forces; they are influences which have shaped human life and have probably created deep human needs that will not change in the foreseeable future. The pathetic weekend exodus to the country or beaches, the fireplaces in overheated city apartments, testify to the persistence of biological hungers which man developed during his evolutionary past. Just as the most domesticated dog or pampered cat retains many characteristics of its wild origins, so does man still exhibit many of the traits and needs of the paleolithic hunter and the neolithic farmer.

A variety of stimuli calling forth an active and creative response during early life may be more important for intellectual and emotional growth than economic factors or even than passive exposure to cultural artifacts. Children developing without challenge in an affluent but highly standardized suburb may be as deprived of opportunities for mental and emotional development as those growing up in a slum or in a modern city-renewal project. Probably most important, and least recognized, is the fact that mere exposure to a stimulus is not by

242

itself sufficient to stimulate growth. Human beings are enriched by their environment only to the extent that they respond positively to it. Information of any sort is of little use per se. Information is *formative* only if it elicits an active, creative response. It is this type of response that becomes incorporated—incarnated one might say—in the physical and mental being of the developing organism and thus continues to manifest itself organically and psychically long after initial exposure to the stimulus.

Intuitively, primitive men have considered themselves part of the environment in which they have lived. They have worshiped rocks, springs, trees, and animals, not as abstract concepts, but as expressions of the cosmic order that generated their own being. This attitude was beautifully expressed by Indian Chief Seattle when he addressed General Stevens, who had been commissioned to administer the Northwestern Territory, where the city of Seattle is now located: "Our dead never forget the beautiful world that gave them being. . . . Every part of this country is sacred to my people. . . . The very dust . . . responds more lovingly under our footsteps than under yours."

The relation to Nature symbolized by Chief Seattle's words is fundamentally antithetical to the spirit of Western civilization, as most vividly illustrated by the social history of North America.

Modern American civilization did not evolve organically out of this continent's soil or historical past. It emerged rapidly from the willful and rational actions of men who were primarily concerned with the political, social, and economic aspects of life. The American land appeared to them as a wilderness to be conquered for the creation of a new society. This conquering attitude was even more pronounced among the European immigrants who flocked to the New World during the 19th century in search of fortune; they were interested in exploiting the land for profit and did not identify themselves with it emotionally. The first phase of American history is thus a saga of conquest, the enemy being Nature itself. During the second phase, the national enterprise was devoted to exploitation of mineral resources and creation of industries. After mastering the wilderness, the pioneering spirit strove to master all other manifestations of Nature. The American way of life, now spreading all over the world, is based on

243

the myth that man is the Lord of the Creation. This has become a credo and almost a religion of the world's masses and of their leaders.

Much of our anxious concern about the environment comes from a belated awareness that, in reality, mankind cannot much longer safely remain separated from the natural order of things. Sir Rabindranath Tagore once wrote that the great adventure of European civilization had been the love of the land, an "active wooing of the earth." At heart we still worship nature, but with a sense of guilt. We realize that by despoiling the earth we jeopardize not only our biological future but also the whole system of natural relationships which are at the basis of human values. Vaguely, we feel the biological need of reestablishing a harmonious accord between man and nature.

Conquest, or mastery, is not the only, as it is certainly not the best, manner for dealing with natural forces. In fact the accelerating "takeover" by today's stark technological philosophy may lead mankind unknowingly into catastrophe. It would not be the first time that trends in organic development initially favoring biological success led finally to disaster for the species. Even technological innovations that emerge as responses to social demands and therefore appear adaptive at first can become destructive in the long run—as we have seen in the case of biological homeostatic responses. Like the wisdom of the body, the wisdom of society is often a shortsighted wisdom.

In the long run, man might be more successful biologically and find greater meaning to life if he tried to collaborate with natural forces instead of conquering them. Ideally, he should try to insert himself into the environment in such a manner that his technologies and ways of life relate him more intimately to nature. He might thereby become once more part of nature instead of its uneasy overlord.

All components of nature are interrelated and all living forms are organized into a highly integrated web which cannot be disrupted without drastic consequences. It is the interdependence of all living things and their complex relation to the physical environment that constitutes the scientific basis of conservation. Their ethical overtone is a commitment to the sanctity of life. Conservation means much more than providing amusement grounds and comfortable camps for weekenders. Its ultimate goal is to help man retain contact with the natural forces under which he evolved and to which he remains linked physiologically and emotionally.

The view that man must learn to collaborate with natural forces instead of conquering them may appear unrealistically romantic and, in any case, incompatible with the aggressive genius of Western civilization. Yet there are reasons to believe that it is the crude philosophy of the conquest of nature that is unrealistic and will soon prove antiquated as well. Before long, all parts of the globe will have been colonized by man and the supply of many natural resources will have become critical. Careful husbandry, rather than exploitation, will then be the key to survival. Capturing energy from nuclear or solar sources and developing stations in outer space or on ocean bottoms will not modify significantly the limitations imposed on human life by the limitations of the planet earth. Man emerged on the earth, evolved under its influence, was shaped by it, and biologically will remain bound to it. He may dream of stars and attempt to reach them, but biologically he is of the earth, earthy.

The limitations of the spaceship earth will inevitably require that man's relationships to his physical environment be based upon ecological concepts. Curiously this view is often taken to imply a completely stable, static system. In the words of a thoughtful sociologist, "I have some concern lest the ecologist's delight in the well-balanced, smoothly-functioning, steady-state ecosystem of the pond be projected uncritically to the earth and its human population."

If the ecological view of man's relation to his environment really implied a "steady-state ecosystem," it would indeed be disheartening because it would mean the end of the human adventure. But this need not and cannot be so. The physical structure and forces of the environment are forever changing, slowly, but inexorably. Furthermore, all forms of life are continuously evolving and thereby making their own contribution to environmental changes. Finally, it seems to be part of man's nature to search endlessly for new environments, or at least for new adventures. There is no chance, therefore, of maintaining a status quo. Even if there were enough learning and wisdom to achieve at any given time a harmonious state of ecological equilibrium between mankind and the other components of the spaceship earth, it would be a

245

dynamic equilibrium. Such a dynamic system would be entirely compatible with man's continuing development. The only question is whether his development will be the outcome of blind forces engendered in a fight to the death between man and nature, or whether man can guide it by deliberate, rational choices.

Admittedly, human evolution and much of human history have been the result of accidents. Even deliberate actions have had unforeseen consequences; in fact, most of the environmental problems of Western civilization derive from discoveries and decisions focused on the solution of other problems. Internal combustion engines, synthetic detergents, medicinal drugs, and pesticides were introduced with a useful purpose in mind, but some of their side effects have been calamitous. We shall, we may hope, eventually develop ways to predict or recognize early the objectionable consequences of social and technological innovations, but this kind of piecemeal social engineering will be no substitute for a philosophy of the environment. If the goal of our civilization is merely to achieve greater safety in doing more and more of the same, only bigger and faster, tomorrow will only be a detestable extension of today.

Creating the future demands more than foresight; it requires vision. Like animal life, human life is affected by evolutionary forces that blindly shape the organism to its environment. But human history involves, in addition, the unfolding of visionary imaginings. The philosophers of enlightenment had imagined the modern world long before there was any factual basis for their vision. They prepared the blueprint for most of what is new and desirable in the modern world because they had the faith that knowledge, social reforms, and scientific technology could someday liberate human beings from fear and destitution. Throughout human history, progress has been the fruit of visionary imaginings. This is true for the physical as well as the social environment; these two determinants of human life cannot be separated.

Man derives satisfaction from two very different kinds of environment. One is primeval nature. We shall have less and less of it as the world population increases; but we must preserve as much of it as possible lest we lose that awareness of our biological origins that is essential to our sanity. The other environment is one which man has

246

toiled to create and in which, through trial and error, he has achieved a kind of harmony between himself and nature. What we long for is rarely nature in the raw; more often it is a landscape suited to human limitations and shaped by the emotional aspirations of centuries of civilized life. The charm of the New England or Pennsylvania Dutch countryside is not a product of chance. Nor did it result from man's conquest of nature. Rather it is the expression of a subtle process through which the natural environment was humanized but in accordance with its own individual genius.

The priceless gift of vision enables mankind to plan for future aesthetic rewards. One need only envisage the marvelous parks and gardens of Europe to realize the creative force of a long-range view in social improvement. Those parks and gardens stemmed from that extraordinary sense which is peculiar to man, the imaginary vision of things to come. Several books by the great landscape architects of the 18th century show drawings of the European parks as they appeared at the time of their creation, with naked banks of newly created brooks and lakes, among puny trees and shrubs—landscapes without substance or atmosphere. Yet, it is obvious that their designers had composed the expanses of water, lawns, and flowers to fit the silhouettes of trees and the masses of shrubbery not as they existed when first put together, but as they were to become with the passage of time. And because men thus visualized the future and planned for it centuries ago, millions of human beings today have the great European parks and classical gardens for their enjoyment.

While the parks and gardens of the past still delight our senses, other kinds of landscapes must be conceived to meet present and future needs. Where the country roads of the past, lined with rows of trees, provided poetic and practical shelter for the man on foot or horseback and for coaches, a modern highway must be designed in such a manner that horizons, curves, and objects of view are related to the physiological needs and limitations of motorists moving at high speed.

Needless to say, envisioning an environment suitable for the total life of an immense technological society is vastly more complicated than visualizing the future appearance of a park or designing a parkway. But certain principles hold true for all environmental planning.

On the one hand, the genetic endowment of *Homo sapiens* has changed only in minor details since the Stone Age, and there is little chance that it can be significantly, usefully, or safely modified in the foreseeable future. This genetic stability defines the potentialities and requirements of man's nature. It also determines the physiological limits beyond which human life cannot be safely altered by social and technological innovations. In the final analysis, the frontiers of cultural development are determined by man's own biological frontiers, which are determined by the genetic constitution he acquired during his evolutionary past.

On the other hand, as we have seen, mankind has a large reserve of potentialities that become expressed only to the extent that circumstances are favorable. The physical surroundings condition not only the biological aspects of phenotypic expressions but also their mental aspects. Environmental planning can thus play a key role in enabling human beings to realize their possibilities. One can take it for granted that latent potentialities have a better chance to be actualized when the physical environment is sufficiently diversified to provide a variety of stimulating experiences and opportunities especially for the young.

The immense role—for good and for evil—played by adaptive responses makes it urgent to develop techniques for studying environmental problems not only as static phenomena in the "here and now," but also in their dynamic expressions extrapolated into the future.

It is as imperative for environmental sciences as for social sciences to develop methods for the study of dynamic systems because the patterns of man's biological and psychic responses change at least as rapidly as the social patterns. Environmental practices do not develop or function in a social void. They can fulfill their purpose—to improve health and happiness—only if they are fitted to the needs and resources of the community, as well as to the special conditions created by the total environment, and these are characteristically in a state of flux. From great estate to municipal park, from slow-paced country road to multi-lane parkway, from city playground to national recreation area, from village to city, and from suburb to satellite community, the environment must endlessly evolve in response to changing human needs and aspirations. The concept of an optimum environment is unrealistic because it implies a static view of man's biological and social nature. Planning for the future demands an ecological attitude assuming evolutionary change and a continuous creative activity on the part of man.

Through a reasoned approach it should be possible to arrive at a formulation of existentialism compatible with human freedom, value judgments, and scientific sophistication. Scientific knowledge, per se, cannot define or impose values. But certainly it can help in predicting the likely consequences of various social and technological practices. It thus provides a rational basis for decision. We may not at once abandon values that science shows are likely to prove destructive— only a minority of smokers have given up cigarettes since the Surgeon General's report—but we may cling to them less tenaciously for knowing the penalties apt to accrue and be readier to accept new values demonstrably to our longrun advantage.

The view that man shapes himself through decisions that shape his environment was expressed in a picturesque way by Winston Churchill in 1943 while discussing the architecture best suited for the new Chambers of the House of Commons. The old building that had been bombed out of existence during the war had been uncomfortable and impractical. Yet, Mr. Churchill urged that it be rebuilt exactly as it was before the war instead of being replaced by a more efficient one equipped for greater comfort and with better means of communication. He argued that the style of parliamentary debates in England had been conditioned by the physical characteristics of the old House, and that changing its architecture would affect the manner of debates and, as a result, also the structure of English democracy. Mr. Churchill summarized the concept of endless feedback between man and the total environment in a sentence that could well serve as the motto for this symposium. In his words, "We shape our buildings, and afterwards our buildings shape us."

## NOTE

[1] In his book, Charles Abrams expressed the same thought in the following words: "In interviewing an architect in 1948 who was then planning the Cleveland zoo, I was struck by the quantity of research that goes into the study of animal habits. The

249

general instructions to the architects were to retain the natural values of sites, simulate the natural habitats of each animal, and guarantee freedom from unnecessary distractions as well as absolute privacy for copulation. Specialists from all over the world were consulted on the eating, sleeping and mating habits of each species, and the findings were reduced to detailed reports which were carefully studied before a line was drawn. No comparable studies, to my knowledge, have ever been made on the human animal in its urban surroundings nor are we even as much concerned as the Zoo architect about the human habitation. The sciences of urban anthropology and human nidology, particularly as they bear on the human female, are not even at their beginnings." (*The City is the Frontier;* New York, 1965.)